CHURCH DOGMATICS

For further resources, including the forewords to the original 14-volume edition of the *Church Dogmatics*, log on to our website and sign up for the resources webpage: http://www.continuumbooks.com/dogmatics/

KARL BARTH
CHURCH DOGMATICS

VOLUME II

THE DOCTRINE OF GOD

§ 28–30

THE REALITY OF GOD I

EDITED BY
G. W. BROMILEY
T. F. TORRANCE

t&t clark

Published by T&T Clark
A Continuum Imprint
The Tower Building, 11 York Road, London, SE1 7NX
80 Maiden Lane, Suite 704, New York, NY 10038

www.continuumbooks.com

Translated by G. W. Bromiley, J. C. Campbell, Iain Wilson, J. Strathearn McNab, T. H. L. Parker, W. B. Johnston, Harold Knight, J. L. M. Haire, R. A. Stewart

British Library Cataloguing-in-Publication Data
A catalogue record for this book is available from the British Library

ISBN13: 978-0-567-36379-4

Typeset by Interactive Sciences Ltd, Gloucester, and Newgen Imaging Systems Pvt Ltd, Chennai
Printed and bound in Great Britain by CPI Antony Rowe, Chippenham, Wiltshire

PUBLISHER'S PREFACE TO THE STUDY EDITION

Since the publication of the first English translation of *Church Dogmatics I. 1* by Professor Thomson in 1936, T&T Clark has been closely linked with Karl Barth. An authorised translation of the whole of the *Kirchliche Dogmatik* was begun in the 1950s under the editorship of G. W. Bromiley and T. F. Torrance, a work which eventually replaced Professor Thomson's initial translation of *CD I. 1*.

T&T Clark is now happy to present to the academic community this new *Study Edition* of the *Church Dogmatics*. Its aim is mainly to make this major work available to a generation of students and scholars with less familiarity with Latin, Greek, and French. For the first time this edition therefore presents the classic text of the translation edited by G. W. Bromiley and T. F. Torrance incorporating translations of the foreign language passages in Editorial Notes on each page.

The main body of the text remains unchanged. Only minor corrections with regard to grammar or spelling have been introduced. The text is presented in a new reader friendly format. We hope that the breakdown of the *Church Dogmatics* into 31 shorter fascicles will make this edition easier to use than its predecessors.

Completely new indexes of names, subjects and scriptural indexes have been created for the individual volumes of the *Study Edition*.

The publishers would like to thank the Center for Barth Studies at Princeton Theological Seminary for supplying a digital edition of the text of the *Church Dogmatics* and translations of the Greek and Latin quotations in the original T&T Clark edition made by Simon Gathercole and Ian McFarland.

London, April 2010

HOW TO USE THIS *STUDY EDITION*

The *Study Edition* follows Barth's original volume structure. Individual paragraphs and sections should be easy to locate. A synopsis of the old and new edition can be found on the back cover of each fascicle.

All secondary literature on the *Church Dogmatics* currently refers to the classic 14-volume set (e.g. II.2 p. 520). In order to avoid confusion, we recommend that this practice should be kept for references to this *Study Edition*. The page numbers of the old edition can be found in the margins of this edition.

CONTENTS

§ 28–30

§ 28 [257]

THE BEING OF GOD AS THE ONE WHO LOVES IN FREEDOM

God is who He is in the act of His revelation. God seeks and creates fellowship between Himself and us, and therefore He loves us. But He is this loving God without us as Father, Son and Holy Spirit, in the freedom of the Lord, who has His life from Himself.

1. THE BEING OF GOD IN ACT

God is. This is the simple statement which we have to develop and explain in this chapter on the basis and in the application of what we have learnt in the previous chapter about the fulfilment, the possibility and the limits of our knowledge of God. In so doing we confront the hardest and at the same time the most extensive task of Church dogmatics, behind which also there lies concealed the hardest and at the same time the most extensive task of the whole of Christian preaching. The task consists in defining the subject of all the statements that are here necessary and possible. The problem of definition as such lies behind us (at least, as far as scientific development and statement is concerned). That was our concern in the doctrine of the knowledge of God. It is self-evident that this problem can never leave us, that it will again accompany us at every step on the next stage of our journey (and on what further stages will we be free from it?). But the result of the considerations that we took up there will have to be authenticated, as we now try to complete the definition of the subject of which we have already given an account as such; as in the framework and in accordance with the doctrine of the knowledge of God we now try actually to say that God is. This statement and the object of the task confronting us is not just one particular "theologoumenon" among others. Strictly speaking this cannot be said of any single article of faith and therefore of dogmatics. Strictly speaking, in dogmatics and in Church preaching every single statement is at once the basis and the content of all the rest. But inevitably this is true in a very particular way of this statement, in which we define completely [258]
the subject of all other statements.

Dogmatics, in each and all of its divisions and subdivisions, with every one of its questions and answers, with all its biblical and historical assertions, with the whole range of its formal and material considerations, examinations and condensations, can first and last, as a whole and in part, say nothing else but that God is. According to the measure that it does this, it serves the Church as criticism of its conduct and as counsel and suggestion for its conduct. Inasmuch as it says, or does not say, that God is, it decides not only on its own usefulness or uselessness, but also on its scientific value or lack of value. In every train of thought, in every sentence which directly or indirectly serves the purpose of saying this, dogmatics does what it ought to do, what its very existence demands and justifies. And conversely, in every train of thought or statement which does not serve this purpose, in which it does not say this either directly or indirectly, in which directly or indirectly it says something other than that God is—in every such form, however enlightening or fruitful it may be in other respects, it will most certainly be guilty of aberration, leading the Church into error instead of to the truth, and compromising itself and its right to exist.

This is the case because the Church too, whose commission the science of dogmatics has to serve in its own sphere and manner, lives by the fact and only by the fact that it can hear the word that God is, and because first and last it has this and only this to say to itself and the world in the execution of its commission—the fact that God is. What God according to His Word wills with men and from men is that they should and must hear, believe, know and reckon with this; in great things and small, in whole and in part, in the totality of their existence as men, they should and must live with the fact that not only sheds new light on, but materially changes, all things and everything in all things—the fact that God is. That this is so—that God wills to let men live with this fact of His own being, and that what God wills happens—is not, of course, the concern of the Church. Indeed, it is not the concern of any man or of any other creature. God Himself sees to it in His Word. But the Church has to serve the Word in which He Himself does see to it. For the Church lives by the Word of God and for the Word of God. It is, therefore, the Church's commission, which the science of dogmatics has also to serve in its own way, that taught and bound by the Word of God and for the sake of it (for it has no other *raison d'être*[EN1] than to serve the Word of God), it has to say that God is. It is, therefore, to be said of it (and above all of it) that it does what it ought to do, what exclusively but also unconditionally is required of it, what exclusively but also unconditionally justifies its existence, when it says that God is. Because it lives itself by the Word of God and for the Word of God, it knows that what must be said in all circumstances, what it is necessary in all circumstances for men to hear, so that they live with this fact in the totality of their existence, but what it can never in any circumstances say of itself (for the Church has never said it of itself), is the fact that God is. It is true to its commission when taught and bound by the Word of God and for the sake of it, it says this directly or indirectly but unequivocally to itself and to the world. For whatever else it can say, if it is to be said properly, directly or indirectly, it must be this. It would also be true to say that it too (and especially) makes itself impossible if it does not say this, or if directly or indirectly it says something else.

So hard and so extensive is the statement that God is, that we may well ask whether a particular development and explanation of this statement, as if it were an individual statement and not the statement of all statements, is not
[259] wholly superfluous and impossible. Should we not be content with the definition of the subject which we make when we adopt the statements which according to the Word of God are necessary for the description of the action and working of this subject? To this we make the following answer. If the Word of God forbids the question of God's being as a particular question, or leaves us in doubt about this particular question, it means that it gives us no real revelation of God. It does, of course, reveal to us perhaps a very significant and effective action and working, but it keeps from us, and therefore does not

[EN1] reason for existence

reveal, the fact that it is, and how far it is, the action and the working of God. This action and working becomes and is significant and effective with a significance and effectiveness qualitatively different from any other action and working in virtue of the fact that it is God's action and working. It is not because it is proclaimed and believed in itself, nor because there is proclaimed and believed a creation, reconciliation, and redemption, but because the whole is proclaimed and believed as God's action and working, that there is proclaimed in Jesus Christ, in Holy Scripture, and in the Church, the Word of God as true revelation. Moreover, the true revelation does not remain silent on the particular question of God's being—quite apart from the fact that it is in its entirety one single answer to the question. It is the whole truth. It authorises us and commands us quietly and candidly to halt at this point and to consider specifically what we are saying when we make this hardest and most comprehensive statement that God is. And because this is the case, we shall be guilty of an omission which will recoil on us if we hurry over the statement that God is, as if it were only the common truth in all other statements, as if it were not worth our while to give particular account of its particular truth.

It was, therefore, an act of rashness, of which he rightly repented, when in his *Loci* of 1521 Melanchthon, the first dogmatician of the Evangelical Church, thought he should so suppress the special doctrine of God in order to turn at once to the statement of the *beneficia Christi*[EN2]. He did this on the ground that: *mysteria divinitatis rectius adoraverimus, quam vestigaverimus. Immo sine magno periculo tentari non possunt*[EN3]. To this we must say that surely the *beneficia Christi*[EN4] also belong to the revealed *mysteria divinitatis*[EN5] which are only to be investigated at some risk; that the *beneficia Christi*[EN6] cannot be properly investigated if some consideration of the *mysteria divinitatis*[EN7] as such has not been undertaken in its proper place; that the danger of every human *vestigare*[EN8] of divine truth, here as well as elsewhere, is not to be avoided as such; that here as well as elsewhere it can be met in the fact that *vestigare*[EN9] is not separated from *adorare*[EN10], i.e., that here as well as elsewhere attention is paid (only) to God's revelation. The second mistake that Melanchthon committed later was if anything worse than the first. It consisted in this. When he later decided to take up again in his *Loci* the doctrine of God, he began to create it from another source than from the revelation of God, namely, from an independently formed and general idea of God. He therefore began to consider the *mysteria divinitatis*[EN11] apart from their connexion with the *beneficia Christi*[EN12]. In this he fell right into the *magnum periculum*[EN13] of which he had been afraid in 1521, and was all the more guilty of the very error which in his first act of rashness he had

---

EN 2 benefits of Christ
EN 3 We should more properly adore the mysteries of God, than investigate them. Indeed, we cannot attempt the latter without great danger
EN 4 benefits of Christ
EN 5 mysteries of God
EN 6 benefits of Christ
EN 7 mysteries of God
EN 8 investigation
EN 9 investigation
EN10 adoration
EN11 mysteries of God
EN12 benefits of Christ
EN13 great danger

[260] had a right instinct to avoid as opposed to late medieval Scholasticism, thus affording a disastrous example to the whole of Protestant orthodoxy. We must be at pains to avoid both these errors of Melanchthon.

Although we cannot allow as such the objection to the possibility of a special doctrine of God, there is something to be learned from it. When we ask questions about God's being, we cannot in fact leave the sphere of His action and working as it is revealed to us in His Word. God is who He is in His works. He is the same even in Himself, even before and after and over His works, and without them. They are bound to Him, but He is not bound to them. They are nothing without Him. But He is who He is without them. He is not, therefore, who He is only in His works. Yet in Himself He is not another than He is in His works. In the light of what He is in His works it is no longer an open question what He is in Himself. In Himself He cannot, perhaps, be someone or something quite other, or perhaps nothing at all. But in His works He is Himself revealed as the One He is. It is, therefore, right that in the development and explanation of the statement that God is we have always to keep exclusively to His works (as they come to pass, or become visible as such in the act of revelation)—not only because we cannot elsewhere understand God and who God is, but also because, even if we could understand Him elsewhere, we should understand Him only as the One He is in His works, because He is this One and no other. We can and must ask about the being of God because as the Subject of His works God is so decisively characteristic for their nature and understanding that without this Subject they would be something quite different from what they are in accordance with God's Word, and on the basis of the Word of God we can necessarily recognise and understand them only together with this their Subject.

In the preceding chapter we have already had to resist the threatened absorption of the doctrine of God into a doctrine of being: and we shall have to do this again. Yet we must not yield to a revulsion against the idea of being as such, which for some time had a part in modern Protestant theology (occasionally with an appeal to Melanchthon), even as late as the extraordinarily informative book of H. Cremer, *Die christliche Lekre von den Eigenschaften Gottes*, 1897; 2nd edn. 1917. God is not swallowed up in the relation and attitude of Himself to the world and us as actualised in His revelation. The dignity and power of His works, of His relation and attitude, depends much more on the fact that as distinct from them, without being any other than the One who manifests Himself in them, He is Himself; that, while He reveals Himself in them, He remains at the same time superior to them. We keep this constantly in mind as we take up the concept of being at this point with complete impartiality.

At the same time we must be quite clear on the other side, that our subject is God and not being, or being only as the being of God. In connexion with the being of God that is here in question, we are not concerned with a concept of being that is common, neutral and free to choose, but with one which is from
[261] the first filled out in a quite definite way. And this concretion cannot take place arbitrarily, but only from the Word of God, as it has already occurred and has

been given to us in the Word of God. This means that we cannot discern the being of God in any other way than by looking where God Himself gives us Himself to see, and therefore by looking at His works, at this relation and attitude—in the confidence that in these His works we do not have to do with any others, but with His works and therefore with God Himself, with His being as God.

What does it mean to say that "God is"? What or who "is" God? If we want to answer this question legitimately and thoughtfully, we cannot for a moment turn our thoughts anywhere else than to God's act in His revelation. We cannot for a moment start from anywhere else than from there.

We stand here before the fundamental error which dominated the doctrine of God of the older theology and which influenced Protestant orthodoxy at almost every point. For the greater part this doctrine of God tended elsewhere than to God's act in His revelation, and for the greater part it also started elsewhere than from there. It is of a piece with this fact that with a surprisingly common thoughtlessness it was usual to begin by deducing the doctrine of the Trinity—theoretically maintained to be the basis of all theology—from the premises of formal logic. In the vacuum which this created, there was no place for anything but general reflections on what God at any rate could be—reflections arising from specific human standpoints and ideas as incontestable data, and then interwoven rather feebly with all kinds of biblical reminiscences. In this way there was created a doctrine of God which could have either no meaning or only a disastrous one for the remaining contents of dogmatics. And also in this way there was created, involuntarily, the basis on which an anti-Christian philosophy (and at the same time and later a heretical theology) could only too easily attack the dogma of the Trinity, and with it all the decisive articles of faith and its knowledge of the Word of God. It was certainly right to define the essence of God: *Essentia Dei est ipsa Deitas, qua Deus a se et per se absolute est et existit*[EN14] (Polanus, *Synt. Theol. chr.*, 1609, *col.* 865). But even in the definition of this *a se et per se*[EN15] there ought never to have been an abstraction from the Trinity, and that means from the act of divine revelation. In all the considerations that are brought before us in this chapter we must keep vigorously aloof from this tradition, remembering that a Church dogmatics derives from a doctrine of the Trinity, and therefore that there is no possibility of reckoning with the being of any other God, or with any other being of God, than that of the Father, the Son and the Holy Spirit as it is in God's revelation and in eternity. So then, as dogmatics describes and explains God as the One who is, it cannot make any free speculations about the nature of His being. Whatever may be the standpoints and ideas that are adduced, in this context it has always to win and explain their particular sense in the light of this revelation—the revelation of the being of the triune God.

What God is as God, the divine individuality and characteristics, the *essentia*[EN16] or "essence" of God, is something which we shall encounter either at the place where God deals with us as Lord and Saviour, or not at all. The act of revelation as such carries with it the fact that God has not withheld Himself from men as true being, but that He has given no less than Himself to men as

---

[EN14] The essence of God is his deity, by which God is and exists absolutely from himself and through himself

[EN15] 'from himself' and 'through himself'

[EN16] essence

the overcoming of their need, and light in their darkness—Himself as the
[262] Father in His own Son by the Holy Spirit. The act of God's revelation also carries with it the fact that man, as a sinner who of himself can only take wrong roads, is called back from all his own attempts to answer the question of true being, and is bound to the answer to the question given by God Himself. And finally the act of God's revelation carries with it the fact that by the Word of God in the Holy Spirit, with no other confidence but this unconquerable confidence, man allows being to the One in whom true being itself seeks and finds, and who meets him here as the source of his life, as comfort and command, as the power over him and over all things.

Therefore our first and decisive transcription of the statement that God is, must be that God is who He is in the act of His revelation. Hence we have already repeated this sentence in our chapter heading with the concept of "The Reality of God," which holds together being and act, instead of tearing them apart like the idea of "essence." It will be noticed that even in this transcription and comprehension the statement speaks of the being of God and therefore answers the particular question of the subject of all the other articles of the creed. We are in fact interpreting the being of God when we describe it as God's reality, as "God's being in act," namely, in the act of His revelation, in which the being of God declares His reality: not only His reality for us—certainly that—but at the same time His own, inner, proper reality, behind which and above which there is no other.

If we follow the path indicated, our first declaration must be the affirmation that in God's revelation, which is the content of His Word, we have in fact to do with His act. And first, this means generally—with an event, with a happening. But as such this is an event which is in no sense to be transcended. It is not, therefore, an event which has merely happened and is now a past fact of history. God's revelation is, of course, this as well. But it is also an event happening in the present, here and now. Again, it is not this in such a way that it exhausts itself in the momentary movement from the past to the present, that is, in our to-day. But it is also an event that took place once for all, and an accomplished fact. And it is also future—the event which lies completely and wholly in front of us, which has not yet happened, but which simply comes upon us. Again, this happens without detriment to its historical completeness and its full contemporaneity. On the contrary, it is in its historical completeness and its full contemporaneity that it is truly future. "Jesus Christ the same yesterday and to-day and for ever" (Heb. 13^{8}). This is something which cannot be transcended or surpassed or dispensed with. What is concerned is always the birth, death and resurrection of Jesus Christ, always His justification of faith, always His lordship in the Church, always His coming again, and therefore Himself as our hope. We can only abandon revelation, and with it God's Word, if we are to dispense with it. With it we stand, no, we move necessarily in the circle of its event or, in biblical terms, in the circle of the life of the people
[263] of Israel. And in this very event God is who He is. God is He who in this event is subject, predicate and object; the revealer, the act of revelation, the revealed; Father, Son and Holy Spirit. God is the Lord active in this event. We say "active"

in this event, and therefore for our salvation and for His glory, but in any case active. Seeking and finding God in His revelation, we cannot escape the action of God for a God who is not active. This is not only because we ourselves cannot, but because there is no surpassing or bypassing at all of the divine action, because a transcendence of His action is nonsense. We are dealing with the being of God: but with regard to the being of God, the word "event" or "act" is *final*, and cannot be surpassed or compromised. To its very deepest depths God's Godhead consists in the fact that it is an event—not any event, not events in general, but the event of His action, in which we have a share in God's revelation.

The definition that we must use as a starting-point is that God's being is *life*. Only the Living is God. Only the voice of the Living is God's voice. Only the work of the Living is God's work; only the worship and fellowship of the Living is God's worship and fellowship. So, too, only the knowledge of the Living is knowledge of God.

We recall in this connexion the emphatic Old and New Testament description of God as "the living God." This is no metaphor. Nor is it a mere description of God's relation to the world and to ourselves. But while it is that, it also describes God Himself as the One He is. "As I live" or "As the Lord (or God, or the God of Israel) liveth" is not for nothing the significant formula for an oath in the Old Testament. God is "the living fountain" (Jer. 2^{13}, 17^{13}), "the fountain of life" (Ps. 36^{9}). The Father has life in Himself (Jn. 5^{26}). Christ is "the author of life" (Ac. 3^{15}), even "the life" (Jn. 14^{6}, Phil. 1^{21}, Col. 3^{4}, 1 Jn. 1^{2}), and "eternal life" (1 Jn. 5^{20}), "alive for evermore" (Rev. 1^{18}). The Holy Spirit is life (Jn. 6^{63}, Rom. 8^{10}). All this is clearly in contradistinction to the gods and idols who "have no life" (Jer. 10^{14}, Ac. 14^{15}). Thus it was quite right when the older theology described the essence of God as *vita*[EN17], and again as *actuositas*[EN18], or more simply as *actus*[EN19]. What was meant was: as *actus purus*[EN20], indeed *purissimus. Domine, cui esse et vivere non aliud atque aliud est, quia summe esse atque summe vivere idipsum es ...* [EN21] (Augustine, *Conf.* 1, 6, 10). In speaking of the essence of God we are concerned with an act which utterly surpasses the whole of the actuality that we have come to know as act, and compared with which all that we have come to know as act is no act at all, because as act it can be transcended. This is not the case with the act of God that happens in revelation. Of course, when we have said this, we have still not said everything that we must say about God when we describe Him as act, or as living. But we must always say this of Him too (and if we are concerned to understand who God is, we must say it first of all) that He is act or He is living. *Vita Dei est tale attributum, quo Deus semetipsum perfectissime actual per actus intrinsecos et immanentes cognoscendi et volendi seque semper actuosum demonstrat*[EN22] (Quenstedt, *Theol. did. pol.*, 1685, 1 *c.* 8, *sec.* 1, *th.* 22). Polanus is surely right: *Propriissime solus Deus vivere dici potest*[EN23] (*op. cit., col.* 986). Thomas Aquinas had said the same (*Summa theol.* 1, *qu.* 18,

---

EN17 life

EN18 super-activity

EN19 act

EN20 pure act

EN21 purest. O Lord, whose being and life are not different things, since you are the self-same, utmost being and utmost life

EN22 The life of God is such an attribute by which God most perfectly acts in fulness through his intrinsic and imminent acts of knowing and willing, and shows himself always to be full of activity

EN23 Most properly speaking, only God can be said to 'live'

art. 3 c): *vita maxime proprie in Deo est*[EN24]. God really lives. And the definition of Polanus is also instructive (*op. cit., col.* 985): *Vita Dei est essentialis Dei proprietas seu ipsa divina essentia vivens, per quam Deus actuose vivere et se ipso omnia agere et vi agitandi movendique praeditus esse ac proinde aliis quoque vitam indere significatur*[EN25].

[264] But we must be more precise. When on the basis of His revelation we always understand God as event, as act and as life, we have not in any way identified Him with a sum or content of event, act, or life generally. We can never expect to know generally what event or act or life is, in order from that point to conclude and assert that God is He to whom this is all proper in an unimaginable and incomprehensible fulness and completeness. When we know God as event, act and life, we have to admit that generally and apart from Him we do not know what this is. So then, when we know God as event, act and life, He is definitely something different—to be distinguished from what we are accustomed to understand by these views and concepts. God's revelation is a particular event, not identical with the sum, nor identical with any of the content of other existing happenings either in nature or in human history. It is a definite happening within general happening: so definite that, while it takes part in this happening, it also contradicts it, and can only be seen and comprehended together with it in its contradiction, without the possibility of a synthesis, apart from the synthesis proclaimed and already fulfilled in itself. So, too, the action of God that takes place in revelation is a particular action, different from any other happening, even in contradiction to it. *Actus purus*[EN26] is not sufficient as a description of God. To it there must be added at least "*et singularis*[EN27]." The fact that in God the source, reconciliation and goal of all other happenings are together real and discernible, is another matter, which as such is only true in the separation of this action from every other happening. God is also the One who is event, act and life in His own way, as distinct from everything that He is not Himself, even though at the same time He is its source, reconciliation and goal. God is not merely differentiated from all other actuality as actuality generally and as such, or as its essence and principle, so that, while He is differentiated from all other actuality, He is still connected to it—and the idea is both immanent in the phenomenon and transcendent to it. He is, of course, differentiated from it in this way too. His work in the creation and preservation of the world can also up to a point—but only up to a point—be described in this way. But the particularity of His working and therefore His being as God is not exhausted by this dialectical transcendence which, however strictly it may be understood, must always be understood with equal strictness as immanence. On the contrary, without prejudice to and yet without

[EN24] life is utterly proper to God

[EN25] The life of God is the essential property of God, or his own divine living essence, through which God is shown to live in fulness of activity, and to do all things in himself, and to be possessed of the power to act and move, and therefore also to grant life to others

[EN26] pure act

[EN27] 'and singular'

dependence upon His relationship to what is event, act and life outside Him, God is in Himself free event, free act and free life.

We were careful not to understand the biblical description of God as "the living God" as a simile. But again, it is not a mere simile in Holy Scripture when God is described as wrath, mercy, patience, repentance, pleasure, pain, or the like, or as remembrance and forgetting, speech and silence, coming and going, presence and absence; and when God's action as attested in deeds is of such a kind as to make it necessary in describing it to apply such [265] categories. As we remember from the doctrine of the knowledge of God, not only some but all human standpoints and concepts, even those used by Scripture, are "anthropomorphisms." It is, then, quite arbitrary to describe these in a special way as *attributa metaphorica*[EN28] (Polanus, *op. cit., col.* 1231 f.), so that they have first to be divested of their full meaning to make the truth of God visible. In their fulness they are especially adapted to describe the special life and being of God, although quite useless to describe the highest ideal in Plato's teaching, or the *πρῶτον κινοῦν*[EN29] of Aristotle. What is described in these views and concepts is the saving contradiction of God found in His revelation, which is more than a mere difference that can be removed dialectically. It is the particularity of revelation amid all other happenings, the particularity of the divine reality as against all other. It is the undialectical transcendence, the free achievement, the free act, the free life of the divine being. And it is not something that can be juggled away by a new idealistic interpretation if at this point we are really to speak of the being of the triune God in His revelation, and not of any other being.

But we must take a further step forward. What is the particularity, what is therefore the specific freedom, of the event, act and life of God in His revelation? We are obviously speaking with a double meaning when in describing God we speak of event, act and life. Event, act and life could refer to an event in nature, or a transcendent happening, to be investigated after the fashion of what we know as natural events. Now it is true that we cannot simply neglect to seek the being of God along this line if we consider ourselves bound to speak of the God of revelation. Therefore, in the attempt to speak here more unequivocally, we must exercise some care. The differentiation of the divine happening from the non-divine does not coincide in Holy Scripture with the distinction between nature and grace, soul and body, inner and outer, visible and invisible. On the contrary, the event of revelation as described for us in Scripture has everywhere a natural, bodily, outward and visible component—from the creation (not only of heaven but also of earth), by way of the concrete existence of the people of Israel in Palestine, the birth of Jesus Christ, His physical miracles, His suffering and death under Pontius Pilate, His physical resurrection, right down to His coming again and the resurrection of the body. We cannot give a new meaning to this component without explaining away the specific sense of this revelation, and therefore the revelation itself, without giving over the field to another reflection foreign to the basis and message of the Church. And this state of affairs cannot be a matter of indifference for the description of the being of God. Whoever describes this as absolute "spirit,"

EN28 metaphorical attributes
EN29 first mover

and by this absoluteness understands an as it were chemical purity as against "nature," must ask himself whether at the very source of his consideration of the matter he has not fallen into a misunderstanding of the most fundamental character and with the gravest consequences, confusing the reality of God with the reality of the spiritual world—a reality to be distinguished no less from the reality of God than from that of the world of nature.

[266] *Si Deus est Spiritus, nihil ergo de eo terrenum aut carnale cogitandum. Deinde ex amalogia spiritualium essentiarum simpliciumque de natura eius iudicium aliquomodo fieri potest*[EN30] (Polanus, *op. cit., col.* 860). Here the confusion has already taken place, or is irresistibly about to do so.

According to Holy Scripture heaven—or supernatural, imperceptible, spiritual reality—is not in any way to be identified with God, even in its highest sublimations and pinnacles. It is fundamentally God's creation, as earth is. It is creative only in the quite narrow, relative and figurative sense in which we can speak of creation within a created world. If we are not tied by the superstitions of a spirit-nature system which confuses theology with metaphysics, and if we understand that what we know as spirit is in itself and as such no less a creation than what we call nature, then we are free to discern that the nature of God, when we describe it as spirit, cannot for that reason be described (like that of the angels) to the exclusion and denial of nature.

We must keep well in mind that Holy Scripture not only speaks of God's wrath, mercy, etc., but also—to the even greater confusion of all spiritualisers—very obviously and emphatically of His face, His eyes, His mouth, His ears, even His nose, His back, His arm, His hand, His right hand, His finger, His feet. Can it really be maintained that all that is meant *non theologice, sed oeconomice: secundum captum nostrum et ex imbecillae cognitionis nostrae sensu*[EN31] (Polanus, *op. cit., col.* 1231 f.)? Are the decisive and in truth very meaningful trinitarian descriptions of God as "Father" and "Son" also not to be understood *theologice*[EN32]? Is it not to be understood *theologice*[EN33] that we are to be called God's children? How can anyone think to explain Holy Scripture when he treats these concepts figuratively, setting over against them something "purely spiritual" as what is really intended? Does the understanding of all the connexions marked by these concepts not depend to some extent on this—that the reality of the natural component of the divine being indicated in them should in its place and in proper proportion be taken just as seriously as the undeniable spiritual reality? It is at this point that we can appreciate how the orthodox doctrine of God, as determined by that of the philosophy of pagan antiquity, paved the way for the later Enlightenment with all that that involved.

It is not, of course, that we have to confuse and confound Creator and creature on this side, ascribing to God our created nature. As God's thoughts are

---

[EN30] If God is Spirit, then nothing should be thought of him that is earthly or carnal. Henceforth, by the analogy of spiritual and simple essences, judgment about his nature can be undertaken in a different way

[EN31] not theologically, but economically: according to our power of comprehension, and out of the sense of our weak intellect

[EN32] theologically

[EN33] theologically

not our thoughts, as His Spirit is not our spirit, so obviously His eyes are not human eyes, nor His hands human hands. But it does mean that what is said naturally about God is not to be arbitrarily translated into something spiritual. The divine being must be allowed to transcend both spirit and nature, yet also to overlap and comprehend both, as attested in His revelation according to the testimony of Holy Scripture. We have to enquire into the event and act and life of God—in His transcendence as against the whole created world, in the order appropriate to the matter—but also in the direction of what we think we know as "natural event." Quite apart from the witness given to Him by Scripture, God could not be understood as the Lord of heaven and earth, as the Saviour of soul and body, as the God of all men, if we could only really under- [267] stand Him by having recourse to these spiritualising abstractions. It is to be noted that it depends on this demarcation from a spiritualising which makes itself systematically absolute, which so to speak obtrudes itself on the Godhead, whether we can seriously and properly speak of God's being as deriving from God's act. If God has no nature, if He is that chemically distilled absolute spirit, He does nothing, and in fact He can do nothing.

The statement of Polanus: *quo quid spiritualius est, eo magis activum est*[EN34] (*op. cit., col.* 860) can only be right in the sense that the "spirit" is the principle of every act, that an act is all the more an act if it is the act of a spirit. But it cannot possibly be right if the reference is to a spirit without nature.

Acts happen only in the unity of spirit and nature. If such a unity is to be denied in regard to God, then—and sooner or later this conclusion has to be drawn one way or another by all who deny it—there is no true, real history of His doings in any genuine sense of the term. There are no decisions and working of God. There is no revelation and reconciliation. There is also no creation and redemption as happening and decision. And, of course, there is no eternal witness of the Son through the Father, no eternal procession of the Holy Spirit from the Father and the Son, no inner life of God. These things are all images and likenesses. They are not strictly and properly true. Their true reality, the truth presumably meant by them, confronts them as the formless, motionless being of a spirit which is open to the serious suspicion that it is nothing but a hypostatisation of our own created spirit. We stand, therefore, at an important and crucial parting of the ways when we assert that we cannot adopt the so-called "purely spiritual" interpretation of the divine being.

Now that we are clear about this, we are free to state the opposite truth that the specific freedom of the event, act and life of God in His revelation and in eternity is, of course, the freedom of the spirit. It is not, therefore, accident or necessity. It does not have the orderliness or fatality of a natural event, although nature is not excluded. It is the freedom of a knowing and willing I, an I which itself distinguishes itself from what it is not, and what it is not from

[EN34] the more spiritual a thing is, the more active it is

itself, an I which controls nature. The particularity of the divine event, act and life is the particularity of the being of a person. We speak of an action, of a deed, when we speak of the being of God as a happening. Indeed the peak of all happening in revelation, according to Holy Scripture, consists in the fact that God speaks as an I, and is heard by the thou who is addressed. The whole content of the happening consists in the fact that the Word of God became flesh and that His Spirit is poured out upon all flesh. In this happening the world of nature and sense is undoubtedly subordinate. It is the servant. It is the component which is not important and necessary for its own sake, but only in its relationship and function.

[268] Therefore, we must be very careful how we state the so-called spirit-corporeality of revelation, however justified it may be against spiritualising. It is a false realism to balance against one another spirit and nature, inner and outer, soul and body, in such a way that their relationship is treated as symmetrical and reversible. In revelation as such the subject treated is undoubtedly spirit. It is for the sake of spirit and only for the sake of it that there is any mention of nature. The well-known phrase of F. C. Oetinger that the end of the way of God is corporeality reveals a historically understandable but essentially doubtful over-simplification, which is only acceptable if we make it read "also corporeality."

In accordance with the happening of revelation we reject a false spiritualising on the one hand and a false realism on the other, and have to understand God's being as "being in person." What is meant is certainly not personified being, but the being that in the reality of its person realises and unites in itself the fulness of all being. In its person means in its unity of spirit and nature. For in this unity, in the due superiority of its spirituality, in the due inferiority of its naturalness, it is not an "It," nor is it a "He" like a created person. It is genuinely (and therefore also for a genuine understanding) always an "I." It is the I who knows about Himself, who Himself wills, Himself disposes and distinguishes, and in this very act of His omnipotence is wholly self-sufficient.

In this formula we are simply interpreting the triune being of God as Father and Son in the unity of the Holy Spirit proceeding from both. This being as such and in its entirety is the being, the *essentia*[EN35], of the Godhead, and whatever else we may have to say about it will have to be understood as a definition of this being. It is in reference to this being that the famous definition of Jn. 4[24]: "God is Spirit," is to be understood; and if we can understand the usual definitions of orthodox dogmatics: *Deus est spiritus independens*[EN36], or *spiritus existens a se ipso*[EN37] or the like (cf. J. Wolleb, *Chr. Theol. comp.*, 1626, 1, 1, 1), as formed in relation to this being, we have no option but to agree with them.

However, before we explain more precisely the spiritual being of God in our second sub-section, we must make the further point that God's being is being which knows, wills and decides of itself, and is moved by itself. Inasmuch as God's being consists in God's act, it reveals itself as being which is self-moved.

[EN35] essence
[EN36] God is independent spirit
[EN37] spirit existing from his very self

It is self-moved in that it differentiates itself both from the abstractly observed being of nature and from the abstractly comprehended being of spirit. Natural being, as far as it can be observable to us as such in this or that material aggregate, is in itself unmoved. We understand it as motivated being only in a series of such aggregates. But in this series, as living nature, it is not observable by us. Comprehensible spiritual being as such is in itself unmoved. We comprehend it as the being of contents, laws and ideas. It has motion only in its relation from individual to individual. But in this relationship it is for us incomprehensible. As such, then, natural and spiritual being means unmoved being. The being of God as we know it from revelation is moved in itself and therefore motivating.

Hence the impossibility of the assertions of a naturalistic or spiritualistic Deism, to which those of a mystical Pantheism have often enough approximated, and in which God is described as the objectivity or the non-objectivity of a being at rest in itself. No matter how strong the emphasis on its other-worldliness the description of this being as supreme or true being does not of itself mean that God is actually described. It means rather that an abstract view of nature or an equally abstract concept of spirit is the measure of all things. The fact that anyone identifies the measure of all things with God does not in this case imply that he is really speaking of God. [269]

Now, of course, there does exist a concrete view of nature and a concrete concept of spirit, i.e., a knowledge of the moved being of nature and spirit as activated by a movement which comes upon both in their mutual relationship from outside, from a third quarter. We have, therefore, to emphasise the further point that God's being is not only moved being, but self-moved being. Nature and spirit, when they are moved, are not moved by themselves, nor is the one by the other, but both from outside. The only point of origin and beginning that is really known to us in this movement of theirs, the third quarter from which they are both moved, is the knowing, willing, appraising, working, and suffering human being. It is because we live that there is a living nature and a living spirit. The concrete view of nature, the concrete, concept of the spirit, is our work. In this work of ours there is achieved a characteristic harmony of both, in which spirit precedes and nature follows, in which spirit is the subject and nature the object, in which nature provides the material, spirit the form. Nevertheless, by the revelation of God, in which God meets us as the Lord of men, we are forbidden and restrained from confusing and comparing the being of God with this working of men. God is not the being moved in and by us which we know or think we know as our movement of nature and spirit. Whatever may be the truth about this movement of ours, if we do not want to be guilty of comparing ourselves with God (and this is precisely what is forbidden and prohibited in God's revelation) we cannot understand this motivated and motivating being of ours as a self-motivated and self-motivating being. It is not only to unmoved nature and unmoved spirit, but to our motivated and motivating being that God's being stands in contradistinction, as the one and only being that is self-motivated.

Hence the impossibility of all those assertions about the nature of God, behind which there is seen to a greater or less extent the moved and moving being of men; his moving of nature and spirit, his special classifying of both together as the measure of all things: "as Pheidias fashioned a Jupiter ... when he gave to his own likeness supreme grandeur, dominance, size and beauty" (J. Wichelhaus, *Die Lehre der h. Schrift*[3], 1892, 332). Again there is no help to be found even in the strongest and most emphatic underlining of this motivation. We can say "man" in the loudest tones. We can ground our statements about man on the most profound metaphysical premisses. But this does not mean that we say "God." By this very act we perhaps again and more emphatically say "man" in distinction and opposition to
[270] God. In fact with this exaggeration we really say "sinful man." Sinful man—according to God's revelation—is man exalting himself, and thinking that by his own efforts he can realise and assert the being of God. Kant speaks forcefully of God. But when he defines God as the necessary postulate of the limit and goal of pure reason, and the equally necessary presupposition of the law-giver and guarantor of practical reason, what else does he do (without adding substantially to his anthropology) but powerfully to speak again and strictly about man (about the depth of the nature of his rational capacity)? Again, Hegel speaks forcefully of God. But when he describes Him as the process of absolute spirit, which exists eternally in itself, eternally proceeds from itself, and existing in itself and outside itself is eternally the same, this is indeed a forceful and profound description of the movement of nature and spirit which proceeds from ourselves and returns to ourselves. But it is not a description of God, whose movement is infinitely more than our self-movement even when the latter is hypostatised, i.e., projected into eternity, and by whose movement this hypostatisation and projection is necessarily forbidden and prevented. Schleiermacher speaks forcefully of God when he describes Him as the source of the absolute dependence of our consciousness, and therefore not only the ground of all religion, but at the same time and as such the ulterior ground of our whole self-consciousness, the mysterious centre of our intelligent and active existence. Schleiermacher more plainly perhaps than any of his spiritual confreres knows how superfluous is a particular concept of God to describe the moving power of spirit and nature, and above all of man as such. In fact, Schleiermacher takes such little account of a force moving us from outside, and above all self-moved, that he purposed to give his system a final form in which it would be a clear presentation of the self-motivated Christian-religious self-consciousness as such: an undertaking which—in view of the instruction it would have given us we can only say—unfortunately his death prevented from further prosecution. A. Ritschl, too, spoke forcefully of God (as his contemporaries saw it). For in impressive distinction from all ancient and modern theoretical metaphysics, he aimed exclusively at the practical, ethico-religious significance of the idea of God. Nevertheless, it can be truly said that we come out of the frying-pan into the fire when we have to be told by him that God is the power "in and over the world" "which man reverences, because it maintains his spiritual self-feeling against the restraints that arise from nature" (*Theol. und Metaphysik*, 1881, 11). Religion is concerned with the solution of the paradox "in which man finds himself as a part of the world of nature and yet as a spiritual personality, which demands of him that he should be lord of the world" (*Rechtf. und Vers.*[4], Vol. 3, 1895, p. 189). Christianity as the highest religion mediates to man a sure appraisal both of himself as a definite spiritual personality, made for the attainment of the supreme good, and also of the world as a contained "whole," and in this way the Christian idea of God is "the ideal link" between our self-consciousness on the one hand and our world-view on the other (*loc. cit.*, p. 190 f.). It will be clear that the attainment of this self-consciousness, the formation of this world-view, and the constitution of the "ideal link" between both, is not so very different from what man ordinarily achieves in his relation to nature and spirit that it is seriously worth while to speak seriously of God at this final point. If God "in and over the world" is only a higher degree of the

movement which we know well enough as our own, it is hard to see to what extent beyond this He is necessarily self-motivated, and therefore to what extent there necessarily has to be a particular idea of God.

Just think what is implied if God's being is understood as self-moved being. It implies that the movement of nature and spirit, which occurs in His revelation and is effected by it, does not lead back to any self-movement of man. It cannot be enervated by the consideration whether the man to whom it is [271]
related may finally and in the last resort be alone in it with himself. God's revelation draws its authority and evidence from the fact that it is founded on itself apart from all human foundations. God's commandment, God's grace and God's promise have a unique force because they are without reference to human strength or weakness. God's work is triumphant because it is not bound to our work, but precedes and follows it in its own way, which may also be the way of our work. God's righteous demand on man, and His faithfulness in covenant with him, are irresistible and irrevocable because for their confirmation they need only God Himself and no corresponding relation of man. All this is compromised and even belied, not only if we think of God's being as unmoved, but even if we think of it as anything other than self-moved. The fact that God's being is event, the event of God's act, necessarily (if, when we speak of it, we turn our eyes solely on His revelation) means that it is His own conscious, willed and executed decision. It is His own decision, and therefore independent of the decisions by which we validate our existence. It is His conscious decision, and therefore not the mechanical outcome of a process the rationality of which, in so far as we can speak of such a thing, will have to be sought outside itself. It is His willed decision, and therefore not an event occurring through external causes or only in an external relationship. It is His executed decision—executed once for all in eternity, and anew in every second of our time, and therefore in such a way that it confronts what is not divine being, not as a mere possibility, but always as a self-contained, self-containing reality. Certainly God's being in this its self-motivation is spirit. But it is divine Spirit. Certainly it is nature. But it is divine nature. Certainly it is both in the unity and togetherness of a person. But this person is the divine person, whom we must see at once to be distinguished from other persons by the fact that He is self-motivated person. No other being exists absolutely in its act. No other being is absolutely its own, conscious, willed and executed decision. Only in the illusion of sin can man ascribe this being to himself or to the content of the world as a projection of himself. Whenever God confronts him in His revelation, this illusion is destroyed, and this being is denied to him and to the whole world. In the light of the judgment and grace which come to him in God's revelation, man must ascribe this being to God and to God alone. Now, if the being of a person is a being in act, and if, in the strict and proper sense, being in act can be ascribed only to God, then it follows that by the concept of the being of a person, in the strict and proper sense, we can understand only the being of God. Being in its own, conscious, willed and executed decision,

and therefore personal being, is the being of God in the nature of the Father and the Son and the Holy Spirit. Originally and properly there is no other beside or outside Him. Everything beside and outside Him is only secondary.
[272] It exists only on the basis of His gracious creation and providence, conditioned by His gracious reconciliation of the sinner, and with a view to His future redemption. And it can be known only by God's Word and revelation. We cannot speak of "personalising" in reference to God's being, but only in reference to ours. The real person is not man but God. It is not God who is a person by extension, but we. God exists in His act. God is His own decision. God lives from and by Himself.

God is. The first and basic general definition of this statement has now been given. Whatever else we may have to say must always correspond to this first definition. Anything contradictory will necessarily be false. Every statement of what God is, and explanation how God is, must always state and explain what and how He is in His act and decision. There is no moment in the ways of God which is over and above this act and decision. There is no evasion of this act and decision of the living quality of God. There is only the apprehension of this quality in virtue of the fact that we are apprehended by Him in His revelation. But this means that it is not merely this quality in its supreme form, *par excellence*[EN38], but basically and properly it is so in a unique sense: *propriissime solus Deus vivere dici potest*[EN39]. If we have life on the basis of His creation and in hope on the ground of the resurrection of Jesus Christ, our quality of life can never be confused with His, or compared or contrasted with it as commensurate. The validity of every further statement about God, as a statement about the living God, depends on the avoidance of this confusion, or this comparison and contrast, between His life and ours. But this will happen automatically if the positive content of the rule which has emerged is clear to us, if every further statement what and how God is is always linked with the fact that God is He who is not only to be found alone in His act, but is to be found alone in His act because alone in His act He is who He is. If we keep this clearly in mind, if all our thoughts are always grasped by God's action, because in it we have to do with God's being, we may be sure that they cannot err, and become either openly or secretly thoughts about ourselves.

2. THE BEING OF GOD AS THE ONE WHO LOVES

It would be dangerous and ambiguous if we tried to prolong the definition of the divine essence as His being in act generally, and therefore, the establishment of the form of this essence—His actuality or His life. Once said, the fact that God's being is absolutely His act will not be restated, but taken seriously in

---

EN38 above all others

EN39 most properly speaking, God alone can be said to live

the insight that this act of His, which is His being, is not actuality in general and as such, but that in His revelation and in eternity it is a specific act with a definite content. It is personal being in the originality and uniqueness that is applicable only to Him. It is the being of a person, distinguished not by its [273] formal completeness, but by its peculiar, distinctive act as such. We must now enquire further what is this act of His, the divine act which is the divine being, so that we have to conclude from it what is divine, i.e., what it is to be God, what makes God God, what God's "essence" is. Following the considerations of the first section this much is established, that God is what He is absolutely by Himself, and not by anything else that would confer divinity upon Him. Therefore the act that becomes visible to us in God's revelation, in which He is who He is, and from which we must conclude what and how He is, can only make manifest in fact that He is who He is. If it does not make this manifest, it has definitely not made manifest what is divine, what is the essence of God. But the act that is visible in God's revelation is not so constituted that we can conclude from it no more than the tautology "God is God." This very tautology as such we find clarified and explained in God's revelation. For it is nothing less than God's self-revelation. It is the revelation of the name by which He wills to be known and addressed by us, the name which does not add a second and extrinsic truth to the first intrinsic truth of His intimate, hidden essence, but which is the name and the criterion and the truth (i.e., the disclosure and description of the particularity) of His innermost hidden essence. This essence of God which is seen in His revealed name is His being and therefore His act as Father, Son and Holy Spirit. The fact that He makes Himself visible in this name is the solution of the tautology. From this name of His we have to conclude what and how He is in His act and therefore in His being: what is divine, what is the character of Him who is God, what makes God God, what therefore His "essence" is. The fact that we cannot go behind His livingness for a definition of His being means in fact that we cannot go behind this name of His, because in the very revelation of His name there occurs the act which is His being to all eternity. However (in order to define this revealed and eternal being) we can, we may and we must ask what this name has to say to us about the particular being of God in His act.

As it is revealed to us as the definition of that which confronts us in His revelation, this name definitely has this primary and decisive thing to say to us in all its constituents—that God is He who, without having to do so, seeks and creates fellowship between Himself and us. He does not have to do it, because in Himself without us, and therefore without this, He has that which He seeks and creates between Himself and us. It implies so to speak an overflow of His essence that He turns to us. We must certainly regard this overflow as itself matching His essence, belonging to His essence. But it is an overflow which is not demanded or presupposed by any necessity, constraint, or obligation, least of all from outside, from our side, or by any law by which God Himself is bound and obliged. On the contrary, in itself and as such it is again rooted in Himself

[274] alone. Yet important as it is, we will postpone this explanation and keep to the positive statement that God is He who in His revelation seeks and creates fellowship with us, and who (because His revelation is also His self-revelation) does this in Himself and in His eternal essence. Creation itself, i.e., the establishment and maintenance of a reality really distinct from Himself, of which man confronted by God may find himself the spiritual-natural unity, is already a seeking and creating of fellowship. This seeking and creating is heightened in the work of revelation itself, which is not so much a continuation of creation as its supersession, and is identical with the reconciliation of sinful man in the incarnation, death and resurrection of the Son of God. This seeking and creating finds its crown and final confirmation in the future destiny of mankind as redeemed in Jesus Christ, in his destiny for eternal salvation and life. What God does in all this, He is: and He is no other than He who does all this. But what is it that He does in virtue of His triune name, and therefore in this whole act of God seen in His revelation? If it is right and necessary to bring together the purpose and meaning of this act in order to understand it, and therefore to understand God, we must now say that He wills to be ours, and He wills that we should be His. He wills to belong to us and He wills that we should belong to Him. He does not will to be without us, and He does not will that we should be without Him. He wills certainly to be God and He does not will that we should be God. But He does not will to be God for Himself nor as God to be alone with Himself. He wills as God to be for us and with us who are not God. Inasmuch as He is Himself and affirms Himself, in distinction and opposition to everything that He is not. He places Himself in this relation to us. He does not will to be Himself in any other way than He is in this relationship. His life, that is, His life in Himself, which is originally and properly the one and only life, leans towards this unity with our life. The blessings of His Godhead are so great that they overflow as blessings to us, who are not God. This is God's conduct towards us in virtue of His revelation. There is no lack of contrariety in this conduct. It establishes and embraces the antithesis between the Creator and His creatures. It establishes and embraces necessarily, too, God's anger and struggle against sin, God's separation from sinners, God's judgment hanging over them and consummated on them. There is death and hell and eternal damnation in the scope of this relationship of His. But His attitude and action is always that He seeks and creates fellowship between Himself and us. For large stretches it may be for us doubtful, dark and incomprehensible. For large stretches it will seem to us like the very opposite of this relationship. It will reveal itself as such through judgment and grace, through dying and making alive, through veiling and unveiling. It will always be the light that shines out of darkness when it is revealed to us as such. We shall have to learn ever and again
[275] what it really means to say that God seeks and creates fellowship between Himself and us. In itself, first and last, it will always be this and no other relationship. God wills and does nothing different, but only one thing—this one thing. And this one thing that He wills and does is the blessing of God, that which

distinguishes His act as divine, and therefore also His person as divine. This one thing is therefore the divine, the *θεῖον*, the essence of God in the revelation of His name, which is the subject of our enquiry. That is to say, we shall find in God Himself, in His eternal being, nothing other than this one thing. As and before God seeks and creates fellowship with us, He wills and completes this fellowship in Himself. In Himself He does not will to exist for Himself, to exist alone. On the contrary, He is Father, Son and Holy Spirit and therefore alive in His unique being with and for and in another. The unbroken unity of His being, knowledge and will is at the same time an act of deliberation, decision and intercourse. He does not exist in solitude but in fellowship. Therefore what He seeks and creates between Himself and us is in fact nothing else but what He wills and completes and therefore is in Himself. It therefore follows that as He receives us through His Son into His fellowship with Himself, this is the one necessity, salvation, and blessing for us, than which there is no greater blessing—no greater, because God has nothing higher than this to give, namely Himself; because in giving us Himself, He has given us every blessing. We recognise and appreciate this blessing when we describe God's being more specifically in the statement that He is the One who loves. That He is God—the Godhead of God—consists in the fact that He loves, and it is the expression of His loving that He seeks and creates fellowship with us. It is correct and important in this connexion to say emphatically His *loving*, i.e., His act as that of the One who loves.

The tempting definition that "God is love" seems to have some possible support in 1 Jn. 4[8], [16]: *ὁ θεὸς ἀγάπη ἐστίν*[EN40]. But it is a forced exegesis to cite this sentence apart from its context and without the interpretation that is placed on it by its context, and to use it as the basis of a definition. We read in v. 9: "In this was manifested the love of God towards us, because that God sent his only-begotten Son into the world, that we might live through him" Again we are told in v. 10 (with a remarkable similarity of predication): "Herein is love, not that we loved God, but that he loved us, and sent his Son to be the propitiation for our sins." And finally in v. 15: In this we have knowledge and faith in the love that God has for us, that we confess "that Jesus is the Son of God." The love of God, or God as love, is therefore interpreted in 1 Jn. 4 as the completed act of divine loving in sending Jesus Christ. If we want to follow M. Dibelius in describing v. 8 and v. 16 as an "equation of God," we must at least go on to say that as such (as the equating of God with an abstract content of His action) it is at once resolved again, being replaced by a declaration of God's act as such. This finding is confirmed by a right understanding of Jn. 3[16]: "God so (Vulg.: *sic*) loved the world, that he gave his only-begotten Son, that whosoever believeth in him should not perish, but have everlasting life."

If, then, we now take the decisive turn, directing our attention to the definition and content of the divine being as it confronts us in God's revelation, and [276] if as our first step we take up the concept of love, it is not because we think that somehow we already know generally what love is as the content of an action which is genuinely good, and that on the basis of this knowledge we can equate

[EN40] God is love

God with this content. The proper procedure is very different. By the reality of the divine act we are summoned to give an account of the essence of this act, and thereby of the essence of God Himself. And led by Holy Scripture itself, we may and must venture to bring the concept of love (the peculiar and final meaning of which we admit we do not know in what is otherwise a tempting application) into the service of our present task, the declaration of the act and therefore of the being of God. We must recognise quite frankly the possibility that in this use "love" may take on a meaning which is fulfilled in a way which breaks up and reforms its meaning in the tempting application. Intentionally we have not begun with a definition of love, but with the resolve to let the act of God visible in His revelation speak for itself—God is in His act the One who seeks and creates fellowship with us. If we define this action of His as the love of God, and therefore God as the One who loves, and (in the proper sense) as love, our gaze must always be directed strictly on the fact, i.e., on God's act, and must not be allowed to wander under the influence of a concomitant and supposititious general idea of love. If we say with 1 Jn. 4 that God is love, the converse that love is God is forbidden until it is mediated and clarified from God's being and therefore from God's act what the love is which can and must be legitimately identified with God. The elucidation of this love is our present task.

1. God's loving is concerned with a seeking and creation of fellowship for its own sake. It is the fellowship of the One who loves with the loved himself, and therefore that which the One who loves has to impart to the loved and the loved has to receive from the One who loves. God is not, therefore, the *Good* first, and then the One who loves, because He does not keep this *Good* to Himself but communicates it to others. God is the One who loves, and as such the *Good* and the sum of all good things. God is good in the fact that He is Father, Son and Holy Spirit, that as such He is our Creator, Mediator and Redeemer, and that as such He takes us up into His fellowship, i.e., the fellowship which He has and is in Himself, and beyond which as such there is no greater *Good* which has still to be communicated to us through His fellowship with us. Loving us, God does not give us something, but Himself; and giving us Himself, giving us His only Son, He gives us everything. The love of God has only to be His love to be everything for us.

"He that spared not his own Son, but delivered him up for us all, how shall he not with him also freely give us all things" (Rom. 8^{32}). Even the knowledge and confession on which so
[277] much weight is laid, especially in the Johannine writings, are not concerned with the light and the life, or the way and the truth, which are given us through the Son of God. Nor are they concerned with the gifts, although these are named specifically enough and sufficiently highly praised. But they are concerned with the Giver of these gifts, and therefore with the Son of God as such. For this reason, in the Synoptics the kingdom of God is not an independent reality, but is absolutely bound up with the revealed Messiah, with His Word and His deeds, with faith in Him. This kingdom cannot in any sense be separated from its King. Therefore the answer of the man beloved of God, according to Psalm $73^{23f.}$, is as follows: "Nevertheless I am continually with thee: thou hast holden me by my right hand. Thou shalt

guide me with thy counsel and afterward receive me to glory. Whom have I in heaven but thee? And there is none upon earth that I desire beside thee. My flesh and my heart faileth: but God is the strength of my heart, and my portion for men. For lo, they that are far from thee shall perish: thou hast destroyed all them that go a-whoring from thee. But it is good for me to draw near to God: I have put my trust in the Lord God, that I may declare all thy works." Paul speaks similarly: "For I am persuaded, that neither death, nor life, nor angels, nor principalities, nor powers, nor things present, nor things to come, nor height, nor depth, nor any other creature shall be able to separate us from the love of God, which is in Christ Jesus our Lord" (Rom. 8[38f.]). Shed abroad in our hearts by the Holy Spirit, the love of God as such is the only ground of the hope that maketh not ashamed, and so worketh tribulation and patience (Rom. 5[4f.]). We overlook this if, like Thomas Aquinas, we tie the love of God to the definition: *A mare nihil aliud est, quam velle bonum alicui*[EN41] (*S. theol.* I, *qu.* 20, *art.* 2 *c*), and then have to continue: *Amans sic fit extra se in amatum translatus, inquantum vult amato bonum et operatur per suam providentiam sicut et sibi*[EN42] (*ib. ad.* 1). Correctly, i.e., biblically, this sentence as a description of the love of God must read: *Amans sic vult amato bonum et operatur per suam providentiam sicut et sibi, inquantum, fit extra se in amatum translatus*[EN43]. For it is in this *translatio*[EN44], or rather *communicatio*[EN45], as such that the Good is bestowed on the other when the matter concerns the ways of God, and not *vice versa.* Because and as God loves, His will is a *velle bonum alicui*[EN46], for it is only because God loves that there is any *aliquid*[EN47] or *aliquis*[EN48] at all, towards whom His will can be or is directed. As there is such another, and as God's will is in fact directed on it, as, therefore, He holds fellowship with it, as He loves it, He wills its good. Because and as He is who He is, because and as it is His will which is directed towards this other, and therefore because and as He loves, His will is good will. If we look for God's good behind His love in a *summum bonum*[EN49] that is separate from His love, in the act of determining this *summum bonum*[EN50] we can hardly avoid a relapse into the concept of a pure unmoved being, and will have to defend it in face of the divine witness of revelation. The polemic with which G. Thomasius defended this patristic and scholastic definition of the essence of God: that the definition "God is love" supposes "a positively good content of the self-communicating" and personal life and that otherwise it would be "a bad volatilisation of the self" (*Christi Person und Werk*[3], 1886, 1, 31), is fallacious in both its arguments. The "positively good content" of God's personal life does not exist behind or apart from His communication, but consists in the fact that it is the self-communicating life as such. And the fact that there is no volatilisation of the divine self is due to the fact that God is in Himself as Father, Son and Holy Spirit the self-communicating life. Along the same lines the definition of H. Lüdemann must also be corrected: "The love of God is His self-communication: but He is His innermost self as *summum bonum*[EN51]. Because He loves the world, He wills that it should have a share in His completeness" (*Dogm.*, 1926, II, 261). No, but His innermost self is His self-communication, and loving the world,

[EN41] To love is nothing other than to will good to another

[EN42] Thus the one who loves becomes external to himself and is transformed into the beloved, inasmuch as he wishes good to the beloved and acts in his concern as if for himself

[EN43] The one who loves thus wills good to the beloved and acts by his care as if to himself, inasmuch as he is taken out of himself and taken into the beloved

[EN44] 'being taken into'

[EN45] communication

[EN46] willing good to another

[EN47] 'anything else'

[EN48] 'anyone else'

[EN49] ultimate good

[EN50] ultimate good

[EN51] ultimate good

He gives it a share in His completeness. And when R. Seeberg (*Chr. Dogm.*, I, 1924, 254) demurs that we cannot possibly characterise the whole activity of God towards the world as
[278] love, but that this description applies only to the "specifically Christian experience of God," it must be remembered that according to Jn. 3^{16}, in virtue of the "specifically Christian experience of God" (which is surely not merely one with others, and cannot be restricted in its reference), God has in a very definite way loved the world, so that we cannot really approve Seeberg's substitution of the omnipotence of God for His love in this connexion.

2. God's loving is concerned with a seeking and creation of fellowship without any reference to an existing aptitude or worthiness on the part of the loved. God's love is not merely not conditioned by any reciprocity of love. It is also not conditioned by any worthiness to be loved on the part of the loved, by any existing capacity for union or fellowship on his side. If he has such a thing, it is itself the prior creation of the love of God. It is not and does not become the condition of that love. It is the object of the divine pleasure which follows the preceding love. The object of the love of God as such is another which in itself is not, or is not yet, worthy of this His pleasure. The love of God always throws a bridge over a crevasse. It is always the light shining out of darkness. In His revelation it seeks and creates fellowship where there is no fellowship and no capacity for it, where the situation concerns a being which is quite different from God, a creature and therefore alien, a sinful creature and therefore hostile. It is this alien and hostile other that God loves. Fellowship with him as such is the fellowship which He seeks and creates. This does not mean that we can call the love of God a blind love. But what He sees when He loves is that which is altogether distinct from Himself, and as such lost in itself, and without Him abandoned to death. That He throws a bridge out from Himself to this abandoned one, that He is light in the darkness, is the miracle of the almighty love of God.

For this reason the Son of Man is "sent to the lost sheep of the house of Israel" (Mt. 15^{24}), and "come to seek and to save that which was lost" (Lk. 19^{10}). "They that are whole need not the physician, but they that are sick. I came not to call the righteous but sinners to repentance" (Lk. 5^{31}). According to Lk. 15 it is the lost sheep, the lost coin and the lost son that are the object of the Messiah's work; while to the Pharisees Jn. 9^{41} must be quoted: "If ye were blind ye should have no sin: but now ye say, we see: therefore your sin remaineth." This is how it is with the love of God that is shed abroad in our hearts—God commends it towards us "in that, while we were yet sinners, Christ died for us" (Rom. 5^{8}). Little justice is done to this aspect by the definition of Polanus: *Amor Dei est essentialis proprietas seu essentia Dei, qua oblectans sese in eo quod approbat, ei bonum vult. Hoc enim est amare: oblectare se eo quod placet, eique bonum velle et praestare*[EN52] (*Synt. Theol. chr.*, 1609, *col.* 1094). We have already discussed the inadequacy of the formula *bonum velle*[EN53] which is openly borrowed from Thomas Aquinas. Equally in need of correction is the other assertion that the particular constituent and motiv-

[EN52] The love of God is the essential property or the essence of God, by which delighting himself in that which he approves, he wills good to it. This is love: to delight oneself in that which is pleasing, and to will and demonstrate good to it

[EN53] good will

ating element of the divine love is a preceding pleasure in the loved. How can God love us if it really depends on an *approbatio*[EN54] that is our due? The same holds of the definition of Quenstedt: *Amor Dei est, quo ipse cum obiecto amabili se suaviter unit*[EN55] (*Theol. did. pol.*, 1685, I, *c.* 8, *sect.* 1, *thes.* 30). It is as *amatus*[EN56] that the loved of God becomes *amabilis*[EN57]. He does not become *amatus*[EN58] because he is *amabilis*[EN59]. Those who make definitions like this are not thinking of the cross of Christ, of the sin of the chosen and elect people of Israel, of the justification of the ungodly (Rom. 4^{5}), and of faith in Him who quickens the dead and calls [279]
those things that are not as though they were (Rom. 4^{17}), but of a general concept of love, which in itself is highly controversial. In reality the basis of the love of God lies outside the man loved by Him and in God Himself. "I love them that love *me*" (Prov. 8^{17}). "He that loveth *me* shall be loved of my Father (Jn. 14^{21}, cf. 23)."For the Father himself loveth you because ye have loved *me*, and have believed that I came forth from God" (Jn. 16^{27}). And Jesus says of Himself: "Therefore doth my Father love me, because I lay down my life, that I might take it again" (Jn. 10^{17}). Therefore the idea of an *objectum amabile*[EN60] cannot be normative when we are concerned with the relationship of the love of the Father for the Son, with which "thou hast loved me before the foundation of the world" (Jn. 17^{23-26}), and above all of the love which is the event in the triune God Himself to all eternity. Certainly God is *objectum amabile*[EN61] to Himself. But He is not eternal love because He finds Himself worthy of love. He is worthy of love, and blessed in Himself, because in His life as Father, Son and Holy Spirit, He is eternal love.

3. God's loving is an end in itself. All the purposes that are willed and achieved in Him are contained and explained in this end, and therefore in this loving in itself and as such. For this loving is itself the blessing that it communicates to the loved, and it is its own ground as against the loved. Certainly in loving us God wills His own glory and our salvation. But He does not love us because He wills this. He wills it for the sake of His love. God loves in realising these purposes. But God loves because He loves; because this act is His being, His essence and His nature. He loves without and before realising these purposes. He loves to eternity. Even in realising them, He loves because He loves. And the point of this realisation is not grounded in itself, but in His love as such, in the love of the Father, the Son and the Holy Spirit. And as we believe in God, and return His love, it is not to be understood from itself, but only from His loving as such.

"Because the Lord loved you, and because he would keep the oath which he had sworn unto your fathers, hath the Lord brought you out with a mighty hand and redeemed you out of the house of bondmen, from the hand of Pharaoh, king of Egypt" (Deut. 7^{8}). "From afar" the Lord appeared to His people in the wilderness and said: "I have loved thee with an

---

EN54 attestation
EN55 The love of God is that by which he cheerfully unites with a lovely object
EN56 loved
EN57 lovely
EN58 loved
EN59 lovely
EN60 lovely object
EN61 lovely object

everlasting love: therefore with loving kindness have I drawn thee" (Jer. 31^{3}). "Not a messenger nor an angel, but he himself saved them: in his love and pity he redeemed them" (Is. 63^{9}). In this light it is difficult or impossible to agree with the doctrine of the love of God as developed by A. Ritschl. Ritschl's general definition of the love of God is to the effect that it is "the constant will which summons another spiritual, and therefore similar, person to the achievement of its own supreme destiny, and in such a way that the one who loves follows his own final purpose" (*Unterricht*, § 12: *Rechtf. u. Vers.*[4], Vol. 3, 1895, 263 f.). In accordance with this view the kingdom of God, i.e., the "moral association of the human race through the motive of universal love," "as the final purpose of the world and the *summum bonum*[EN62] for created souls," is the necessary correlative of the divine self-purpose. According to Ritschl, it is as God wills both—this final purpose of the world, and in and with it His own peculiar purpose—that He is love: and as He wills both constantly, that He is eternal love. "If therefore God loves eternally the community of His kingdom (Eph. 1^{4}, ^{6}), He also loves the individuals that are bound up in it in so far as He purposes to take them up into the kingdom of
[280] God. If these are presumed to be sinners, God loves even sinners in the light of their ideal destiny, for the realisation of which He chooses them" (*op. cit.*, p. 303). Ritschl was of the opinion that the way of thinking thus described is "not at all difficult." It has "its analogy in the self-reliance and the self-judgment which is ours in the exacted moments of our moral volition, in which we experience the power of our self-determination for good with the disregard of all the hindrances that are present in and outside us" (*op. cit.*, p. 269). We might say that this way of thinking is in fact only too easy, because its object is too similar to the well-known working of our human self-consciousness in its elevated moments. Riveted in this way to his own purpose and that of the loved, man himself may love (although he, too, may often love in other ways than this). But we are not to describe in this way the love which not only realises a purpose of its own and that of another, but also has its purpose in itself, the divine love. If God is riveted in this way, as though He were not God before and without His realising this double purpose, even this event cannot be understood as the divine realisation of divine purposes. He rather stands in a half-light which makes it possible to understand it without any previous mention of the name of God, as the action of human self-consciousness, so that what according to Ritschl is meant to be the analogy is the true reality intended. If we dissolve what God does in love into inflexibility of purpose, we shall find it hard to rediscover the divine essence of this action, that which distinguishes it as a holy and gracious, a laudable and sanctifying action. We shall find it hard to differentiate it from the pragmatism of all other possible events, and declare it as the sovereign action of this subject. If we keep this task in view we will postulate of the divine loving that in a reality which is unsearchable it has in itself not only its blessing and its ground, but also its purpose.

4. God's loving is necessary, for it is the being, the essence and the nature of God. But for this very reason it is also free from every necessity in respect of its object. God loves us, and loves the world, in accordance with His revelation. But He loves us and the world as He who would still be One who loves without us and without the world; as He, therefore, who needs no other to form the prior ground of His existence as the One who loves and as God. Certainly He is who He is wholly in His revelation, in His loving-kindness, and therefore in His love for us. He has not withheld Himself from us, but given us Himself. There-

---

[EN62] highest good

fore His love for us is His *eternal* love, and our being loved by Him is our being taken up into the fellowship of His eternal love, in which He is Himself for ever and ever. All the same it is a "being taken up." It is not part of God's being and action that as love it must have an object in another who is different from Him. God is sufficient in Himself as object and therefore as object of His love. He is no less the One who loves if He loves no object different from Himself. In the fact that He determines to love such another, His love overflows. But it is not exhausted in it nor confined or conditioned by it. On the contrary, this overflowing is conditioned by the fact that although it could satisfy itself, it has no satisfaction in this self-satisfaction, but as love for another it can and will be more than that which could satisfy itself. While God is everything for Himself, He wills again not to be everything merely for Himself, but for this other. While He could be everything only for Himself (and His life would not on that [281] account be pointless, motionless and unmotivated, nor would it be any less majestic or any less the life of love), He wills—and this is for us the ever-wonderful twofold dynamic of His love—to have it not only for Himself, but also for us. It does not belong to us to have being, and when we have it it does not belong to us in this being of ours to be the objects of the love of God. We might not be at all, and we might be without being the objects of His love. God does not owe us either our being, or in our being His love. If we are, and if we are objects of the love of God, that means that we on our side are debtors to God, without God owing anything to us. If He loves us, if He has preferred our being to our not-being, our lovableness to our unlovableness, that is for us the ever-wonderful dynamic of His love. It is grace and not nature. For it takes place in the whole intervention of the divine action and being. We cannot go back behind this event. We should not seek and think of God anywhere else than in this act, or as any other than as the One who is at this point and in this way. Just because we must hold fast to this, it must be clear that the fact that we can actually hold on to this rests on the overflowing of the divine love. The eternal correlation between God and us, as shown in God's revelation, is grounded in God alone, and not partly in God and partly in us. It means that we are tied to God, but not God to us. So in the highest and last degree (and this is true of what has been said about the goodness, the basis and the purpose of the divine love) the concept of God's love surpasses and oversteps the common concept of love that we ourselves can produce and presuppose. Here especially the common concept must be interpreted according to the particularity of this object. In this connexion especially, we must beware of an unreflecting inversion and therefore of a definition of the divine love on the basis of a common concept of love. If we are not careful at this point we shall inevitably rob God of His deity.

What we have to avoid can be grasped in a crude form from some of the famous aphorisms of Angelus Silesius:

I know that without me God cannot an instant be.
He needs must perish at once were death to come to me.

God owes as much to me as the debt that I must pay,
I give my help to Him, He keeps me in my way.

The blessedness of God, His life without desire,
He doth as much from me, as I from Him acquire.

What God eternally doth ever wish or long,
He looketh on in me, as in His likeness strong.

God truly nothing is, therefore something to be,
Choosing myself for Him, He hath to be in me,

[282] God loveth me alone, He holdeth me so dear,
That if I love Him not, He dieth of anxious fear.

Nought is but I and thou, and if we two are not,
Then God is no more God, and Heaven itself is nought.

The *Cherubinischer Wandersmann* in which these pious blasphemies are to be read (Rainer Maria Rilke has the same sort of thing on his conscience) is published with the imprimatur of a Roman Catholic bishop, and we may well ask whether this bishop was an imbecile or whether he had a secret understanding with the modern rogue. What is beyond question is that this is the impossible way of talking about the relations of God and man, and yet it is incontestably possible, and even necessary, in a train of logic in which—in view of the indispensable requirement of all human love, a beloved object different from the one who loves—we try to tie the love of God to the existence of an object of this kind, and to exhaust it in the relationship to this other. For example, we find in A. E. Biedermann the definition that the love of God is "the self-determination for the self-positing of the absolute world-process, and the immanence of the absolute God as its basis" (*Chr. Dog.*, 1896, 636). But in this sentence, if it is to be acceptable at all, we have to stress the word "self-determination" so strongly that there can be no simultaneous mention of an absolute God and an absolute world-process. The equation of both under an "absolute" necessarily involves an understanding either of God as the world-process or of the world-process as God. And either way the actuality of God's love as seen in His revelation is forsaken and forgotten in favour of a general concept of love (which is not incontestable in itself, like Hegel's). For the same reason the definition of E. Böhl (*Dogmatik*, 1887, 61) is perhaps suspect when it is applied to God. It is to the effect that love is "the inclination, the aspiration, the desire of one essence for another, the procession of a personality from itself, with the desire to go over to another or to take up the other into itself .... It cannot be alone, but it desires its like." Yet when, loving us, God does not withhold Himself, but gives Himself, this is love, His love, and therefore beyond all our concepts true love, just because it does not involve a transfer of God's person to us or of ours to God's. For when God loves us He is true to Himself. Indeed He is supremely true to Himself when He loves us. In this respect E. Böhl has very rightly seen and said: "Only relatively can the All-highest make creatures the objects of his love .... Otherwise we are forced to the position that because God is love, He must always have around Him the creatures to whom He has shown this love. We are thus forced to accept an eternal existence of the world side by side with God—which is a negation of the creaturely, of that which is only willed and created by God. It does not belong to the completeness of this divine love that it communicates itself to a mortal, created essence. It is quite another question if of His own free will God chooses to make the world the object of His love" (*op. cit.*, p. 62). On the other hand we have to ask whether certain passages in the work of H. Cremer already men-

tioned (e.g., pp. 19 f., 25) do not go beyond what is legitimate in the emphasis on the being of God in its relation to us. When Cremer writes (p. 25) "that we are eternally the object of God's love, or, more specifically, that it is the essence of God's manifestation to us eternally to will and be Himself, not for anyone, not in *abstracto*[EN63] for any possible object, but wholly and utterly for us, and for us alone," we have to observe that we certainly will never see clearly enough and can never say strongly enough that in loving us God has given and gives Himself to us, and gives Himself fully, since this loving is His own being and essence. How can we ever say too much here, when God has loved and loves and will love us in His own Son? On the other hand, we must not allow the completeness of His being in love for us to blind us to the fact that we do not speak of His, the divine love, if we try to deny it the movement that is proper to it in itself, even though it is not an attitude to us. The fact remains that God is He who gives everything life and breath and all things, and who there- [283]
fore does not need the service of men's hands to be who He is (Ac. 17^{25}), the Father of lights, from whom every good and perfect gift *ἄνωθέν ἐστιν καταβαῖνον*[EN64] (Jas. 1^{17}), the *μακάριος καὶ μόνος δυνάστης*[EN65] (1 Tim. 6^{15}), whose word is therefore to be understood as "the gospel of the glory of the blessed God" (1 Tim. 1^{11}). It is in the light of these texts that the older theology spoke with emphasis not only of the love but also (and to some extent much more so) of the blessedness (*beatitudo*) of God: *qua nullius indigus et omnium bonorum complementum se ipso fruitur et in se acquiescit*[EN66] (*Syn. pur. Theol.*, Leiden, 1642, *Disp.* 6, 43). *Nam ipse per se et sua natura semper ab omnibus malis liber, semper omnibus bonis affluens est, semper hanc suam felicitatem perfecte cognoscit, semper sibi αὐτάρκης et sufficiens, semper se ipso contentus est, nullo nostro bono eget* (Ps. $50^{7f.}$ was often quoted at this point) *eoque nihil extra se appetit*[EN67] (Polanus, *Synt. Theol. chr.*, 1609, *col.* 996). And Augustine had already adduced the differentiation that in so far as it has as its object something other than God, the divine loving is not to be described passively like ours as *frui*[EN68], but actively as *uti*[EN69], by which *ille usus, qui dicitur Dei, quo nobis utitur, non ad eius sed ad nostram utilitatem refertur, ad eius autem tantummodo bonitatem*[EN70] (*De doctr. chr.* 1, 31–32). We have to add only that this very blessedness of God itself is to be understood as the blessedness of His love. *Beatitudo in actu consistit*[EN71] (Polanus, *op. cit.*). But God's act is His loving. It is His blessedness in so far as it is His essence even apart from us. But He wills to have this same essence, not merely for Himself alone, but also, having it for Himself, in fellowship with us. He does not need us and yet He finds no enjoyment in His self-enjoyment. He does not suffer any want and yet He turns to us in the overflow of the perfection of His essence and therefore of His loving, and shares with us, in and with His love, its blessedness. This blessedness of the love of God is founded on the fact that He is Father, Son and Holy Spirit and as such loves us: as our Creator, Mediator and Redeemer, as love itself, the One who loves eternally. It is as well to make all this clear because it reminds us of the mystery of the divine love which transcends all thought, of its

---

EN63 in the abstract

EN64 comes down from above

EN65 one who alone is blessed and mighty

EN66 according to which, being in want of nothing he enjoys fulness of all goods in his very self, and rests in himself

EN67 For he himself, through himself and his nature, always free from all evils, is always abounding in every good; he always perfectly knows his own happiness; he is always content in his very self, always self-sufficient and satisfying to himself. He needs no good of ours ... and thus strives for nothing outside himself

EN68 enjoyment

EN69 employment

EN70 that employment (which is ascribed to God and according to which he employs us) is directed not to his utility but to ours, and only then to his goodness

EN71 blessedness consists in act

divinity which is different from all other love and eternally surpasses all other love, and of the fact that as we have to do with God's being in God's revelation, we have to do with the one true love to which all other love can only bear witness, not of itself, not by an indwelling power of witness, but only because our creaturely loving is confronted in God's revelation with this one true love, and that we, who love as creatures, are claimed in God's revelation as the objects of this divine, this one, true loving.

This, then, is the particular actuality of the being of God, the content of that which we have previously described in its form as God's acting and living. This is the nature of God disclosed in the revelation of His name. God loves. He loves as only He can love. His loving is itself the blessing which as the One who loves He communicates to the loved. His loving is itself the ground of His loving. His loving has its aim and its purpose in itself. His loving in the turning of the One who loves to a loved different from Himself is an overflowing of the loving with which God is blessed in Himself. This is how God loves. And genuinely and properly this is how only God loves. And this loving is God's being in time and eternity. "God is" means "God loves." Whatever else we may have to understand and acknowledge in relation to the divine being, it will always have to be a definition of this being of His as the One who loves. All our further insights about who and what God is must revolve round this mystery—the mys-
[284] tery of His loving. In a certain sense they can only be repetitions and amplifications of the one statement that "God loves." Even in the question of the mystery of God to be raised in the third sub-section, we cannot for a moment lose sight of the fact that we have to speak of God's loving, of the mystery of that loving, and of its difference and particularity as God's loving. The consideration of the mystery of His freedom cannot lead us in any other direction. It cannot lead us to another god who is not the One who loves. We must also focus on this same centre when we come to discuss the doctrine of the attributes of God, and we try to find a common explanation of the divine loving as such and the divine freedom as such. Everything will depend on our not losing the basic definition that we have now found, that God is the One who loves. What follows must all be in fact a development of this basic definition.

Before we proceed, however, alongside this basic definition of the divine being, we have to repeat and underline a definition on which we touched in a general way, as then required, in the first sub-section but which must now be made more express and exact than it was there. In the light of the definition of His being as a being in act we described God as a person. We must now show, from the closer definition of the divine act, that this was not an arbitrary postulate (from the concept of an act as distinct from that of a mere happening). The One who (in His own way) loves us, who (in His own way) seeks and creates fellowship between Himself and us, also informs us what a person is, in that (in His own way! not as if we knew of ourselves what it is, but in such a way that we now come to recognise it for the first time) He acts as a person. The definition of a person—that is, a knowing, willing, acting I—can have the meaning only of a confession of the person of God declared in His revelation, of the One who loves and who as such (loving in His own way) is *the* person. God is what man in himself never is, what man himself can only understand as he looks to Him, admitting that of himself he does not know what he means when he says it. Man is not a person, but he becomes one on the basis that he is loved by God and can love God in return. Man finds what a person is when he finds it in the person of God and his own being as a person in the gift of fellowship afforded him by God in person. He is then (in his own way as creature) a person wholly and exclusively in the fellowship of Him who (in His way as Creator) is it in Himself. Therefore to be a person means really and fundamentally to be what God is, to be, that is, the One who loves in God's way. Not we but God is I. For He alone is the One who loves without any other good, without any other ground, without any other aim, without any other blessedness than what He has in Himself, and who as He does so is Himself and as such can confront another, a Thou. Without being limited or bound by this other, He can be this other's limit and bound, the very ground of his being, [285] and in such a way that He can meet this other on his side as a Thou, and can be understood and addressed by this other as Thou. He is therefore capable of fellowship—capable of fellowship on the basis of His own power and act, capable of fellowship and capable of achieving fellowship in Himself and without the need of this other, but at the same time capable of fellowship and capable of achieving fellowship with reference to this other. This means really and fundamentally to be I. The being and therefore the loving of God has alone this character of being I.

For "such self-determination ... is the completest self-affirmation; such activity complete self-activity, complete life in which the subject, its own being and life, coincides with the determination and activity of others, so that life proceeds from life, life produces and creates life" (Cremer, *op. cit.*, p. 21).

For this reason the original and proper knowing and willing and doing that distinguishes an I from an It, and an act from a mere happening, is the property and the prerogative, not of the human, but of the divine being as the One who loves. It is only the divine loving that truly knows, truly wills and truly acts, because in it the knowing and willing subject, its object, and the seeking and creating of fellowship with it, are one, quite irrespective of the existence of another different from itself, and as such they are the ground of existence of this other and the definition of its relationship to this other. Thus to know, to will, and to act like God as the One who loves in Himself and in His relationship to His creation means (in confirmation of His I-ness) to be a person. God is a person in this way, and He alone is a person in this way. He is the real person and not merely the ideal. He is not the personified but the personifying person—the person on the basis of whose prior existence alone we can speak (hypothetically) of other persons different from Him. When He meets us in His revelation as the One who loves, He meets us as the One who is unique.

What do we know of our own selfhood before God has given us His name, and named us by our name? What do we know of what it means to say Thou before God has named us in this way, and in thanks and praise and prayer we for our part have called Him Thou? What do we know of what speaking means before God has spoken with us? or what hearing means, before we have heard God? or what acting means, before God in Jesus Christ has been manifested as the One who acts for us? or what suffering means, before God, and He again in Jesus Christ, is known as the One Who suffers for us? or what might and lordship are, without the recognition of His might and His lordship in His Word? We are thinking and speaking only in feeble images and echoes of the person of God when we describe man as a person, as an individual. Consciously or unconsciously it is thanks to the love of God in His revelation that we can describe man in this way, and consciously or unconsciously it is not the being of man, but the being of God as the One who loves, i.e., the reflection of God in men unfolded by His Word, which there confronts us as reality.

[286] The One, the person, whom we really know as a human person, is the person of Jesus Christ, and even this is in fact the person of God the Son, in which humanity, without being or having itself a person, is caught up into fellowship with the personality of God. This one man is therefore the being of God making itself known to us as the One who loves.

It is not the case then—and this is the decisive result of the whole consideration—that we have to blush when we adopt the language of Scripture and talk of God, not in abstract terms as the "highest good" or the "absolute" or "omnipotence" or "omniscience" and the like, but personally as One who is all these things as the knowing, willing and acting I; when in fact we take the metaphor "God is love" and as in 1 John 4 we understand it personally: He is the One who loves. This personal way in which Scripture speaks is not in any way childish or naive or anthropomorphic (or at least it is no more so than all the terms and concepts we use in the service of faith and proclamation on the basis of and in obedience to God's revelation). The personal way in which Holy Scripture speaks corresponds absolutely and exclusively to the fact that God is not something, but someone, the One from whom man merely holds in fee the possibility of being one himself. We have to blush (because then we are talking with false childlikeness, immaturity and impropriety) only if words again slip out in which we do not reckon with the personality of God or do not take it seriously.

But again, it is not the case that this manner of speech stands under the proviso that it is allowed or even commanded us as an element of our anthropomorphic manner of expression, but that we have to remember that beyond this manner of expression of ours God is not really one person but one thing, e.g., the impersonal absolute, the highest good, the world-spirit or world-cause or the like. The fact that in knowing God we cannot comprehend Him because we know Him only as men and not as He knows Himself, has nothing whatever to do with a proviso of this kind (according to which the esoteric claims finally to know Him as He knows Himself). If we know God only in a human way, even in this limit we know Him on the basis of His revelation as the One He is. He is the One who loves, surpassing all our concepts and ideas of love, but still the One who truly loves, and therefore One—person. As One, as person, He surpasses all our concepts and ideas of person, but still He reveals what one, a person, really and truly is. We are therefore allowed and commanded within the limits of what is human to speak the truth when we speak of Him as the One, as personal; the truth, beyond which there is no greater, because in the mystery of His ways which we cannot unravel, God is none other than the One as whom He has made Himself manifest and comprehensible to us in His revelation.

Finally it is not the case that this application of the personal manner of [287] speech to God means the recognition of a paradox in the nature of God that we cannot unravel, because on the one hand we must necessarily understand God as the impersonal absolute, but at the same time (and in unavoidable logical contradiction to this) we must also understand Him as person. In this connexion we must notice that the paradox of the nature of God that we cannot unravel is not in any sense that of a logical tension between two concepts which we can perceive and control as such, as if we knew what "absolute" is on the one hand and "personality" on the other, as if the difficulty consisted only in bringing both together, and as if God's reality were just the overcoming of this difficulty. No: the (to us) inexplicable paradox of the nature of God is the fact that He is primarily and properly all that our terms seeks to mean, and yet of themselves cannot mean, that He has revealed Himself to us in His original and proper being, thus remaining incomprehensible to us even in His revelation, yet allowing and commanding us to put our concepts into the service of knowledge of Him, blessing our obedience, being truly known by us within our limits. It is the paradox of the combination of His grace and our lost condition, not the paradox of the combination of two for us logically irreconcilable concepts. Recognising the true, divine paradox, we shall not see together or put together God's personal-ness and God's absolute-ness in the way that we are often forced to do, with and without logical contradictions, when we describe created realities, but we shall hold to the fact that God has revealed Himself to us as He who He is, that is, as the One who loves and therefore as One—person. There is, then, nothing that we can say to this (whether logically compatible or incompatible). Fixing all our attention on its unique particularity we can say only the one thing with all that it involves—that He is the One. We can say it only in such a way that it corresponds to what He has said to us already in His Word, which will do justice, of course, to what may be truly signified by the "absolute." But we cannot say it as if the truth that He is the One seems to be dialectically delimited and completed by the fact that He is "absolute," as if in order to describe God we must dilate on His personality and His absoluteness in a kind of vacuum, as if God is truly and properly God only in the dialectical conquest of this antithesis. He is God (within the limitations of our human knowledge) as the One who (in His own way) loves, and therefore as the One, and He is all that He is inasmuch as He is this One: not subsequently in His being as the one thing, not in a simultaneity as the one person and the one thing, nor yet in a synthesis beyond this antithesis, but simply inasmuch as (in His own way) He is the One.

From this standpoint we can survey the discussion of the personality of God which has played such a prominent part in the theology of the 19th century and to some extent of the 20th as well.

[288] Its origin is to be found deep down in the doctrine of God of the time of orthodoxy, and even of the Middle Ages. We have already mentioned the common practice in this doctrine of placing the doctrine of the Trinity after the development of a concept of the nature and attributes of God in general. This arrangement led to the temptation of speaking of God apart from His revelation and therefore apart from His being as the One who loves, on the basis of a free appraisal of what can be called divine. The result was an involuntary movement away from the school of Scripture into that of heathen antiquity. The nature of God was defined as a neuter furnished with every conceivable superlative, as the *ens perfectissimum*[EN72] and the *summum bonum*[EN73], which as such, as the *actus purus*[EN74] of the spirit, is also the *primum movens*[EN75]. And it was no easy matter to bring together the concept of the existence of this *Deus unus*[EN76] and that of the biblical *Deus triunus*[EN77]. The presupposition that this God was one person, not one thing, but all things as the One, was clear and effective in the Reformers and tacitly self-evident in their successors, but it had no real basis and no prominent place in all this older doctrine of God, either from the concept of nature and attributes already mentioned, or even from the doctrine of the Trinity. Indeed, the doctrine of the Trinity only gave rise to further obscurity. For the more the term *persona*[EN78] (*modus subsistentiae*, manner of being) came to be equated with a "person" (in our meaning of the word) and therefore (in complete contradiction to the intentions of the trinitarian doctrine of the early Church) the more the idea gained currency of three personalities in God, the less could the being of God be understood as the One who loves, and therefore as the One, in terms of the one life of the threefold God in His revelation and in Himself. In this situation theology was assailed by the inrush of the so-called Enlightenment, the product of the rising anthropology of the new age, with its reduction of the idea of God to the eternal truth of the theoretical and practical aesthetic ideas of human reason, or in the last resort to this parental reason as such (thought of as hypostatised). It was fairly easy to re-recognise this image supposedly identical with the Godhead in the orthodox doctrine of the nature and attributes of God, or to interpret this older doctrine of God according to the measure of this image. For essentially constructed according to the directions of heathen antiquity, what else was it but a hypostatisation of the world of ideas, or of the idea of all ideas, which may just as well and perhaps better be named reason rather than God.

This equation or inversion is, of course, the work of the Idealism of the turn of the 18th and 19th centuries, which appeared to supersede but in reality crowned and completed the Enlightenment. It is from the theological school which made this stimulus most consistently its own, viz., that centred on Hegel, that there came the first conscious and express attack

---

[EN72] most perfect being
[EN73] highest good
[EN74] pure act
[EN75] first mover
[EN76] one God
[EN77] triune God
[EN78] person

against the idea of the personality of God, which the older theology of the Enlightenment, not yet conscious of the extent of its method of reduction, or not yet intellectually and morally mature, had on the whole failed to do, in spite of the constant accompaniment of Spinozism. If God is in reality only the highest idea, or the origin of all theoretical and practical aesthetic ideas, or "the spirit," if we know Him as we know this spirit, and in it the source of all rationality, and in this the absolute or the highest good of men, it is very hard to see why and how He can and may be One, why and how He can and may be person. What a person is, was now thought to be known from the knowledge of self as person. Person is the individual manifestation of the spirit, its individualisation, which as such is limited, but contingently necessary. How, then, could God be a person? The esoteric or explicit meaning of this question was: How could God be limited? How does the infinity of the spirit tally with the finiteness that is prescribed for it with the concept of personality? *Omnis determinatio est negatio*[EN79] was echoed in every kind of tone from Spinoza. Personality means a *determinatio*[EN80], and therefore a *negatio*[EN81] incompatible with the absolute. Thus the absolute or God cannot be personality. "As persons we know and feel ourselves only in our difference from other similar persons outside ourselves, from whom we differentiate ourselves, that is, as finite; in this realm of finitude, and fashioned for it, the concept of personality [289] logically seems to lose every meaning apart from this, and a nature which has no other like itself outside itself seems unable to be a person. To speak of a personal God or a divine personality seems from this point of view to be a combination of ideas, one of which in the last resort excludes and supplants the other. Personality is a self-contained self-hood over against another which it differentiates from itself; absoluteness is the uncontained and unlimited which excludes from itself nothing but the exclusiveness inherent in the concept of personality. Absolute personality is a *non ens*[EN82] which we cannot even conceive" (D. F. Strauss, *Die christliche Glaubenslehre*, Vol. 1, 1840, 504 f.). "The concept of personality cannot be taken up by a finite spirit in such a way as to be abstracted thereby from the moment of finitude. Personality is rather the specific form of subsistence of the human spirit as finite, on which the sensuous basis of subsistence constructs both for the form and for the content of personality a constitutive moment ... The assertion of the personality of God is thus only the shibboleth of a still imaginative Theism. This notion is, however, to be lifted by strict thought into the pure concept of the absolute spirit that is alone adequate for God, which presupposes no finite existence in God Himself, but which is in His being in Himself the absolute pre-supposition for the totality of all finite existence" (A. E. Biedermann, *Chr. Dog.*, 1869, 639). That reflection on the nature of "personality," and the conditions which are indispensable for its rise and continuance, make it impossible to speak of a" personality of God," is still asserted with great force by H. Lüdemann (*Chr. Dog.*, Vol. 2, 1926, 168).

It is to be observed that this critique was able to invest itself with the form of an almost Calvinistic and puritanical concern for the purity and pre-eminence of the thought of God over against its confusion with a (or rather with *the*) fundamental self-determination of man. Nor is it possible to doubt the subjective sincerity in this respect of the battle waged by the Hegelians. Not without the collusion of the older orthodoxy, there had been an emergence and penetration of confusion between the idea of God and the idea of spirit generally. And this had become so incontestably self-evident through the classical Idealism of the philosophico-theological thinkers of the 19th century that even the acutest exponents of Christian doctrine—even a theologian like Biedermann, who undoubtedly in his day strove

---

EN79 every determination is a negation
EN80 determination
EN81 negation
EN82 non-being

honestly and with great and penetrating scholarship to evolve a Church tradition that would without doubt build up and not destroy the Church in the modern situation—were not capable of the insight that by the glorification of an absolute spirit they served a God who, measured by the biblical revelation, was alien, and who indeed, measured by the same standard, was not divine but created. Since they did not know any other god than this (at least as theologians), it necessarily remained hidden from them that it was extremely logical to deny this god personality, and that this logical consistency merely proved they had completely lost sight of the object of an Evangelical theology. The absolute spirit which had become the object of their theology was in fact not person and could not be thought of as such. In this they were quite right in their defence against all their less consistent opponents. As a result of the prejudice arising from this confusion and therefore arising from the true nature of their whole approach, they could not, of course, see the esoteric or implicit meaning of the question—How could God be person? Thus they were unable to assert the decisive reason why their God could not be a person. For indeed, why does the absoluteness and infinity which is predicated of this God necessarily cause the very idea of personality to appear as the essence of finitude and therefore exclude it? The explanation—and surely there is a powerful positive pathos hidden behind what seem to be the purely negative assertions of these theologians—is that in their thinking the place where they should speak earnestly, genuinely and realistically of personality was already occupied, and in fact solemnly and conclusively
[290] occupied, so that the claim could not be allowed a second time. If personality was self-evidently denied to what was conceived and described as "God," it was no less self-evidently attributed to the subject of this conception and description, namely, to the conceiving, describing man. What did it matter that in distinction to its "God" this subject was referred to the sphere and manner of finitude, if at the same time it was decked with this predicate, if it was understood as the subject which is always capable of itself of conceiving and describing the absolute spirit, the supreme good, infinite being? The subject which has the merit and the power of being subject of this predicate—does it not fulfil the concept of personal being, the nature of the true I? Is it not the true knowing and willing I? What difference does finitude make to it, if it stands in this relation to the infinite, with such creativeness, direction and control, if the infinite as such is obviously the predicate of the finite subject? The infinite, the God who is subject to his control in this way, obviously cannot be in any way unsettling, menacing or critical, in spite of the subject's finitude. Behind and above His whole infinity there towers all the time the comforting certainty that the finite being itself, as subject of this infinite predicate, is undoubtedly the person at work, supreme in thought and definition over this infinite. This work must obviously abide by only one rule if the finite subject is to remain secure. Under no circumstances may the predicate be conceived or described as the subject (in the same, or perhaps in a basically superior sense, as compared with the human subject), and therefore under no circumstances may God be conceived or described as person. This would be an admission that God's infinity is His own and not that of man. It would involve a denial and abandonment of the presupposition that God is the content of the human concept of reason. It would mean a serious calling in question of that which is based solely on human self-consciousness, and therefore of the final reality of human personality. Man would be finally stripped of his own creative role in relation to the visible and the invisible, and therefore to all things. This was what must never under any circumstances be allowed to happen according to the most sacred convictions of the generations cradled in the Enlightenment, Romanticism and classical Idealism. The predication of God as personality was necessarily for them the absurdity of which no philosopher or theologian must under any circumstances be guilty. For this predication meant an end of the predicating subject. This predication could not meaningfully be understood as a predication at all, but only as the recognition of something which precedes all human predi-

cation, as the end of the control under which the neutral infinite so comfortably contemplates and governs itself as man's own infinite, realising itself in the act of his finite personal being. This was the end of all things, which was not allowed to come to pass. The whole advance of the new age, embraced in the equation of God and the idea of reason, was a defence against the destroying of human self-consciousness through the reality or even the mere possibility of a divine self-consciousness materially different. In this destruction there could be discerned only an inrush of primitive barbarity into the preserve of the newly discovered and already self-evident "religion within the limits of pure reason." On these grounds, therefore, the Hegelian theologians necessarily had to deny firmly and strenuously the personality of God. In this position they were very experienced and from their own standpoint rightly vigilant apologists of the neo-Christian Church which since 1700 had begun more consciously and decisively to come together and consolidate. They knew the true enemy and the danger involved. Only from this point of view is their opposition to the personality of God really intelligible. It was irresistibly powerful because it moved in purely analytical statements, because it merely repeated the so-to-speak commonly held presupposition that man is the person who, thinking the idea of his reason, has the power to think God, and that for this reason, and in confirmation of it, God is to be thought of as absolute and infinite, but cannot under any circumstances be thought of as person and therefore as the superior rival of man. On the premisses of the Enlightenment, Romanticism and Ideal- [291]
ism this opposition to the personality of God cannot be avoided, because it is absolutely vital. If we begin with this equation, willingly and wittingly or not we have already contested the fact that God is a person, and we cannot later recant. For with this equation we have attributed true and proper personality to man as the subject of the idea of reason, thus taking the step which necessarily brings us into insoluble contradiction with belief in the personal God.

The weakness in all the modern vindications of this belief is that they have taken up their position on the same premisses as their opponents, namely, on the equation which their opponents must necessarily hold. Naturally, there has been no lack of answers to the suggestions of the Hegelian theologians. Ought not personality to be ascribed to God for the very reason that man describes the truest and the best of his own existence with this concept, and therefore has to complete with it his final, supreme and indeed decisive predications of the absolute spirit? H. Siebeck has argued it in this way. The inner development of man comes up against a climax which consists in his knowing himself as a unit over against the world—on the one side as part, on the other side as the centre of the world. Understanding himself in this latter sense, he can regard the world as the means of his self-preservation and self-participation. Indeed, personality sees its moral uniqueness as founded on the basis of the world-whole; the world must be planned for the emergence of personality. And therefore the idea of God must be constructed on the analogy of personality (*Lehrb. der Rel. Phil.*, 1893, 168 f.). "The essence of the personal is projected from experience into the transcendent" (*op. cit.*, p. 363). Siebeck indeed conceded that all the marks of empirical personality, when directed to an absolute essence, incur the loss of their discursive conceivability. But he thought he could set his mind at rest about this by the consideration that without the true personality of God all religious history would have to be explained away as an illusion, and by the specially attractive assertion that all powerful spiritual movements of history have always been born out of the rich depths of the life of particular, spiritually strong personalities (*op. cit.*, pp. 364 f.). H. Lotze argued similarly: "No other form of being than that of personality can satisfy (or even be considered for the purpose) the longing of the soul to grasp as reality the highest which it is given to sense." So firmly is it convinced that living, self-possessing and self-enjoying individuality is the imperative precondition and the only possible source of every good and all good things, so much is it filled by secret disdain of all apparently lifeless existence, that we always find embryo religion in its myth-forming beginnings busy transfiguring natural reality into spiritual: it has never on the other hand felt any need to bring spiritual life back to blind reality as a more solid base" (*Mikrokosmos*[3], Vol. 3, 1880, 563 f.). In the same way R. Rothe has explained that it is "a narrow-minded delusion to think that we must regard the blessed God as so superior that He must be denied everything that constitutes the peculiar excellences of human nature" (*Ethik*, Vol. 1, 1867, 122). Again, A. Ritschl could say that the recognition of the personality of God discloses" the value which religion asserts for the human spiritual life" (*Rechtf. u. Vers.*[1], Vol. 3, 1874, 173). It is clear from all these considerations that they have a common hypothesis with those who deny the personality of God, namely, that God is to be understood as the content of the highest human values. But on this common ground they cannot hold their own against the criticism levelled from the other side.

For one thing, they are *technically* impossible. If it is not to be denied or superseded, infinity of spirit or good or being, so far as these are thought of as the content of a human idea, does not tolerate any other finitude than that which is proper to the subject of this idea as such, but which must therefore be thought of as necessarily superseded in the predicate of this subject and therefore denied. If the absolute is the absolute of human idea, the concept
[292] of an "absolute personality" has to be described with Strauss (*op. cit.*, p. 505) as nonsense, or with Biedermann (*op. cit.*, p. 643) as a *contradictio in adiecto*[EN83]. For it constantly gives to the predicate the creative finitude which as such can only belong to the subject. The subject will then be defended only too self-evidently against the threatened competition with an eagerness for the purity of its predicate, and it will be all too easily demonstrated that it ill becomes the mark of the subject to be elevated to the predicate. We cannot very well proceed, as Lotze wanted, by first reducing the antithesis of Ego and non-Ego, which constitutes human personality, to the antithesis of the spirit to its manifestations (even though these arise at the instigation of an external world of reality), and then turning round and postulating an unlimited spirit which, being "itself everything that is," does not need any such external cause to be in perpetual activity and therefore to be personality. "When we describe the inner life of the personal God, the current of His thoughts, His feelings, His will, as one which is eternal and without beginning, never at rest, and never excited to movement from any stationary position, we demand of our power of imagination no greater task than is sought of it by any materialistic or pantheistic viewpoint" (Lotze, *op. cit.*, pp. 569–80: *Grundzüge der Rel. Phil.*[3], 1894, 39–43). That materialistic and pantheistic views claim the power of the imagination in all sorts of ways is cold comfort in view of the dilemma in which we find ourselves in regard to this vindication of the personal God. For it is not clear whether the absolute is absorbed by personality, or personality by the absolute, or perhaps each by the other. The reader is left in a complete fog with regard to the really vital question whether, in spite of assurances to the contrary, he is not confronted here by a materialistic or pantheistic viewpoint. It was a bad omen for the prospects of modern Protestant theology that (from Rothe to Ritschl and in part even to the present day) it found this Lotzian vindication of the personality of God particularly masterly and helpful.

Secondly, this vindication, and the similar attempts of his associates, had the fatal peculiarity that they exposed the distinctively postulatory character of the whole modern doctrine of God in what is undoubtedly a very compromising way. As L. Feuerbach wrote, long before Lotze and Siebeck: "Theology is anthropology, i.e., in the object of religion which we call in Greek *Theos*, in English God, there expresses itself nothing other than the nature of man; or, the God of mankind is nothing other than the deified nature of man" (*Das Wesen der Religion*, 1848, Lecture 3). "Christianity reproached heathenism for idolatry, Protestantism

---

[EN83] contradiction in terms

reproached Catholicism, or early Christianity, for idolatry, and Rationalism now reproaches Protestantism, at least the older orthodox Protestantism, for idolatry, because it worships a man as God, and therefore an image of God—for that is what man is—in place of the original, in place of real being. But I go further and say: Rationalism itself, indeed, every religion and every cult which sets up a God, i.e., an unreal being, a being different and separated from real nature, the real being of man, and which makes it an object of worship, is the worship of images and consequently idolatry ... For God did not create man in His image, as the Bible has it, but, as I have shown in *Das Wesen des Christentums*, man created God after his image. And even the rationalist, the so-called believer in thought and reason, creates the god whom he worships in his image; the living archetype, the original of the rationalist god is the rationalist man. Every god is a being of the imagination, an image and in fact an image of man, but an image which man places over against himself, and imagines as an independent being" (*op. cit.*, Lect. 20). "Because for the Christian the spirit, the feeling, thinking, willing being, is his highest being and his ideal, he makes it also his first being, i.e., he changes his spirit into an objective, existing outside him, and different from him .... Is the eternal spirit not just the spirit of man desiring to be eternal, complete? ... Does not man wish to be free from the confines of the flesh? does he not wish to be omniscient, omnipo- [293]
tent, omnipresent? Therefore is not this god, is not this spirit, the realised desire of man to be eternal spirit? Have we not, therefore, objectivised even in this god the nature of man? ... Is, therefore, their god, their eternal spirit, anything other than the image and pattern of what they themselves want to become, the original and copy of their own nature as it is to be unfolded in the future? ... The eternal spirit is nothing but the generic concept of the spirit which is symbolised as an independent being by the power of imagination at the command of human wishes and human impulses towards happiness" (*op. cit.*, Lect. 28). We can see how here the mystery of the modern doctrine of God—that the being of God is the predicate of the human subject—was long ago carelessly exploded by a philosopher who derived from the school of Idealism, but was no longer interested in the Church. We may well wonder that his objection did not make more impression on those who denied the personality of God in so far as he also and particularly attacked their positive assertions. But we must wonder even more how its defenders, with their references to the longing of the human heart, the infinite value of human personality, the import of the history of religion, the meaning of personality in spiritual and world history, with their quite open and express projection of human self-consciousness into the transcendent, could expose themselves so openly to this objection of Feuerbach without apparently taking any account of its existence. It was of little value to the cause advanced that the character of the newer theology as a higher anthropology could be silenced and suppressed, as was thought possible by an ecclesiastically-minded modern like Biedermann. But it was unparalleled naivete that it should be shouted abroad as was done, not by the deciders, but by the protagonists of the personality of God. The only possible result was to make more suspect the statement which they wanted to advocate, and indeed, to compromise with this addition the whole common doctrine of God as eternal spirit.

But let us suppose that their attempt had not been vitiated by its technical impracticability. Let us suppose the real possibility of distinguishing it from a self-admission of the illusion of the modern doctrine of God. Let us suppose that it had genuinely proved what it set out to prove, namely, that the eternal spirit, rightly equated with God, is as such also person, therefore itself subject, the knowing and willing I in real difference from the human I. Let us suppose that we are really prepared to venture this predication of the supreme being (the consistency with which even Lotze was prepared to do it is not beyond question). Granted these things, how very disloyal we are to the whole intention of the modern doctrine of God! What perspectives we open up in relation to the human subject as the ostensible measure of all things when we do not oppose to it the neutral absolute which can be leisurely surveyed

and mastered, but a divine I endowed with this absoluteness! If we concede the personality of God, we are flagrantly guilty of the absurdity which means the invasion of the sanctity of the unity of life which binds God and the world together in man, thus involving the end of the modern self-consciousness with which it was hoped to unite the Christian faith, and indeed to represent and commend the Christian faith as its deepest wisdom. Only the dullness and the stupidity of the thought-processes of these protagonists of the personality of God could hinder the onset of this end of all things. If anyone had suddenly taken seriously the matter with which at bottom Lotze and Siebeck only played, if anyone had once begun to think of God and speak of God to the effect that God as such was the true, speaking, acting person, if anyone had done this (and it could not happen otherwise), not on the basis of speculative considerations, but on the basis that God is actually present in His revelation, there would have been achieved in the eighties and nineties of the 19th century the fundamental disturbance at any rate of theological, and in that way indirectly of philosophical and, again indirectly, of general thinking, which would have taken from the development
[294] self-evidently adopted and continued from the 18th century its self-evident character. This did not happen. The reaction represented by Lotze and others could not be effectively dangerous to the modern self-consciousness because it shared its hypotheses. It could actually have been a danger, but the time was not ripe, and therefore it could not have any historical success. But we cannot, of course, deny that in its total weakness it was objectively a symptom of the fact that, although contrary to the prevailing doctrine and irreconcilable with its basic hypotheses, the recollection of the biblical concept of God had not disappeared altogether. Its influence was still felt even within the (to it) strange surroundings of modern anthropological thought, and by this curious detour *via* the concept of human personality.

The fact that the problem remained in spite of their own intentions and systematisation had to be admitted in a most extraordinary way even by the two classical antagonists of the personality of God, Strauss and Biedermann, to the detriment of the clarity and logic of their position. The result was that at the apex of their critique they both showed leanings to a certain compromise. The exposition of Strauss (*op. cit.*, pp. 523 f.) concludes with the statement that God is not just "general substance" to whose being the self-insertion of personality does not belong. He is certainly not a person beside and above others. But He is "the eternal movement of the general, continually making itself subject, achieving objectivity and true reality only in the subject, and in so doing abolishing the subject in its abstract self-hood." As eternal personality, He allows that which is other than Himself, nature, to proceed from Himself, so that it can return to Himself as self-conscious spirit. His personality must not be thought of as individual personality but as comprehensive personality. Instead of personifying the absolute, we must learn to understand it as that which eternally personifies itself. When Strauss says this, is he really saying anything different from what Lotze later thought he was saying *against* him? It is true that with this perversion of the Hegelian doctrine of the Trinity he did not even remotely attain the biblical concept of the personal God, but directly denied it. It is also true that with this "comprehensive personality" he destroyed his own technical concept (he had already defined the absolute so as to exclude irrevocably the concept of personality). But these facts cannot allow us to overlook how strongly and openly in his thought another conception of the nature of God was at work, one which rested on different presuppositions and asserted itself contrary to his intentions. This actual and involuntary compulsion of the problem can be seen even more clearly in the case of Biedermann (*op. cit.*, p. 645 f.). After an exemplary proof that the concept of an "absolute personality" must necessarily disintegrate into its several parts, the one necessarily excluding the other, he goes on in this astonishing way. It is still legitimate to postulate an absolute personality. Indeed: "If we think of God rightly and fully as absolute spirit, then, if we can conceive of Him at all, we can do so only as absolute personality." The pantheistic images of a life-force

or world-soul poured out through the universe are inadmissible according to Biedermann. God is absolute spirit and therefore impersonal in concept; but He is absolute personality in our conception, in the "intercommunication of religion" which "goes on between the infinite and the finite spirit within the finite human spiritual life, and which therefore must reach its final conclusion in the form of the latter." Obviously, this proviso is no compensation for the damaging, or indeed the removal, of the biblical concept of God by the previous denial of the personality of God. No compensation is possible on the basis of the modern anthropological presupposition, because the presupposition itself is ultimately responsible. The God who speaks and acts and therefore exists in His revelation is as little to be recognised in the "representation" of Biedermann (whatever its content, and however biblically filled out) as in the gnosticising picture which Strauss finally thought he could sketch positively as the nature of God. The reason for this is that ultimately and irrevocably the "representation " of [295]
Biedermann can be only a representation. It can have only subjective truth. This "only" makes Biedermann's doctrine of God ecclesiastically untenable, in spite of the concession with which it finishes. Whatever else He may be, the God who, though He may be person in subjective truth, is in objective truth not person but an impersonal absolute is not to be compared with the God of the biblical revelation. Moreover, in the case of Biedermann we must seriously ask whether by this concession he has not destroyed his own technical concept to the point of unrecognisability. For can the distinction between concept and representation be substantiated in such a way that under the term concept there is described the comprehension of objective truth, under the term representation that of a merely subjective truth, the two being mutually related as higher and lower steps of the same perception? How is this distinction to be made? And supposing it is, how is the relationship to be achieved? Can even the purest concept be more than a representation purified as far as possible from all intuitive evidence, a representation made as mathematical as can be? To what extent in the concept are we really on a higher step of the knowledge of truth? And does not the naive representation have necessarily in itself something of the value and pretension of the concept? To what extent in the representation are we really on a lower step of truth? The difference between concept and representation can at best be only a difference of clarity; and how often must the question be asked whether the representation does not enjoy a higher degree of clarity than the concept? On the other hand, if the difference is maintained on the basis of a particular theory of knowledge, like the difference between objective and subjective knowledge of truth, how can we relate the two as stages in the same knowledge and therefore, e.g., say of the same object that here it cannot possibly have a certain predicate, and there it must of necessity have it? How do we come to speak of stages in the knowledge of truth instead of a contradiction of true knowledge against false and false against true? If, however, either the distinction or the relationship cannot be properly sustained, if there is either only a knowledge directed one way or another at the one truth, or only the contradiction between true and false perception, Biedermann has to reply to the whole might of his own critique if he wants to explain the concept of "absolute personality" as impossible on the level of concept, and yet cling to it on the level of representation. Either there must be conflict on the level of representation, or there must be a solution of the conflict on the level of concept. A third course is possible only if there is a double truth—which Biedermann did not want to maintain. It is remarkable enough that with their concession Strauss and Biedermann were untrue to their own systematisation. It is even more remarkable that in working it out they did exactly the same thing—and against the background of their preceding critique they did it even more impressively—as philosophers who attempted directly to recover the personality of God. Contrary to the intention of the whole of the modern doctrine of God, according to their own understanding and admission the problem of the personality of God as such obviously could not actually be denied—the very problem that they wished to deny

by raising the question. With all the energy of the idealistic reduction and cleansing of the concept of God, with all the power of the desire that lay behind it to defend the human subject against the superior competition that threatened it from the side of the personality of God, they were not actually in a position completely to ignore the fact that, whether they liked it or not, the concept of God had once meant more, and in the Bible which they still read still meant more, than this sum of human ideas and the eternity which belongs to it as such. If with these conscious concessions they attained as little the concept of God as the contemporary defenders of the personality of God, the fact that even as opponents of the
[296] personality of God they ultimately made these conscious concessions bore witness to the fact that the biblical concept of God had not actually disappeared, but that it was always present as a question and a threat, as an error to which justice must somehow be done.

There was, then, a constant vacillation between the intention of this concept of God and the modern doctrine of God, or that of pagan antiquity. The one was affirmed, but there was obviously no ability or desire to sustain it. The other was rejected as untrue, yet its presence had still to be taken into account. There was error, but continual hesitation in error. The error was begun, but the aberration could not be completed. And all this goes to show, as so often in Neo-Protestantism, that it is easy enough to raise trouble and disturbance in the Church by introducing new teaching, but not so easy to break up the Church by raising a consistent counter-doctrine and therefore a counter-Church. Neo-Protestantism in the 18th and 19th centuries certainly tried to lead the Church back to a renewed paganism. But it is self-evident that it did not have the power even to set about this attempt with ultimate seriousness, let alone to see it through. To-day, perhaps, it is to be regarded as an interlude—comparable with Marcionism in the early Church. There is, therefore, no more point now in being as angry with its champions as we sometimes are when we lose sight of the inner weakness of the whole affair. If we know that we cannot accept what is even in the orthodox doctrine of God the customary transposition of the divine being into a neutral absolute, to an anthropocentricity which is secretly at work in response to the revelation of God, we are not forced into this unhappy state of vacillation. If we can abandon the dialectic to which it necessarily gives rise with all its inconsistencies and illogicalities, if we need not feel coerced by it, then we cannot show too much anger against those who are imprisoned in this dialectic. The dispute about the personality of God then becomes a historical matter. As such it is no doubt very interesting, exciting and informative. But it is still merely historical.

We conclude with two terminological elucidations. The first is that in this context everything depends on the statement that God is the One who loves. But nothing at all depends on the statement that He is or He has personality. The second statement is unknown both to the Bible and to primitive and Reformation dogma. It emerged only when the right and important thing that is meant by it began to be problematical on the grounds that we have discussed. It became a battle-cry attacked by the one side and championed by the other. Taken by itself, however, it does not say the right and important thing that it is meant to say. It can say this only in the context of the statement that God is the One who loves, as the express avowal and affirmation of the fact that God is not something, not a thing, but a person, the One, the speaking and acting Subject, the original and real I. But it is as who He is and therefore as the One who loves that He is this. The concept of personality as such is too colourless to form a necessary basis for our description of this absolutely indispensable moment in the nature of God. We can use it, and shall do so, when the need arises. But we can have no essential interest in the modern debate centred on this concept. We can and must, therefore, concede that we can do without it so long as what is intended in it is assured and accepted. In preaching nothing is to be gained by this concept, and nothing lost. The only thing which matters is that God's Word should be proclaimed as the Word of the One, the One who loves; as the Word of which He Himself as such is the Subject and content; and

not as an expression of our own eternity and therefore not as the word of a general, neutral truth or goodness. What will then be proclaimed is not that God is person, but the particular person He is. If this happens, this is all that is needed. And it can and must happen even though the concepts of "personality" and "person" are not employed as such. Secondly, if we accept the concept of the personality of God, we must be conscious of a certain lack of clarity arising from the fact that right up to modern times most people have spoken of divine "persons" in relation to the doctrine of the divine Trinity. What is meant here is the being of [297]
God in the three modes: Father, Son and Holy Spirit. In our treatment of the doctrine of the Trinity we took the view that the concept "person" should be dropped in the description of this matter, because in all classical theology it has never in fact been understood and interpreted in the sense in which we are accustomed to think of the term to-day. The Christian Church has never taught that there are in God three persons and therefore three personalities in the sense of a threefold Ego, a threefold subject. This would be tritheism, which the concept *persona*[EN84], understood as *modus subsistentiae*[EN85], is in fact meant to avoid. The important and true thing intended by the concept of personality in the modern sense as a description of God is, of course, connected not merely closely, but indissolubly, with the doctrine of the Trinity. Being in Himself Father, Son and Holy Spirit, God is in Himself the One who lives and loves, and therefore One, and therefore the One; and as we know Him as Father, Son and Holy Spirit, we know Him always as the One who loves, and therefore as the One who meets us, and addresses us and deals with us as Thou. What we can describe as personality is indeed the whole divine Trinity as such, in the unity of the Father, Son and Holy Spirit in God Himself and in His work—not the individual aspects by themselves in which God is and which He has. Not threefold, but thrice—and thrice not in any self-sufficiency of one of the aspects, but in their being with each other and for each other and in each other, in their succession one to another—the one triune God is the One who lives and loves, and therefore One, the One, and therefore, if we want to call it so, personality. There are not three faces of God, but one face; not three wills, but one will; not three rights, but one right; not three Words and works, but one Word and work. The one God is revealed to us absolutely in Jesus Christ. He is absolutely the same God in Himself. This one God as the Triune is—let us say it then—the personal God.

3. THE BEING OF GOD IN FREEDOM

The being of God is His own. His act is His own. His love is His own. In this His being and act God is who He is. After all our previous considerations, we cannot lay too strong an emphasis on this fact in characterising the divine being. But what do we imply by this emphasis? There are, of course, other beings, other forms of activity; there are also others who love and other persons. Obviously, when we emphasise that it is of God that we are speaking, we are not distinguishing Him only as when, by the use of the personal demonstrative or possessive pronoun, we distinguish one subject from others of the same class. If we say of God "He," "this," or "His," if in each sentence we give the word God explicitly or implicitly the tone and the weight of meaning that befits it, when we allude to Him distinctively in this way we are also affirming something essential, indeed in some sense the one essential thing that is to be

---

[EN84] person
[EN85] manner of being

affirmed of Him. His act is in a unique way His act. His love is uniquely His love. He is uniquely who He is. The essential fact that must be affirmed of God consists in the characterisation of the uniqueness of the form and content of His being, and when we distinguish Him from everything else that exists we are necessarily expressing at the same time this essential fact. Already we have
[298] found that we could not properly speak of God's life and love without constantly referring to the unique mode of His life and love. We speak irrelevantly of God's life and love if we do not constantly make this distinction and reference, if we do not constantly look into the depths of the divine being and keep in view the fact that we have indeed to do with a life and love, yet not with any life and love, but with the life and love of God Himself. This object permits and indeed commands us to speak of a life and love, of a living and loving I, defining, attesting and proclaiming it. But permitting and commanding us to do so, He also requires us to understand and name Him beyond all our insights and ideas as the I who lives and loves in His unique way, to give Him the honour which cannot even remotely accrue to any but the living and loving being known to us, but which we must specifically deny to all other living and loving beings known to us, because it is properly and originally His honour alone, because we can truly understand all other life, love and being only in virtue of His creation and therefore as the reflection and echo of His life and love. Only when we glimpse the depth in which He lives and loves and has His being, have we truly recognised and understood His being as love and therefore as divine.

We now turn to the question of this depth in the divine being. So far we have asked and answered it provisionally, but for good or ill it must now engage our attention directly if our reflection upon the life of God is not to be incomplete. We must know what we are thinking and doing when we do not speak of the life and love of God without reference to their uniqueness, without drawing this vital distinction. We must know what is meant by the special divine character which is to engage our attention when we make this reference and this distinction. We must enquire about the determination of the divine being which makes it necessary for us to study this divine essence. The difficulty and the doubtfulness of this question are obvious. As regards its difficulty, how are we even to frame a question concerning the special and distinctive essence of the divine being, let alone know how to answer it? As regards its doubtfulness, are we not here necessarily disregarding the revealed being of God and asking about something else supposedly lying behind it? Must we not therefore base our answer upon another presupposition, perhaps that of a presumed universal knowledge of God? We take up at once the challenge of this second question. This is, of course, the very thing which must not happen under any circumstances. Even when we enquire about the special and distinctive element in the life and love of God, we are not enquiring about the content of a universal idea of the divine, as though we could glean from this instruction concerning the special and distinguishing essence of God. We make our enquiry on the assumption that the object of this universal idea of God, i.e., of any idea of God formed otherwise than in view of God's revelation in Jesus [299] Christ, is necessarily other than He who is Lord and salvation, and therefore the object of the faith of the Church and the only true God. We are not trying to discover a characteristic mark of divinity which this God will have in common with other gods. We are not concerned with any idea of the divine under which we will subsume the only true God with other gods. We are well aware that, if we do this, we shall be enquiring in fact not about the idea of God, but, in common with the worshippers of those other gods, about the idea of man, about the sum of his wishes and longings, about the highest embodiment, in absolute form, of our own being. Therefore now as before we do not enquire in disregard of God's revelation, but with our attention concentrated upon it and only upon it.

It is the fundamental weakness of the work of H. Cremer, which we have mentioned more than once and which is so bravely progressive in its basic direction, that formally at least it remains the slave of tradition in that it reckons ultimately with the existence and authoritativeness of an idea of God known also to the heathen, of a universally current predicate of divinity, although this does of course receive its content only through the subject Jesus Christ, the sole true revelation of God, and must therefore be understood and interpreted in the light of this revelation (*op. cit.*, pp. 32 f.). The energy with which Cremer tried to argue this point of view ought not to pass without due appreciation. But is not the biblical message concerning God—even in regard to the predicate of divinity, in regard to what distinguishes God's life and love as His, as divine—much more than a special interpretation of a universal idea of God which the prophets of *Yahweh* shared with the prophets of Baal, the apostles with the exponents of the mystery religions? Does not the predicate "divine" as well as the subject "God" belong to that other text which the prophets and apostles and they alone have read? Has not the predicate become new in the sense that it can be received only in this its newness, and no longer—or only polemically—with reference to its old, universalised significance?

No change of theme was involved when we spoke first of God's life and then of God's love, first of His being in act and then of His being as the One who loves. It was not as if we knew first and in general of God's life as such and only then provided this generalised subject with its specialised predicate, that it is the life and ruling of love. But God's life itself and as such is in all its depths the loving of God, and only in preparation for this insight, only in development of the prior logical assertion that God is an acting Subject, did we linger for a moment (but in fact only for a moment) to reflect upon God's being in act, which is in no sense act in general but the concrete, specific action of His love. And so, too, when we enquire into the unique and distinctive divinity of God, the characteristic depth of His being, it does not imply the introduction of a new theme, as though we were looking behind the wings of the theatre, as though having answered the question: Who is God? we could now ask *in abstracto*[EN86]: What is God? For as God is not an it but a He, so He is not a He

[EN86] in the abstract

who has first to partake in an it in order to be this He. In God there is no it that
[300] is not Himself. There is nothing general that is not His particular being in the uniqueness of its act and therefore its living and loving. Now that we are asking: What is God? what is His divinity, His distinctive essence as God? we can only ask again: Who is God? For He has what He is, not only in Himself and as a concomitant and attribute of His being, but because He is, and is everything that He is. Strictly speaking, there is no divine predicate, no idea of God, which can have as its special content what God is. There is strictly speaking only the divine Subject as such and in Him the fulness of His divine predicates. Properly speaking the idea of God can have only this divine Subject as its content and the divine predicate must be sought only in this Subject as such, outside of which it can have no existence and cannot therefore become the content of an idea. If we now seek to discover what God is, our enquiry will not be presumptuous, foolish and blasphemous only if we at once allow it to be taken out of our hands and rightly framed; only if we are aware that with the greatest childlikeness, which in this connexion is also the greatest, the only possible profundity, we are again asking: Who is He? We need only stand on the ground which we took up from the beginning—the question of the reality of God in the actuality of His revelation where He is faithful to Himself and where we are therefore confronted by His being as it is in itself—and the question of the depths of His being, of His unique and distinctive divinity, loses the dubiousness which seems at first to cling to it. Nor in this case need its apparent difficulty cause us any further trouble. It is as difficult (but not more so) as any other question which God's self-revelation raises for us and which we have to answer in the light of it. We can indeed know what we are thinking and doing when we are speaking of God's living and loving as of something distinctive. It is necessary and right and also not impossible for us to be clear about it. We have only to remember that we have to enquire about the distinctiveness of this particular living and loving, not from the point of view of universal criteria and standards, but in view of the reality revealed to us by God Himself.

And we must also recollect that in formulating our question directly we do not approach it empty handed. For we could not complete our consideration of the life and love of God as such without realising at every step the peculiar and distinctive characteristics of this divine living and loving. We understood the being of God as moved, although self-moved, as life living from its own centre. We understood His loving to be loving for its own sake, an unconditioned, utterly sovereign love, positing its own basis and purpose. Without this more concrete determination, without this characterisation of the uniqueness of His living and loving, we are obviously not speaking of God's living and loving, but of life and love generally, and therefore definitely not of God. We
[301] must now take this particular determination as our present point of departure. It was indicated in the title of the section and this third sub-section by the idea of freedom. This does not mean that with this idea we can grasp and exhaust by a long way all that is to be said in answer to our question. It can only suggest

the direction in which we are to look. But it can do that. God's being as He who lives and loves is being in freedom. In this way, freely, He lives and loves. And in this way, and in the fact that He lives and loves in freedom, He is God, and distinguishes Himself from everything else that lives and loves. In this way, as the free person, He is distinguished from other persons. He is the one, original and authentic person through whose creative power and will alone all other persons are and are sustained. With the idea of freedom we simply affirm what we would be affirming if we were to characterise God as the Lord. But His lordship is in all circumstances the lordship of His living and loving. Our present question is that of the mode of His lordship and therefore of His living and loving—of the divine characteristics by which, as He who lives and loves, He manifests His sovereignty. This mode is characterised by the fact that it is absolutely God's own, in no sense dictated to Him from outside and conditioned by no higher necessity than that of His own choosing and deciding, willing and doing. If we enquire how, according to His revelation in Jesus Christ, God's lordship differs in its divinity from other types of rule, then we must answer that it is lordship in freedom. It would be senseless to ascribe this characteristic to other kinds of sovereignty, or to any other living and loving but that of God. There are other sovereignties, but freedom is the prerogative of divine sovereignty. Freedom is, of course, more than the absence of limits, restrictions, or conditions. This is only its negative and to that extent improper aspect—improper to the extent that from this point of view it requires another, at least in so far as its freedom lies in its independence of this other. But freedom in its positive and proper qualities means to be grounded in one's own being, to be determined and moved by oneself. This is the freedom of the divine life and love. In this positive freedom of His, God is also unlimited, unrestricted and unconditioned from without. He is the free Creator, the free Reconciler, the free Redeemer. But His divinity is not exhausted in the fact that in His revelation it consists throughout in this freedom from external compulsion: in free utterance and action, free beginning and ending, free judgment and blessing, free power and spirit. On the contrary, it is only manifest in all this. For He has it in Himself quite apart from His relation to another from whom He is free. He in Himself is power, truth and right. Within the sphere of His own being He can live and love in absolute plenitude and power, as we see Him live and love in His revelation.

There is no plainer description of the divinity of God than the phrase which occurs so
frequently in the Pentateuch and again in the Book of Ezekiel: "I am the Lord." It is followed
hard by that other, analytical phrase: "I am the Lord your (or thy) God," and it has its exact [302]
New Testament parallel in the "I am" of the Johannine Jesus. It is, of course, obvious that in
this biblical "I am" the Subject posits itself and in that way posits itself as the living and loving
Lord. In doing so, this Subject is God. He who does this is the God of the Bible. Because He
is the One who does so, everything outside Him depends on His good-pleasure or its oppos-
ite. Because of it, His throne is high and lifted up (Is. 6^{1}), being prepared in the heavens by
Himself (Ps. 103^{19}) above the cherubim (2 Kg. 19^{15}). Because of it His eyes look down upon

the earth (Ps. 11[4], 33[13f], 102[19]). Because of it there is none like Him (Ex. 8[10], 15[11]; Ps. 86[8], 89[8].) He alone is God and there is no other (Deut. 4[35]; 2 Kg. 19[15]; 1 Chron. 17[20]). He is the Lord of Lords, the King of Kings (1 Tim. 6[15]; Rev. 17[14], 19[16]). He is the alpha and the omega, the beginning and the end, the first and the last (Is. 44[6]; Rev. 1[8], [17], 21[6], 22[13]). Thus we read in Rom. 11[35f.]: "Who hath first given to him, and it shall be recompensed unto him again?" **ὅτι ἐξ αὐτοῦ καὶ δἰ αὐτοῦ καὶ εἰς αὐτὸν τὰ πάντα. αὐτῷ ἡ δόξα εἰς τοὺς αἰῶνας**[EN87].

The loftiness, the sovereignty, the majesty, the holiness, the glory—even what is termed the transcendence of God—what is it but this self-determination, this freedom, of the divine living and loving, the divine person? If later on we shall not be able to portray fully the attributes of divine love except with close attention to their divinity, i.e., their divine excellence, conversely we shall have to understand this divinity of God in all its aspects as the sum of His freedom.

By freedom we denote what was called in the theology of the early Church the *aseitas Dei*[EN88]. In content, the idea is already to be seen in the fondness of the Greek fathers for compounds with the word **αὐτός**[EN89] to express the attributes of God: To God belongs **αὐτουσία, αὐτοζωή, αὐτοαγαθία**[EN90]; He is **αὐτάρκης, αὐτοκράτωρ, αὐτόθεος**[EN91], etc. It was formulated for the first time by Anselm of Canterbury : *summa natura ... per se ipsam et ex se ipsa est, quidquid est*[EN92] (*Monol.* 6); *summa veritas ... nulli quidquam debet nec ulla ratione est, quod est, nisi quia est*[EN93] (*De verit.* 10) ... *te tibi omnino sufficiens et nullo indigens quo omnia indigent, ut sint et ut bene sint*[EN94] (*Proslog.* 22). And specifically: *Ille igitur solus a se habet, quidquid habet*[EN95] (*De casu diab.* 1) Similarly, the older Protestant dogmaticians frequently included in their definition of God a characterisation such as: *a se ipso ab aeterno existens*[EN96], or something of the sort. This feature was usually defined as the divine *independentia*[EN97], about which W. Baier (*Comp. Theol. pos.*, 1686, I, *c.* 1. 6) made the (in itself correct) statement: *Per hoc enim sicut Deus ab aliis rebus omnibus adaequate distinguitur, ita nihil est, quod a Deo, tanquam proprium et determinatum conceptum prius concipere possis, quam quod non sit ab aliis adeoque a se et necessario exsistat*[EN98]. But the replacement of the term *aseitas*[EN99] by *independentia*[EN100], and the content of the explanation, reveal that the tendency was for that

EN 87 Because all things are from him and through him and for/unto him. To him be the glory for ever

EN 88 aseity of God

EN 89 'self-'/ 'auto-'

EN 90 being in himself, life in himself, goodness in himself

EN 91 self-sufficient, powerful in himself, God in himself

EN 92 the highest nature, is through its very self and from its very self, whatever it is

EN 93 the highest truth does not owe anything to anyone and is not by any reason that is, except such as it is

EN 94 altogether satisfying yourself for yourself and lacking in nothing in which all things lack in order to be and to be well

EN 95 Therefore whatever he has, he alone has from himself

EN 96 existing by his own very self, from eternity

EN 97 independence

EN 98 For just as by this is God adequately distinguished from all other things, so likewise there is nothing which you could think in relation to God as a proper and determined concept before the fact that he does not have his existence from other things and therefore exists from himself and of necessity

EN 99 aseity

EN100 independence

which must always be our primary concern when it is a question of the being of God, the positive aspect of God's freedom to exist in Himself, to be less clearly grasped and considered less important than the negative aspect of God's freedom from all external conditions. The inevitable result was to miss the biblical idea of God, to which there was a close approximation in the favourite citation of Exodus 3[14].

Our emphasis in defining the concept must not in any circumstances fall upon this negative aspect. To be sure, this negative side is extremely significant not only for God's relation to the world, but also for His being in itself. We cannot possibly grasp and expound the idea of divine creation and providence, nor even the ideas of divine omnipotence, omnipresence and eternity, [303] without constantly referring to this negative aspect of His freedom. But we shall be able to do so properly only when we do so against the background of our realisation that God's freedom constitutes the essential positive quality, not only of His action towards what is outside Himself, but also of His own inner being. The biblical witness to God sees His transcendence of all that is distinct from Himself, not only in the distinction as such, which is supremely and decisively characterised as His freedom from all conditioning by that which is distinct from Himself, but furthermore and supremely in the fact that without sacrificing His distinction and freedom, but in the exercise of them, He enters into and faithfully maintains communion with this reality other than Himself in His activity as Creator, Reconciler and Redeemer. According to the biblical testimony, God has the prerogative to be free without being limited by His freedom from external conditioning, free also with regard to His freedom, free not to surrender Himself to it, but to use it to give Himself to this communion and to practise this faithfulness in it, in this way being really free, free in Himself. God must not only be unconditioned but, in the absoluteness in which He sets up this fellowship, He can and will also be conditioned. He who can and does do this is the God of Holy Scripture, the triune God known to us in His revelation. This ability, proved and manifested to us in His action, constitutes His freedom.

Just for these reasons it was a retrogression when the idea of God's *aseitas*[EN101] was interpreted, or rather supplanted, by that of *independentia*[EN102] or *infinitas*[EN103], and later by that of the unconditioned or absolute. It is not that these ideas were not serviceable, admissible and even necessary in their place. But in their place means against the background of a positive conception of God's being, which as such (but only as such) includes also a very definite non-being, but which is not exhausted in this non-being, which must be constantly presupposed if this non-being is to be real, if it is to be a divine and not a different kind of non-being. Similarly, the thought of the divine transcendence, if intruded as a substitute, can denote the being of God only when it is remembered that it cannot be exhaustively defined as God's opposition to the reality distinct from Himself, that it can also signify God's positive fellowship with this reality and therefore His immanence within it, that in this connexion, because it has in fact pleased God to establish and maintain this fellowship, it can

---

EN101 aseity
EN102 independence
EN103 infinity

have "immanence" as its primary connotation, and only within this framework and as an explanation of its method denote what the idea immediately and intrinsically suggests, so that it truly describes the being of God only when it describes Him in His own characteristic freedom which He enjoys beyond and above His opposition to the reality distinct from Himself.

If we fail to bear all this in mind, if we view the being of God in its abstractly understood transcendence in accordance with the disastrous suggestions of Neo-Platonism, i.e., as negative from the point of view of the being of the reality distinct from Himself, then we have substituted for the biblical idea of God an idea which is easily recognisable as the highest idea conceivable to man. For what is the idea of the infinite, the unconditioned or the absolute but the idea of our own limits, which suggest to us both our transcendent goal and
[304] origin, but which in themselves can be understood only as our limits and therefore as the negation, the non-being of all that we are? If we interpret this our non-being as pointing to true being, if we make our limits the object of an apotheosis, we are in no sense testifying to God. On the contrary, by this abuse of the name of God, we are affirming our awareness that these limits suggest our transcendent goal and origin. We are expressing the deep appreciation and esteem we feel for this our goal and origin, and for our own ideal image, carefully purged of all imperfection, but still only postulated as far as its being (even its divine being) is concerned.

God's freedom is the freedom proper to and characteristic of Him. It is His freedom not merely to be like the reality different from Himself, but to be as the Creator, Reconciler and Redeemer acting towards it and in it, and therefore as its sovereign Lord. Again, it is His freedom not merely to be in the differentiation of His being from its being, but to be in Himself the One who can have and hold communion with this reality (as in fact He does) in spite of His utter distinction from it.

According to the self-attestation of His revelation, God is free to reveal His existence within the sphere of the reality that is distinct from Himself. Notice that it is *His* existence, therefore the existence of Him whose being is clearly differentiated from the whole realm of this reality. But it is His *existence*, that is to say His being, independent of our thought about it, preceding and providing the basis for our thought, absolutely objective. And it is this His existence within the reality that is distinct from it, so that in this reality to which man belongs, and in all its differentiation from it, it can be recognised by man; so that the divine self-revelation can be apprehended by him and grasped according to the possibilities of his knowledge. Now all this obviously does take place as God's self-revelation takes place, creating and finding faith. Therefore it can all take place—it lies within the scope of God's freedom. He shows and proves in His revelation His freedom to begin with Himself: with Himself, without subtraction from His being, without reserving the secret possibilities of a being beyond that which He is at the point where He begins; to begin with Himself, i.e., not to ground His existence anywhere else but with, or rather in, the life which He here reveals; to begin with Himself in such a way that no thinking can evade the inescapable, incontestable and unforgettable event of this beginning—and to do it here, in the midst of a reality which is as distinct from Him as He is from it, here, then, where, viewed from either angle, His existence necessarily seems impossible. The freedom to manifest it notwithstanding, is shown and proved by God in His revelation. But this is the freedom of His incarnation in Jesus Christ foreshadowed in His election and rule of Israel, the freedom of His Word, the freedom of His Spirit, the freedom of His grace. It is from first to last the freedom with which He proves His own existence, the proof which every human proof of His existence can only repeat if it is really to prove God's existence and not something very different, that is, if, in the last resort, it is not to prove the existence of man from the awareness of [305] his own limitation.

That it fulfils this condition is the peculiar excellence of the—falsely so-called and as a result permanently misunderstood—ontological proof of God's existence by Anselm of Canterbury (*Prosl.* 2–4). Anselm halted on the very frontier of the great Neo-Platonic error of a God whose being consists only in a hypostatised summary of His non-being in relation to all other kinds of being, a God who is certainly conceivable as an idealisation of man, but whose objective existence can only be demonstrated by sophisms. On the very brink of this error he proved the existence of God by the fact that God has demonstrated and does and will demonstrate Himself. For (deserving our gratitude and answering prayer) He constitutes Himself the point of departure which no thought can by pass or elude, and with which all thought must begin. In this event of His self-demonstration God is He *quo maius cogitari nequit*[EN104]. By His holy name, not only His non-existence but even the thought of His non-existence is excluded. Such an error is forbidden man by the fact that God has given Himself to be the object of man's awareness and at the same time has illuminated man's mind to grasp this object.

The freedom in which He proves His existence is the freedom of God in His revelation. And the freedom to exist which He exercises in His revelation is the same which He has in the depths of His eternal being, and which is proper to Him quite apart from His exercise of it *ad extra.* He who begins in this way with Himself in His revelation is He who begins with Himself from eternity, and therefore the One who properly and necessarily exists. And the fact that He is this is what we mean by God's being in freedom.

At this point Catholic dogma (Bartmann, *Lehr. d. Dogm.*[7], Vol. I, 1928, 106 f.; Diekamp, *Kath. Dogm.*[6], Vol. I, 1930, 151 f.) joins issue with a theory of the modernist Hermann Schell. According to Schell, the self-existence of God is to be understood as the divine "self-realisation," "self-constitution" and "self-causation." What he has in mind is the phrase of Jerome: *Deus est causa sui*[EN105]. Objections in formal logic can of course be raised to this statement, that *causa*[EN106] must be something other than the *causatum*[EN107], that it must logically precede it, etc. But these are less decisive than the material point that God as *causa prima*[EN108] cannot be both *causa*[EN109] and *causatum*[EN110], but only *causa*[EN111]. Therefore

---

[EN104] than whom nothing greater can be thought
[EN105] God is his own cause
[EN106] cause
[EN107] caused
[EN108] first cause
[EN109] cause
[EN110] caused
[EN111] cause

"aseity" cannot in any sense be interpreted as God's act of self-realisation, His self-initiation, as though in a certain sense God arose out of Himself. Obviously in relation to God we can speak only of the ground and actuality of His being which is not in need of any special origin and constitution. The God who takes His origin from Himself or is constituted by Himself is in a certain sense limited by the possibility of His non-being and therefore He is not the free God. Yet the special concern of Schell must be recognised. His intention is suspected by Catholic scholastic dogmatics, and on Catholic ground it can, of course, be fulfilled only with difficulty. For it arose out of his opposition to the scholastic equation of God with the unmoved Mover of Aristotle. What he had in mind was a development of the doctrine of the eternal generation of the Son by the Father, and procession of the Holy Ghost from the Father and the Son. If the inner life of God is the life of Father, Son and Spirit, and if therefore His life resides in this process of generation, then it is hardly possible to raise any decisive objection to the description of God by the idea of self-realisation—later Schell spoke with more reserve about self-actualisation and self-expression. But this is true only if we remember two things: (1) that of the three modes of being of God, that of the Father is
[306] not even the object of any self-realisation, which limits the idea in its application to the life of God; and (2) that an eternal self-realisation, which alone is possible in the case of God, can have nothing whatever to do with any idea of God taking His origin from Himself, so that it is at least very inadequately denoted by the expression *causa sui*[EN112]. Thus the expression "self-realisation," in its legitimate use, can mean only the freedom of the divine being which is in need of no origination (not even an origination from itself).

The freedom in which God exists means that He does not need His own being in order to be who He is: because He already has His own being and is Himself; because nothing can accrue to Him from Himself which He had not or was not already; because, therefore, His being in its self-realisation or the actuality of His being answers to no external pressure but is only the affirmation of His own plenitude and a self-realisation in freedom. If, therefore, we say that God is *a se*[EN113], we do not say that God creates, produces or originates Himself. On the contrary, we say that (as manifest and eternally actual in the relationship of Father, Son and Holy Ghost) He is the One who already has and is in Himself everything which would have to be the object of His creation and causation if He were not He, God. Because He is God, as such He already has and is His own being. Therefore this being does not need any origination and constitution. He cannot "need" His own being because He affirms it in being who He is. It is not, of course, that His being needs this affirmation. But He does actually affirm it in this way. And what He creates, produces and causes, what needs origination and constitution in order to be, what can need existence, is not God Himself, or His reality, but the reality which is distinct from Himself. When we say that God is free to exist, we do not say that God lifts Himself, as it were, out of non-existence into existence, that He makes Himself free to exist. What we say is that the mode of existence is proper to Him which is exempt from any limitation by the possibility of its non-existence. He is the One who is in Himself the Existent. By existing in this way He is not subject to

[EN112] his own cause
[EN113] from himself

any necessity, as though He must first exist in order to be who He is. But by His existence He simply reaffirms Himself. It is not that He needs to reaffirm Himself, but that, being who He is, He does in fact reaffirm Himself and His existence. When we say that God begins with Himself, we do not say that He needs a basis in which He must define and delimit Himself in differentiation from what He is not, or from His own non-existence, in order to have His being within this limit. We say rather that He Himself, in being, is His own basis, and that as such He differentiates His being from what He is not, His existence from His non-existence, and even from the very thought of His non-existence, the basis and the differentiation being confirmed in the very act of His being. Again, it is not that His being needs this confirmation, but that the very fact of His being, free from all need, is in fact this confirmation. This is the first primary meaning of God's being in freedom, in aseity.

The insight expressed in this way is endangered when it is thought essential to complete and deepen the idea of the aseity of God by the Catholic dogma that God's being is necessary, that He is to be defined as the *ens necessarium*[EN114]: "It is an intrinsic impossibility that He should not be or should be other than He is." This is said to result from the idea of the pure essence or the primary being of God. But because the deduction is only too easily drawn from this idea, we must treat it with great reserve. At any rate the German word *notwendig* is more than doubtful. For in God and for God there can be no "difficulty" (*Not*) which He has to "turn" (*wenden*), or turn from Himself, by His being. But even in the Latin *necesse, necessarium, necessitas*[EN115] we have a combination of *ne* and *cedere*[EN116] and therefore the implication of something which it is impossible to evade, not to speak of the Greek ἀνάγκη[EN117] which really means "straitness." The case is a good illustration of the fact that our words require a complete change of meaning, even to the extent of becoming the very opposite in sense, if in their application to God they are not to lead us astray. We may perhaps be able to say of pure actuality or primary being that if we are to give the true meaning we must speak of "turning difficulties," or the "inescapable," or being "driven into straits." But we certainly cannot say this of God. We cannot apply the terms to God if defined in this way. Of God we can say only that in the actuality of His being He is its affirmation, that in the actuality of His being His non-being or His being other than He is is ontologically and noetically excluded, that it becomes an absolute impossibility, i.e., an impossibility which has no possibility as its background. As distinct from what is meant by these terms, there is no need as a result of which God has to be. But if God is, it is the effect of His freedom, which knows no necessity, no inevitability, no straitness. The fact that He is (and this is the truth of the statement under discussion) does, of course, settle the fact that He exists eternally. His non-existence or the possibility of His non-existence is negated and becomes inconceivable. But this decision results from His actual being as He who is, and it is in obedience to this empirical decision as He is sought and worshipped in it that we have to say that He cannot be non-existent or other than He is. If we seek to establish the intrinsic impossibility that God could not be, or could be other than He is, i.e., if we seek the necessity of His being, or of His being in this particular way, on any other basis than that of this empirical decision, we have to consider whether we are not concerned with a God who in His need to be is not God but [307]

EN114 necessary being
EN115 necessary, needful, necessity
EN116 not and failing
EN117 compulsion

the postulated apotheosis of our creaturely existence. We have also to ask ourselves whether the confidence with which we think we can speak of the necessity of the existence of this God can resist the challenge of the question which inevitably arises—whether God might not also not be, or be other than He is? The genuine necessity to answer this question negatively can spring only from the God who knows no necessity, who, not needing His own being, simply has being as a matter of empirical fact, thus affirming Himself in fact, although He does not need to, as the One who is. The difference between the false and the true negation of our question consists in the fact that the former proceeds automatically from the development of an idea, but the latter can be won only from the hearing of the divine Word in prayer and supplication, from the experience of the struggle between the flesh and the spirit, from the real overcoming of real temptation. In this respect the way of Catholic dogmatics is obviously an easier and smoother way. But it is not apparent to us how we can follow it in obedience or with what promise of reward. For there can be no hope of reward in wishing to cling to something supposedly higher and better than the God who in freedom lives as He who He is.

When we have established this first proposition that God is He who is free in Himself, we can express His aseity in a second proposition, that He is the One who is free from all origination, conditioning or determination from without,
[308] by that which is not Himself. The fact that in every way He is independent of all other reality does not in itself constitute God's freedom but its exercise. It does not constitute His divinity, but He is divine in it. If He does not need His own being or any basis or limitation in Himself, if He has and is in Himself being, ground and limit in the actuality of His existence and in the freedom proper to Him, how can He possibly need any other being, or need to be grounded or limited by it? God is absolute, i.e., utterly independent of everything that is not He. God is, whether everything else is or is not, whether it is in this way or some other. If there is something other, it cannot precede God, it cannot place God in dependence upon itself, and it cannot limit God or change God. If there is something other, it can exist in its own manner of being only by God and from God. It can exist only in subordination to, and in the service of, God. But God was, is and will be who He is without the being and nature of this other existence having any other possible significance than what God is pleased to assign to it. We can and must say all this too, although we refused to say it first, but were first taught ourselves that God is free in Himself.

For we have to be taught first, by the decision made in His actual existence, that God is free in Himself. This statement has to come first as the content of a knowledge whose object cannot be an idea, but only God Himself in His self-evidencing existence. Otherwise how can the second proposition, that God is free from all external conditioning, be distinguished from a product of our own wishful thinking? Absolute being purged from all subservience to outward conditions may easily signify, as we have seen, the kind of being that we would gladly ascribe to ourselves, and can actually do so with some uncertainty and indefiniteness, in the form of "pure actuality." To what extent is God defined by it and not ourselves? Obviously, to the exact extent that we have first recognised and acknowledged the freedom of God quite apart from this His independence of all external conditions; that we have learnt to respect the empirical affirmation of the divine life as such, and therefore to reckon with Him as with the One who is absolute above and beyond the absoluteness in which He confronts that which is not Himself, and in respect of which we are irresistibly drawn to wish ourselves like Him—we can therefore say at once, to reckon with Him as with the One who is alone absolute in sovereign splendour, whom we therefore cannot equal or try to equal, because we are forbidden and prevented from doing so by His demonstration of His own existence, by the factual affirmation of His being. If this is clear to us, we shall be able to guard against the temptation to self-apotheosis which can so easily arise from the elucidation of this secondary freedom of God. This fundamental presupposition will naturally always have to be very clear to us if we are not to succumb tacitly or openly to this temptation.

And a second point is immediately clear if we allow due validity to this funda- [309] mental presupposition, viz., that the existence of a reality distinct from God and confronting Him in its difference cannot imply any difficulty in relation to the absolute God. It will necessarily imply such a difficulty in relation to the "absolute" which, as man's own reflection, gains its absoluteness only in virtue of this opposition, only through the denial of its conditioning by this distinct reality. The definition of this absolute will always hover between two extremes. On the one hand, it may be consistently affirmed, with the result that the existence of the other is rendered problematical and finally destroyed and the real world recedes into the ghostly light of ultimate unreality. On the other hand, this other may be inconsistently endowed with a degree of independent reality, so that the so-called absolute is subjected to a certain conditioning by this other and its supposed Godhead to a thoroughgoing determination by the subordinate world. This dilemma is removed if the freedom of God is primarily and fundamentally defined as God's freedom in Himself, and only from that point of view understood as His independence of the world, and therefore His absoluteness in the usual sense of the term. In this case the absoluteness of God—that which makes it a genuine absoluteness—does not derive primarily from the mode of His relationship to the world. For this very reason, He can enter into a real relationship with the latter. There can be a real world confronting Him, not threatened with destruction by the divine absoluteness, but, on the contrary, existing as a world precisely because of it. There can be a world which is not to be understood, on the basis of our idea of God, as a *pudendum*[EN118], a contradiction to God, but as something which authenticates His reality and accrues to His glory. In this case, when the world has to be viewed *sub specie aseitatis*[EN119], i.e., in the light of the primary creative freedom of God, there can no longer be any question of aloofness or hostility to the world on the part of the absolute God (or rather of a mysticism which worships

EN118 embarrassment

EN119 within the framework of aseity

an idol under the name of God). God has His absoluteness decisively in Himself. For the same reason, also, there cannot be a being and existence of the other which imperils the divine absoluteness or limits the divine freedom or produces even a partial disturbance of the relation of dependence. The relativity of the other is made necessary (here the term is in place) by God's absoluteness. It is made irrevocably necessary. There cannot, then, be any divinisation of the world or demonisations of this other. If, then, the freedom of God is understood primarily as His own positive freedom, it can and must be understood secondarily in His relationship to that which is other than Himself, which exists through Him and in subordination to Him, as His true immanence as well as His true transcendence.

We must notice in this connexion, too, the danger of a different and purely speculative foundation of this secondary absoluteness of God. "Being itself or pure reality depends on
[310] no one and needs no other in order to be and work, and it can receive no sort of completion of its being through any other" (Diekamp, *op. cit.*, p. 152 f.). This may well be true, but it must not be said of God. For again "pure reality" in itself is not to be equated with God, but only in so far as God is reality is He (as the One He is) anything in the nature of pure reality. Pure reality can also be the reflection of our own existence, and will inevitably land us in the dilemma either of being consistent and having to assert the actuality of the "impure" reality distinct from it, or of being inconsistent and limiting the "pure" by the "impure" reality. This dilemma discloses to us the difference between what is connoted by this idea and God.

Against the background of these presuppositions we will now attempt a general explanation of the divine freedom in this secondary connotation of the idea—as the "absoluteness" of God. The fact that God is free in His relationship to all that is not God means noetically that God cannot be classified or included in the same category with anything that He is not. There exists no synthesis in which the same attribute, whether being, spirit, life or love, can be predicated in the same sense both of God and of something else; in which, therefore, God is to be an element embraced with other elements in the one synthesis. Whenever God is placed side by side with another factor (with the explicit or implicit copula "and" or in some other way), we must clearly realise that there can be no question of a synthesis; that any conceivable synthesis is precluded in advance by the inclusion of the element God along with others; that the element God stands in such a relation to all other elements that the latter, in spite of individual variations, are all characterised as one group; that by their intrinsic difference they are all separated from the divine in such a way that no higher unity is possible between them and God which can be expressed by a higher comprehensive term. If there is here a unity, it is not in any sense a unity which can be expressed by a higher term embracing God and these other elements. If we think and speak of God as an element juxtaposed with others in a series, the very idea or view of the series as such must be fundamentally disturbed (which in this case means reinterpreted) by the fact that the element God is in such a way independent of all the other elements and of the series as such, that, whatever may be the common denominator,

God will not be embraced by it, but will remain detached and independent in regard both to these associated elements and to the common factor which binds them together. *Deus non est in genere*[EN120], as we have seen already.

The theological consequences of this first proposition are so far-reaching, logically, that we can only give one or two examples by way of indication. Because *Deus non est in genere*[EN121], we must take exception to Roman Catholic theology when—in what seems an incomprehensible contradiction to this statement of Thomas Aquinas—it thinks it possible at every opportunity to fall back upon a concept of being which comprehends God and what is not God, and therefore at bottom to explain all the relations between God and what is not God in the form of an exposition of this general concept. Because *Deus non est in genere*[EN122], the doctrine of God in Kant is quite intolerable, for in it the idea of God is put alongside [311] other supreme ideas like freedom and immortality, and with them is subordinated to the crowning idea of reason. Because *Deus non est in genere*[EN123], every theological method is to be rejected as untheological in which God's self-revelation is apparently recognised, but in fact is subsumed beneath a higher term, whether that of truth, or that of divine revelation in general, or that of religion, or that of history, so that it now has to be interpreted in the light of this higher comprehensive idea. We have already seen that the Bible repudiates such comparisons of God with other values, such attempts to transcend God, as though He were not supreme, the alpha and the omega. If we refuse to learn this lesson, if we audaciously attempt such equations and subsumptions, if we dare to bracket God along with other things, then, whatever may happen inside the framework of the system, God Himself cannot be spoken of, at any rate not honestly and seriously. With whatever earnestness and sincerity we may attempt to speak of the God who is embraced by such a system, in the last analysis we are not speaking of God but of the higher synthesis furnished by our controlling idea. The absoluteness of God permits of no such systematisations.

But behind this noetic absoluteness of God there stands decisively His ontic. This is decisive because in God's revelation it is really a question of His ontic absoluteness, from which His noetic absoluteness inevitably follows. God's freedom in relation to all that is not God signifies that He is distinct from everything, that He is self-sufficient and independent in relation to it, and that He is so in a peculiar and pre-eminent fashion—as no created being confronts any other. No created beings are in fact so independent of each other that in spite of this relative mutual independence they have not also to some extent a certain mutual interdependence, in the sense that ultimately none of them would have its being and nature apart from its interlocking with the being and nature of all the others. But God confronts all that is in supreme and utter independence, i.e., He would be no less and no different even if they all did not exist or existed differently. God stands at an infinite distance from everything else, not in the finite degree of difference with which created things stand towards each other. If they all have their being and a specific nature, God in His freedom has conferred it upon them: not because He was obliged to do

---

[EN120] God does not belong to any category
[EN121] God does not belong to any category
[EN122] God does not belong to any category
[EN123] God does not belong to any category

so, or because His purpose was influenced by their being and nature, but because their being and nature is conditioned by His being and nature. If they belong to Him and He to them, this dual relationship does not spring from any need of His eternal being. This would remain the same even if there were no such relationship. If there is a connexion and relatedness between them and Him, God is who He is in independence of them even in this relatedness. He does not share His being with theirs. He does not enter with them into a higher synthesis. He does not mingle and blend Himself with them. He does not transform Himself into them. Even in His relationship and connexion with them, He remains who He is. He creates and sustains this relationship. Through it He holds sway in an absolute supremacy which is unbroken and uninterrupted in the greatest aspects and also in the smallest. He would be
[312] who He is even without this connexion. Every relationship into which God enters with that which is not Himself must be interpreted—however much this may disturb or correct our preconceived ideas of connexion and relationship—as eventuating between two utterly unequal partners, the sheer inequality consisting in the fact that no self-determination of the second partner can influence the first, whereas the self-determination of the first, while not cancelling the self-determination of the second, is the sovereign predetermination which precedes it absolutely.

From this point of view all the conceptions of God must be excluded *a limine*[EN124] and definitively which take the form of what is called pantheism or panentheism. God does not form a whole with any other being either in identity with it or as compounding or merging with it to constitute a synthesis—the object of that master-concept, so often sought and found, which comprehends both God and what is not God. God enters into the closest relationship with the other, but He does not form such a synthesis with it. Therefore neither the conception of an identity of God with the universe in its totality is acceptable, nor that of God's identity with the elementary constituent substance of the universe—a view with which the history of Western philosophy began in Ionia—nor again the conception of God's identity with a world-soul or reason penetrating and informing the universe as an *élan vital*[EN125], or with the essential spiritual reality behind it, whether conceived statically as the inherently changeless principle behind all human mental and spiritual activity, or dynamically as the propelling force behind human intellectual and religious development. The mythology of a merely partial and to some extent selected identity of God with the world, which under the name of panentheism has been regarded as a better possibility than undiluted pantheism, is really in a worse case than is that of the latter. And again, it would be shortsighted, within the framework of panentheism itself, to give too decided a preference to Idealism, as though its two forms of expression, or one of them, were well adapted to compensate for the fundamental error on which they rest, and lead on to the Christian idea of God. Within the framework of these erroneous presuppositions, the Ionian possibility was not bad of its kind. And so it could not fail to come about that in the second half of the 19th century there was an inversion, and a type of panentheism arose which selected as its mythologumen, not the spirit or soul or reason as in an earlier period, but matter, or the atom, or some other symbol for the universe in its naturalistic aspect, identifying this with supreme being or divinity. We

---

[EN124] at the outset
[EN125] spark of life

may abuse this procedure as crass materialism. We may also point out with satisfaction that it is not quite so easy to maintain a materialism purged of all spiritual elements as the more careless materialists supposed. But we must not forget that at least the same applies to the affirmation of a "spiritualism" purged of all material elements; that this crass materialism is in fine only a reaction against the equally crass "spiritualism" previously in the ascendant; and that ultimately both of them had little cause to criticise a simple, undifferentiated and therefore crass pantheism, because after all they only represent action and reaction in the same view according to which God can be identified with another. If, as distinct from pantheism, it is desired to hazard only a partial identification, beyond the chosen sphere of the identification God must still be mingled with something else: in the case of Idealists with the (unavoidable) nature of the universe; in the case of materialists, with the likewise not wholly avoidable spirit. To that extent panentheism in its two forms is more crass, than crass pantheism. It is easy to see, however, that there is no place for mutual recrimination, since in every identification of God with another the fundamental error has been committed which in itself and as such can very well develop in a twofold and threefold dialectic, but on the basis of which there can never be a return to honest and serious thinking and speaking about [313]
God. In this connexion the essential insight is that God cannot in any way be or constitute a synthesis with that which is other than Himself. The Bible speaks of the God who cannot be or do this. It speaks of the absolute God. It is for this reason that it speaks sincerely and seriously of God. And this is what must happen, at any rate in the Christian Church, as a witness against all false gods.

Now the absoluteness of God strictly understood in this sense means that God has the freedom to be present with that which is not God, to communicate Himself and unite Himself with the other and the other with Himself, in a way which utterly surpasses all that can be effected in regard to reciprocal presence, communion and fellowship between other beings. It is just the absoluteness of God properly understood which can signify not only His freedom to transcend all that is other than Himself, but also His freedom to be immanent within it, and at such a depth of immanence as simply does not exist in the fellowship between other beings. No created being can be inwardly present to another, entering and remaining in communion with him in the depths of its inner life. No such being can create and sustain the life of another, seriously leading and governing, binding itself to the other and the other to itself in eternal faithfulness and whole-hearted devotion. The essence of every other being is to be finite, and therefore to have frontiers against the personality of others and to have to guard these frontiers jealously. It lies in the nature of the created being to have to be true to itself in such a way that with the best will in the world it simply cannot be true to another. It is its very nature that it cannot affirm itself except by affirming itself against others. For this reason it is only by simplification and tentatively, i.e., not with basic seriousness, that created beings can be present with each other, communicating and binding themselves to each other, listening to each other. Therefore between all such beings, as there is no genuine transcendence so there is no genuine immanence. A pantheistic or panentheistic alternation between God and another is required to affirm a true immanence even between created beings, instead of between God alone and all created beings. This affirmation needs a good deal of poetic fancy. But God is free. He is also free to be immanent, free to achieve a uniquely inward and genuine immanence of His being in and with the being which is distinct from Himself.

Therefore God can indeed (and this is His transcendence) be sufficiently beyond the creature to be his Creator out of nothing and at the same time be free enough partially or completely to transform its being or to take it from it again as first He gave it. But, if the expression may be allowed, God can do even more than this. He can (and this is His immanence) so indwell the other that, while He is its Creator and the Giver of its life, and while He does not take
[314] away this life, He does not withdraw His presence from this creaturely existence which is so different from His own divine life. Now that it has originated in His will and subsists by His will, He does not detach Himself from it in an alien aloofness, but is present as the being of its being with the eternal faithfulness of which no creature is capable towards another. God can allow this other which is so utterly distinct from Himself to live and move and have its being within Himself. He can grant and leave it its own special being distinct from His own, and yet even in this way, and therefore in this its creaturely freedom, sustain, uphold and govern it by His own divine being, thus being its beginning, centre and end. God can in fact be nearer to it than it is to itself. He can understand it better than it understands itself. He can inspire and guide it at a deeper level than it knows how to do itself—infinitely nearer, better, more deeply, yet not in dissolution but in confirmation of His own divine singularity, and again not in dissolution but in confirmation of the singularity of the creature. The fact that God can do this is His freedom in immanence.

But we must go further. God is sufficiently free to indwell the creature in the most varied ways according to its varying characteristics. The fulness of the movement in which, according to the witness of the Bible, we find God relating Himself to the creature must not therefore be interpreted as inessential and analogical, but as in the strictest sense a reality, because it is in this movement that He shows Himself to be God and not an idol, and therefore free—in contradistinction to the limitedness of a being which, even though it bears the highest attributes, betrays its creatureliness in the fact that its mode of approach and relation to the creature is, from the latter's point of view, inflexible. Of course, God too in His relationship to the world can react only in a certain way and not otherwise—that is, only according to His own standpoint, in correspondence with His divine being, as He determines and wills in His freedom. But in this His freedom, in which He spontaneously binds Himself in a certain way to the world, He remains unbound from the point of view of the world and its specific determinations. His changelessness does not coincide with any one of our constancies. His faithfulness is His own, and not the metaphysical equivalent of any one of the normal features of creaturely existence. His presence in the life and being of the world is His personal and therefore actual presence expressed in continually new forms according to His sovereign decisions.

It is not, then, the rigid presence of a being whose nature we can, so to speak, formulate in this or that principle. God is free to be present with the creature by giving Himself and revealing Himself to it or by concealing Himself and withdrawing Himself from it. God is free to be and operate in the created world either as unconditioned or as conditioned. God is free to perform His work either within the framework of what we call the laws of nature or outside it in the shape of miracle. God is free either to grant His immanence to nature by working at its heart or by exerting His sway at an infinite height above it. God is free to conceal His divinity from the creature, even to become a creature Himself, and free to [315] assume again His Godhead. He is free to maintain as God His distance from the creature and equally free to enter into partnership with it, indeed, to lift the creature itself, in the most vigorous sense, into unity with His own divine being, with Himself. God is free to rule over the world in supreme majesty and likewise to serve in the world as the humblest and meanest of servants, free even to be despised in the world, and rejected by the world. God is free to clothe Himself with the life of the world in all its glory as with a garment; but free likewise Himself to die the death which symbolises the end of all things earthly, in utter abandonment and darkness. God is free to be entirely unlimited over against the world: not bound by its finitude, nor by its infinitude; not confined to its time and space as a whole, nor to any one area of space or period of time. He is equally free to limit Himself: to be eternal in the tiny endlessness of our starry heavens, or of our human conceptuality, but eternal also in our finitude; to be shut up in the totality of our time-space universe, but also in all humility to be confined to this or that time and place as contrasted with other times and places. God is free to ally Himself, within creation, to the spirit as against rebellious nature, but also free to ally Himself with nature in opposition to the undoubtedly more rebellious spirit. God is free to be provoked and to be merciful, to bless and to punish, to kill and to make alive, to exalt us to heaven and to cast us down into hell. God is free to be wholly inward to the creature and at the same time as Himself wholly outward: *totus intra et totus extra*[EN126] and both, of course, as forms of His immanence, of His presence, of the relationship and communion chosen, willed and created by Himself between Himself and His creation. This is how He meets us in Jesus Christ. His revelation in Jesus Christ embraces all these apparently so diverse and contradictory possibilities. They are all His possibilities. If we deny Him any one of them, we are denying Jesus Christ and God Himself. Instead of recognising and adoring God, we are setting up an idol. For we are imposing upon Him—in defiance of the freedom which He has actually proved to us—a bondage which can be only that of our own self-will that would like to deny God and put itself in the place of God. If only the Word of God breaks through the walls of our self-will, our worship of the freedom of God exercised in His immanence can have no bounds. And then the full inadequacy of all pantheism and panentheism will be exposed to us. For what a poor limited God it is, and what a poor and limited world, whose confines wholly or partially overlap in these systems, so that they have to be wholly or partially interpreted as a unity! Once the boundless exaltation of God's freedom in immanence is recognised to be necessary and rendered, there can be no further lapse into these systems.

We must go further still. God is sufficiently free to differentiate His presence infinitely, and decisively, not merely with respect to the variations of the creature, but also in Himself, that is, according to the demands of His own intention with regard to the creature. The relationship and fellowship of God with

[EN126] wholly inward and wholly outward

the world is not bound to a definite scheme, to the *quantum* and *quale*[EN127] of a certain mode of action uniformly proceeding from Him.

Although in His eternal being and action towards the world God is undivided and indivisibly One and the Same, although He is always wholly the One He is, the mode of His action varies. It is one thing in the incarnation of the Word, in the once-for-all and unique assumption of human nature into unity with His eternal Son, into communion with His divine being. It is another thing in the wider kingdom of His grace—in the life of the Church and the children of God, in the power of preaching and the sacraments, in the power of the new conception and birth of man to faith by the Holy Spirit. It is another thing again in the
[316] creation, preservation and government of the existence and nature of the world and man, in virtue of which they are always neutral reality. It is another thing again in the future consummation, in the return of Christ, in the resurrection of the dead, in the last judgment and the end when He will be all in all. He acts and speaks variously in the prophets and apostles, in preaching and sacrament, in Holy Scripture, in the writings of the fathers and the creeds of the Church, differently yesterday, and differently to-day, and differently to-morrow. His communion with the angels is certainly different from His communion with the rest of the world. His communion with men is different from His communion with other spiritual creatures. His dealings with the faithful differ from His dealings with men in general. His manifestations in Church history differ from His manifestations in world history as such. And finally He is always infinitely diverse in His communion with each individual angel, thing, man, or believer, as compared with all the rest.

There is not only the infinite individual variation of the divine action *ad extra*[EN128], to which we first referred, but as its ground in the being and will of God, in His decrees, there is a whole hierarchy of His decisions and acts, the variation of which does not destroy but confirms the oneness of God as a divine unity in contradistinction to the unity of a natural force or spiritual principle. When we say this, we are not speculating. On the contrary, it would be speculation, an illegitimate simplification, a dishonouring of God, not to say this, seeing it is stated so unambiguously in God's revelation. It is fatal for the Church and a threat to the faith of each individual and his eternal felicity to overlook even a single one of the revealed variations of God's immanence, to deny it, to efface it, or to level it out into something generalised which as such certainly cannot be the divine.

We may say that dogmatics especially, which is always concerned to distinguish and discriminate (and necessarily so for the sake of the purity and fulness of Church doctrine), has its authorisation and justification at this point in the concept of God. If we do not like dogmatics because of its inevitable refinements and distinctions, we must consider whether we are not tilting against God Himself. For He has the freedom in all His *opus ad extra*[EN129] to remain the One who He is in an apparently inexhaustible abundance of distinctions which have to be noted. And He can be a valid object of our knowledge only if we do not deny Him this freedom and the apparently overwhelming richness of distinctions within His being, but conscientiously reckon with it at every point, being concerned only to realise and accept Him as He is.

[EN127] quantity and quality
[EN128] outside of himself
[EN129] work outside of himself

The triumph of God's freedom in immanence is seen precisely in this hierarchy of His being and action as it operates in relation to the being which is distinct from Himself. Yet it is not the case—for how otherwise would it be a hierarchy?—that we stand confronted by this richness of the divine being as by an unfathomable ocean of possibilities of any and every kind. According to the testimony of the same revelation which in the first instance simply discloses this richness as such to our gaze, inviting us to take God seriously as God now in this and now in that of His multiple manifestations, the fact emerges that all these possibilities of divine presence and action have a very definite centre, that is, they have their basis and their consummation, their meaning, their [317] norm and their law in Jesus Christ. In the first place, the fulfilled union of the divine and the human in Jesus Christ is, to be sure, one among others of these various possibilities of divine immanence, but over and beyond that, it must be defined, in its once-for-all and unique aspect, as the possibility of all other possibilities. For the Son of God who became flesh in Jesus Christ is, as an eternal mode of the divine being, nothing more nor less than the principle and basis of all divine immanence, and therefore the principle of what we have called the secondary absoluteness of God.

We have seen that the freedom of God, as His freedom in Himself, His primary absoluteness, has its truth and reality in the inner Trinitarian life of the Father with the Son by the Holy Spirit. It is here, and especially in the divine mode as the Son who is the "image of the invisible God" (Col. 1[15]), in God Himself, that the divine freedom in its aspect of communion with the other, i.e., the secondary absoluteness of God, has its original truth. Here it is not yet relationship and fellowship with the other that is outside God, with the created world. We should be repeating the error of Philo and Gnosticism, which was unhesitatingly repudiated by the early Church, if we tried to identify the Son of God with the world, and therefore to introduce the world in some sense as a necessary element, a divine mode, into the life of the Godhead. There could not then be any question of God's freedom in regard to it. But God Himself is the Son who is the basic truth of that which is other than God. As the Son of God this Other is God Himself. But God Himself becomes Another in the person of His Son. The existence of the world is not needed in order that there should be otherness for Him. Before all worlds, in His Son He has otherness in Himself from eternity to eternity. But because this is so, the creation and preservation of the world, and relationship and fellowship with it, realised as they are in perfect freedom, without compulsion or necessity, do not signify an alien or contradictory expression of God's being, but a natural, *the* natural expression of it *ad extra*. The world is, because and as the Son of God is. πάντα δι' αὐτοῦ ἐγένετο καὶ χωρὶς αὐτοῦ ἐγένετο οὐδὲ ἓν ὃ γέγονεν (Jn. 1[3]). ὁ κόσμος δι' αὐτοῦ ἐγένετο[EN130] (Jn. 1[10]). When we now learn that, over and beyond all this, it is said of the same Son of God: σὰρξ ἐγένετο[EN131] (Jn. 1[14]), that therefore, besides being Creator, He became creature, it is clear that in this singular and supreme relationship and fellowship between God and the world realised in the incarnation we have the quintessence of all possible relationship and fellowship generally and as such, and that in the transcendent freedom of God thus expressed we see the archetype and the norm of all the possible ways in

[EN130] Through him were all things made, and without him was not anything made that was made. The world was made through him

[EN131] became flesh

which He expresses His freedom in this relationship and fellowship. As the Son of God takes His place among other creatures, His place is inevitably at their head, controlling them all. He is necessarily the *πρωτότοκος πάσης κτίσεως*[EN132] (Col. 1^{15}), and whatever else is created, is created *δι' αὐτοῦ*[EN133], as well as *ἐν αὐτῷ*[EN134] and *εἰς αὐτόν*[EN135]. And with whatever freedom God expresses Himself in other ways in the sphere of creation, we shall have to recognise in the way in which He exercises His freedom here, and only here, the meaning, the norm and the goal of all the other ways in which He also does it, and quite differently.

Thus in spite of the almost confusing richness of the forms of divine immanence we are led to recognise a hierarchy, a sacred order, in which God is present to the world. We have only to grasp the fact that Jesus Christ is the focus and crown, and not merely the focus and the crown of all relationship and fellowship between God and the world, but also their basic principle, their
[318] possibility and presupposition in the life of the Godhead, and we shall see God's freedom disclose and develop itself. It does not do so as chaos. It does not do so as an ocean of particularities and contradictions. It does not do so as a picture composed arbitrarily and fortuitously, so that one thing is missing here and another might be different there. It does not do so as a pyramid whose apex is the apex and nothing more, based upon elements of a very different nature and origin, with which it unites to form a whole. But it does so as the one work of one unvarying wisdom, which excludes the fortuitous and the contradictory, which does not will at random or juxtapose incompatible elements, but which in the abundance of its effects wills only one thing, namely itself, and which orders all things to its own glory but also to the life and healing of the other which has its being by it and in it. Thus, everything for which God is free and in which God is free will be understood by us as the unity of the freedom of His being if we approach it in this way. It will not confuse us by its manifoldness, but will comfort, warn and rejoice us if we see that it derives from Jesus Christ the Son of God, attesting Him, serving Him and leading to Him, as is in fact disclosed to our sight and hearing in God's revelation. There is no caprice about the freedom of God. The faithfulness which He evinces and proves in His freedom with regard to His creation is His own faithfulness. It cannot, therefore, be reduced to the level of the regularity of a cosmic process. But it is not on this account concealed from us so that as a matter of fact and in practice we do not know to whom and to what we are clinging when we embrace and apprehend by faith this divine loyalty, when we are summoned by it, and consoled by it, and in turn invoke it. But what it purposes and wills is sure, as is the fact that in all its forms it is true steadfastness, responsible dealing and no irresponsible game. The fact is sure that God constantly turns to us, whether He seems near or far, whether He speaks to us in silence and in

EN132 first-born of all creation
EN133 through him
EN134 in him
EN135 for him

secret or whether He addresses us openly, whether He blesses us or punishes us, kills or makes alive. The fact is sure that He is none other than the Creator, the Lord of the Church, the Ruler of our hearts and consciences, the Judge at the last day, the same Lord to me and thee and to His angels and archangels, the same yesterday, to-day and for ever, here and now and in the remotest lands and times, ever diversely manifested in His freedom, yet ever the same, never and nowhere a different God. But we are sure of this fact only because God is Jesus Christ and Jesus Christ is God; only because the divine immanence in all its varied possibilities has its origin in Jesus Christ and therefore its unity in Him, but only in Him, in the diversity of its actions and stages. Therefore we cannot be sufficiently eager to insist, nor can it be sufficiently emphasised in the Church and through the Church in the world, that we know God in Jesus Christ alone, and that in Jesus Christ we know the one God. For this reason we are constantly called to make a decision in this matter, and every [319]
decision to which we are summoned will always be in the last resort a decision on this point. Any deviation, any attempt to evade Jesus Christ in favour of another supposed revelation of God, or any denial of the fulness of God's presence in Him, will precipitate us into darkness and confusion when we realise the abundant variety of the divine presence grounded in the divine freedom, because, without the key to the whole, even though He is undoubtedly present and we objectively meet Him, we will not find Him as God, nor be able to recognise and praise Him as God, for we will meet Him only in the diversity, in the curious details and puzzling contradictions of His presence. We will then have to fall back, according to the best of our knowledge and belief and our judgment from some other point of view, upon another basis of unity for His presence. We will then have to seek God here and there, and objectively we will not be mistaken in our search: for where is He not to be sought, He who has first sought and found us in Jesus Christ? But with what meaning and success can He be sought anywhere when He remains unknown to us in this form, when He is not acknowledged by us here as the one God; here, where He discloses the unity which embraces the manifold richness of His immanent presence, where He has permitted Himself to be found? All other unities of immanence which we seek and think we find cannot constitute the unity of His immanence, because we seek them elsewhere than at the point where God Himself has revealed it, where He has first sought and found us. We are simply making an idol of the ruins of His immanence, which seen and accepted as such does not attest but denies Him, and in the service and worship of this idol we can only more and more blind ourselves to the true God present to His creation.

In this way arise the various heathen religions and the various heresies within Christianity. The religions of heathendom come about because man simply does not know or refuses to know the ground of divine immanence in Jesus Christ. The Christian heresies spring from the fact that man does not take seriously the known ground of divine immanence in Jesus Christ, so that from its revelation, instead of apprehending Jesus Christ and the totality in

Him, he arbitrarily selects this or that feature and sets it up as a subordinate centre: perhaps the idea of creation, or the sacraments, or the life of the soul, or even the kingdom of God, or the regeneration of man, or the creeds or doctrine. There is also a possibility of idolatry by wresting a part or stage of the hierarchy of divine immanence from its connexion with its divine Head and accepting it in itself and as such as the truth and reality of Christ—oblivious of the fact that this immanence both as a whole and in its parts has Christian truth and reality only in so far as it is founded in Jesus Christ and summed up in Him, so that if, as a whole and in its parts, it is affirmed, preached and believed as a centre in itself and alongside of Christ, the Church will inevitably be led back into heathendom and its worship of the elements.

If the freedom of divine immanence is sought and supposedly found apart from Jesus Christ, it can signify in practice only our enslavement to a false god.
[320] For this reason Jesus Christ alone must be preached to the heathen as the immanent God, and the Church must be severely vigilant to see that it expects everything from *Jesus Christ*, and from Jesus Christ *everything*; that He is unceasingly recognised as the way, the truth, and the life (Jn. 14^{6}). This attitude does not imply Christian absolutism or ecclesiastical narrowmindedness, because it is precisely in Jesus Christ, but also exclusively in Him, that the abundance and plenitude of divine immanence is included and revealed. If we do not have Christ, we do not have at all, but utterly lack, the fulness of God's presence. If we separate ourselves from Him, we are not even on the way to this richness, but are slipping back into an impoverishment in which the omnipresent God is not known. The freedom of God must be recognised as His own freedom and this means—as it consists in God and as God has exercised it. But in God it consists in His Son Jesus Christ, and it is in Him that God has exercised it. In all its possibilities and shapes it remains the freedom which consists and is exercised in Jesus Christ. If we recognise and magnify it, we cannot come from any other starting-point but Him or move to any other goal.

Christology, therefore, must always constitute the basis and criterion for the apprehension and interpretation of the freedom of God in His immanence. The legitimacy of every theory concerning the relationship of God and man or God and the world can be tested by considering whether it can be understood also as an interpretation of the relationship and fellowship created and sustained in Jesus Christ. Is it capable of adaptation to the fundamental insights of the Church concerning the person and work of Jesus Christ—the *analogia fidei*[EN136]? Or does it stand in isolation from Christ's person and work, so that it can be brought into connexion with these insights only as an introduction or an appendix, neither deriving from them nor leading back to them. There are strictly speaking no Christian themes independent of Christology, and the Church must insist on this in its message to the world. It is at all events impossible to assert the contrary with reference to God and His freedom. If we appeal to God and His freedom, in the last resort, directly or indirectly, we can expound and elucidate only this one theme.

With this we have said conclusively what is to be said at the close of this subsection and of this whole section. We gave it the title: "The Being of God in Freedom" ; and in it we have spoken of God's aseity and of His primary and

---

[EN136] analogy of faith

secondary absoluteness. We again remind ourselves that in this whole discussion we have not been looking past the revelation of God to a dimension of His being somewhere beyond; we have not been concerned to define a divine predicate, a general idea of God, but the profundity of the revealed God Himself in His aseity, His primary and secondary absoluteness. Woe to us if we had spoken of freedom generally and ascribed this to God as an attribute the meaning of which we could fathom quite apart from the fact that it is a divine attribute! We would then have been engaged in erecting at this very spot the worst of all idolatries. When we say that God is free, the accent does not fall on "free" but on "God." What we mean by freedom in this context, in what legit- [321] imate sense God can be known and understood as He who dwells in freedom, is something which can be disclosed only as we put the question to God Himself and listen to the answer which He gives us. For this reason we started from the living and loving of God, and now again we must point expressly to the fact that we have not strayed from the living and loving of God, but that it is the aseity, the freedom of the divine living and loving, and only to that extent the divinity of this living and loving, the divinity of God, which has occupied this final section. We cannot get behind God—behind God in His revelation—to try to ask and determine from outside what He is. We can only learn and then attempt to repeat what He Himself alone can tell us and has told us—who He is. But He is who He is as the One who loves, not in a substance in which He can be more or less or something other than the living God. We have seen indeed that the life and act of God is the life and act of His love. The only reason we have to distinguish between the living and loving of God is because He is not merely the idea of love but the One who loves in the very act of His existence. It is not that God first lives and then also loves. But God loves, and in this act lives. If we have interpreted the divinity of His act, or the divinity of God, as freedom, we could not and cannot mean by this notion of freedom anything different from Himself as the One who loves. We cannot mean a "universal" in which He merely participates as the One who loves. We can mean and characterise only the manner, the utterly unique manner, of His love. His loving is, as we have seen, utterly free, grounded in itself, needing no other, and yet also not lacking in another, but in sovereign transcendence giving, communicating itself to the other. In this freedom it is the divine loving. But we must also say, conversely, that only in this divine loving is the freedom described by us divine freedom. If we abstract the love of God and therefore the purpose of God, however circumspect we may be, we describe only a world-principle. Therefore we must not think away the love or the person of God for a single moment if we wish to think rightly and truly of God's divinity. God is free. Because this is the case, we must say expressly in conclusion that the freedom of God is the freedom which consists and fulfils itself in His Son Jesus Christ. In Him God has loved Himself from all eternity. In Him He has loved the world. He has done so in Him, in the freedom which renders His life divine, and therefore glorious, triumphant, and strong to save.

[322] § 29

THE PERFECTIONS OF GOD

God lives His perfect life in the abundance of many individual and distinct perfections. Each of these is perfect in itself and in combination with all the others. For whether it is a form of love in which God is free, or a form of freedom in which God loves, it is nothing else but God Himself, His one, simple, distinctive being.

God's being consists in the fact that He is the One who loves in freedom. In this He is the perfect being: the being which is itself perfection and so the standard of all perfection; the being, that is, which is self-sufficient and thus adequate to meet every real need; the being which suffers no lack in itself and by its very essence fills every real lack. Such a being is God. He is this being because He lives as such. It is as we return to life as the fundamental element in the divine being that we also move forward to God's perfections. The one perfection of God, His loving in freedom, is lived out by Him, and therefore identical with a multitude of various and distinct types of perfection. There is no possibility of knowing the perfect God without knowing His perfections. The converse is also true: knowledge of the divine perfections is possible only in knowledge of the perfect God, of His loving in freedom. But because God lives His perfect being the knowledge of His perfections is also a way—the way which in the presence of the living God we must tread. In other words, even in the knowledge of the one perfect God we are confronted by His richness. The real God is the one God who loves in freedom, and as such is eternally rich. To know Him means to know Him again and again, in ever new ways—to know only Him, but to know Him as the perfect God, in the abundance, distinctness and variety of His perfections.

As we understand the one being of God from this angle, we enter the region of that complex of teaching which the older dogmatics treated under the heading "The Doctrine of the Attributes of God," His *appellationes, virtutes, attributa, proprietates* or even *perfectiones*[EN1]. From these suggested terms—while reserving to ourselves the right to make occasional use of the others—we choose the last because it points at once to the thing itself instead of merely to its formal aspect, and because instead of something general it expresses at once that which is clearly distinctive. The fact that God's being has attributes is something which it has in common with the being of others. But that it is identical with a multitude of perfections—if the term is taken strictly—is something which is the "attribute" of God and of God alone.

[EN1] designations, virtues, attributes, properties, perfections

The old problem of the doctrine of the attributes of God is so far-reaching that in this section we must first devote to it a general treatment, and then develop it concretely in the two following sections. [323]

Let us first attempt to define the problem as such. In this connexion our primary affirmation must be that here too it is a question of nothing else but of God Himself. But because we are thinking of God Himself, we are thinking of the One who at the same time, in confirmation and glorification of His oneness, is also many. We are careful not to say: all. There is much which God is not. God is not creature. God is not sin. God is not death. But He is many, not merely something, not merely one. He is who He is and what He is in both unity and multiplicity. He is the One who is this many, and the many who are this One. The One is He who loves in freedom. The many are His perfections—the perfections of His life. Only perfections come under consideration here, for what He is is perfect because He is it. And every sort of perfection which there can possibly be can be only His perfection. How can He be anything except in perfection, and what can be perfect except in Him? But everything which can be described as perfect is so because He is this thing. He not only has it as others might have it. He has it as His own exclusively. And not only so, but He *is* it, so that it has its essential being in Him.

Sed certe quidquid es, non per aliud es quam per te ipsum. Tu es igitur ipsa vita, qua vivis et sapientia qua sapis et bonitas ipsa qua bonis et malis bonus es[EN2] (Anselm of Canterbury, *Prosl.* 12).

Since God is Father, Son and Holy Ghost, i.e., loves in freedom, every perfection exists essentially in Him.

Deo autem hoc est esse, quod est fortem esse, aut iustum esse, aut sapientem esse et si quid de illa simplici multiplicitate vel multiplici simplicitate dixeris, quo substantia eius significetur[EN3] (Augustine, *De Trin.* 4, 6, cf. VI, 7, 8). *Hoc enim est Deo esse quod velle, et hoc velle, quod sapere*[EN4] (*Conc. Tolet.* XV, 688, *Denz.* VI, *No.* 294). *Sicut nefas est putare, quod substantia supremae naturae sit aliquid, quod melius sit aliquo modo non ipsum, sic necesse est ut sit, quidquid omnino melius est quam non ipsum .... Quare necesse est eam esse viventem, sapientem, potentem et omnipotentem, veram, iustam, beatam, aeternam et quidquid similiter absolute melius est quam non ipsum*[EN5] (Anselm of Canterbury, *Monol.* 15). And so Calvin wanted all the attributes of God to be understood as *virtutes*[EN6] of His *aeternitas καὶ αὐτουσία*[EN7] (*Instit.* I, 10, 2).

[EN2] But certainly whatever you are, you are not so through something other than your own self. Therefore you are the very life by which you live, and the wisdom by which you are wise and the very goodness by which you are good to those who are both good and evil

[EN3] With God, being is what being strong or being just or being wise is, and his substance would be of the signified, if one were to say anything of that simple multiplicity or multiple simplicity

[EN4] For it belongs to God to be what he wills, and to will what he knows

[EN5] Just as it is unlawful to think that the substance of the highest nature is something in comparison with which not-itself were better, so it is necessary that it be whatever is altogether better than not-itself. Thus it is necessary that it be living, knowing, powerful and all-powerful, true, just, blessed, eternal and what is absolutely and in the same way better than not-itself

[EN6] virtues

[EN7] eternity and 'being in himself'

To speak of God's attributes as we must and may do, since we are speaking of Him on the ground of His revelation, means therefore to speak again and this time properly, in concrete definition, of His being. It is impossible to have knowledge of God Himself without having knowledge of a divine perfection, and it is impossible to have knowledge of a divine perfection without having knowledge of God Himself—knowledge of the triune God who loves in freedom. For as the triune God, both in regard to His revelation and to His being
[324] in itself, He exists in these perfections, and these perfections again exist in Him and only in Him as the One who, both in His revelation and in eternity, is the same. To grasp and understand this connexion is the special task of the doctrine of God's attributes. In this doctrine we have to attain the insight that God—and here the German language offers a possibility of expression which other languages do not have—is not only the Lord (*Herr*), but the Lord of glory (*Herrlichkeit*), and conversely, that all glory is the glory of God the Lord (*die Herrlichkeit Gottes des Herrn*).

In taking as our point of departure the glory of God we touch on a concept the explanation and exposition of which will form the conclusion to our whole survey of this doctrine and therefore to the doctrine of the reality of God. We cannot well do other than begin at this point with the same concept.

It does not go without saying that with equal emphasis God (or, according to 1 Cor. 2^8 and Jas. 2^1, Jesus Christ) is both the *Lord* and the Lord of *glory* and is recognised and confessed as such. There is always the danger of a cleavage here. The danger is equally great on both sides, and on both sides it jeopardises no less than everything.

God as the Lord can be viewed and understood so to speak in a punctual or linear manner. He is the fully existent One, and perhaps also, according to our definition, the One who is utterly loving and free. But as such He is perhaps a very intensive, yet to some extent also a very slender, not to say impoverished and spectral being. He becomes living for us, He acquires for us abundance of life, vividness and palpable reality, only as He enters into relation with us, as there stands over against Him a world and especially man in his manifold movement, in relation to which He Himself acquires movement. But He cannot be taken with true and final seriousness in this movement and therefore in His glory, His glory cannot be accepted strictly, because all that His revelation appears to affirm in this regard has to be understood only as a divine economy which is grounded more in the nature of the world, and in our own nature, than in the nature of God Himself. This nature itself, as the proper being of God, has to be regarded as standing inscrutably beyond and above this economy. That God is mighty, holy, just, merciful, omnipresent, is affirmed more in relation to an analogical world in which He exists for us than in relation to His being in itself as it is in reality. In this case faith in Him can never completely free itself from ultimate suspicion in face of a Lord whom it pleases to yield Himself to us in this or that form in a kind of sport, without disclosing Himself in reality, without giving us any pledge that in Himself He is not perhaps quite other, and so radically different from the forms of glory in the game played with us that it is not worth while perhaps to take part in this game or this economy. In regard to the glory of God understood in this way, we may well prefer the dark secret of our own existence (as a secret with which we are in [325] any case more intimately concerned) to the whole range of this purely economical glory of God, i.e., to the unknown quantity, the inscrutable being who is concealed by it. In this case, we will be strongly tempted, in spite of the ambiguity of our own life, in spite of the frailty of our own glory, finally to accept these tatters, to try to be our own neighbour, instead of committing ourselves to an enigma in regard to which we cannot conclusively know—if we do so commit ourselves—in whose hands we will rest. It is dangerous and ultimately fatal to faith in God if God is not the Lord of glory, if it is not guaranteed to us that in spite of the analogical nature of the language in which it all has to be expressed God is actually and unreservedly as we encounter Him in His revelation: the Almighty, the Holy, the Just, the Merciful, the Omnipresent, the Eternal, not less but infinitely more so than it is in our power to grasp, and not for us only, but in actuality therefore in Himself. Holy Scripture speaks to us of God in such a way as to give us this assurance. It does not point beyond the whole glory of God to this punctual or linear being, as though the latter is the real and true God, while His glory is only a mode of revelation, a phenomenon. But attesting to us the glory of God, it certifies to us that this Lord of glory is as such the real and true God. In this manner Scripture invites us to serious and true faith in God Himself and not merely to committal to the economy or sport of a great Unknown, even though he may be called the One who loves in freedom. To attest and expound this biblical unity of the Lord with His glory is the business of the doctrine of the divine perfections.

But the task must also be viewed from the other angle. The glory of God can be seen and understood in a way which dissipates and dissolves it because it has no Lord. It then consists in a collection of mighty potencies by which man sees himself surrounded and about which, on the basis of revelation, he must believe that in them all he is confronted by the divine. He must believe in an omnipresent One who penetrates all things. He must believe in His infinite and irresistible power. But he must also believe in a holiness and justice governing both himself and the world—a norm by which he is measured and to which he is responsible without ever being able to satisfy it. Besides all this he must believe further in a goodness and mercy, in a patience reigning over all, in a wisdom which orders all things for the best, holding them together and leading them to a goal, and finally in an eternity from which man springs and towards which he moves. What a strange, obviously inscrutable, incoherent and self-contradictory world of ultimates this is in which he thus finds himself!—and so much the more so the more seriously he takes now the one, now the other of these divine potencies, the more sincerely he wishes to lay it to heart that in all of them he has to do with the Deity. Really with the Deity?

[326] Really with God Himself? That is just the question—whether the whole so-called glory of God is not really a world of conceptual forces, of principalities and powers, which in the last resort, as the objectified projection of human wishes and fears, is no less but much more of the world, in a certain sense, than the rest of the world and man himself. Where and who is God in this His supposed glory? Is He more than a collective name for all sorts of ultimate values which as such will still be divine without Him? How mistaken is our understanding of this glory when the recognition that it is God's glory is only a meaningless appendix to the real view, according to which it is only the cosmos, or rather the chaos, of certain hypostatised principles! What servitude, in this case, is the alleged worship of God and so-called piety! What rebellion is concealed behind our submission! What a desire to break free from our bondage to masters whose claim to rule is obviously compromised by their plurality, and who can in any case be so easily handled that man tries to make himself independent of them all, attributing to himself the power to decide what is holy, righteous, good and eternal, and what in all this is really the One! Again it is inevitably dangerous and ultimately fatal to faith if God is not the Lord of glory, if we have no guarantee that everything which in heaven and on earth is truly glorious, and therefore all power, goodness, justice and wisdom, are not distinct from Him but are in fact Himself. Here again, everything is made plain to us in Holy Scripture. In testifying to us of God's glory, Holy Scripture does not refer us to this and that, to all sorts of potencies about which we must subsequently allow ourselves to be persuaded that they are God's representatives and servants. But according to Scripture, all the glory of God is concentrated, gathered up and unified in God Himself as the Lord of glory. While in Holy Scripture God has quite definite attributes and an abundance of perfections, we are never concerned merely with these attributes or perfections as such, but with them as His, and therefore always directly with Himself. Therefore Holy Scripture can summon us to a faith which does not consist in the affirmation of all sorts of ultimate values, but in the affirmation of a single genuine sovereignty established over us—an affirmation which has nothing in common with slavish submission, which contains no fear and therefore no seed of revolt in itself. There is revolt against this Lord only in the form of a return to slavery, to the unreal worship and piety which we think ourselves called upon to render to a diffused glory which is not that of God. To show the biblical unity of all glory with its Lord is the task of the doctrine of God's perfections viewed from its second angle.

It should be noted that in this matter we have an exact parallel to the concern of the doctrine of the Holy Trinity. In this doctrine the one God in His three modes of being corresponds to the Lord of glory. As it is of decisive importance to recognise the three modes of being, not only economically as modalism does, but, according to the seriousness
[327] of the divine presence and power in the economy of His works, as modes of being of the one eternal God Himself, so it is equally important to understand that God in Himself is not

divested of His glory and perfections, that He does not assume them merely in connexion with His self-revelation to the world, but that they constitute His own eternal glory. Again, as it is of decisive importance not to dissolve the unity of the Godhead tritheistically into three gods, but to understand the three modes of being strictly as the modes of being of the one God with whom we have to do in all His works, so it is of equal importance to interpret God's glory and perfections, not in and for themselves, but as the glory of the Lord who alone is able to establish, disclose and confirm them as real glory. The attributes or perfection of God are as it were the letters of the divine Word. It becomes a Word only through the sequence and unity of these letters. But again, it is only in this sequence and unity that the letters can constitute the Word. In the same way the doctrine of God's perfections consists at every point only in the development and confirmation of the doctrine of His being. We can in fact only continue to say that He is the One who loves in freedom. Yet in the doctrine of God's perfections there must be this development and confirmation of the doctrine of His being. It must therefore tread this path.

We next turn our attention to the question of the possibility, legitimacy and necessity of speaking here of perfections (in the plural), of the glory of God as a multiplicity of perfections, and therefore of the latter in their individuality and diversity. This possibility, legitimacy and necessity are not at all self-evident.

That there exists objectively in God Himself a multiplicity of this kind, and therefore individuality and diversity, contradicts what we have indicated as the characteristic relation of simplicity and plenitude in the being of Him who is the Lord of glory. And in the history of Christian doctrine it has been disputed more or less consistently and expressly, but very definitely in substance. The multiplicity of attributes as contrasted with the simplicity of the being of God has always been affirmed to be improper. The simplicity of the divine being has always been held to be the only true description of that being. We must discriminate between an extreme and a more moderate or mediate form of the opposition which confronts us, but it cannot be ignored that we have to meet it equally decisively in both its forms.

The extreme expression of it is seen in the strict nominalistic thesis as represented by Eunomius in antiquity and William of Occam and Gabriel Biel in the Middle Ages. According to this all individual and distinct statements about the being of God have no other value than that of purely subjective ideas and descriptions (*conceptus, nomina*) to which there is no corresponding reality in God, who is pure simplicity. According to Eunomius God is in fact to be characterised only as *nuda essentia*[EN8]. Schleiermacher too is probably to be understood in the sense of this extreme opposition—which in the form of a thesis of Meister Eckhart (*nulla distinctio in ipso Deo esse potest aut intelligi*[EN9]) was condemned as heretical by Pope John XXII in 1329. For as he sees it, all attributes which we distinguish in God (whose being is exhaustively defined in the concept of causality) do not denote something distinctive in God but something distinctive in the way we relate our pure feeling of dependence to Him at various stages of our religious self-consciousness (*The Chr. Faith*, § 50). Corresponding to the absolute unity of God we can see in His attributes only an expression, which our

---

[EN8] bare essence

[EN9] no distinction can be or be understood in God himself

thinking cannot avoid, of the Godhead which in itself is absolutely one (R. Seeberg, *Chr. Dogmatik*, I, 1925, 399).

According to the main stream of theological tradition which holds the balance in this matter, the emphasis—in distinction to this strict nominalism—falls less upon the negation,
[328] upon the "only," than upon the positive point that the statements concerning a multiplicity of perfections in God are statements expressing our vision of God. They may be made quite decidedly in regard to the characteristic limitations of the human understanding face to face with this object. Thus Irenaeus defined the attributes of God as *earum virtutum quae semper sunt cum Deo appellationes, quemadmodum possibile est et dignum hominibus audire et dicere de Deo*[EN10] (*Adv. o. h.* II, 13, 9). Thomas Aquinas wrote as follows: *De Deo loquentes, utimur nominibus concretis, ut significemus eius subsistentiam, quia apud nos non subsistunt nisi composita: et utimur nominibus abstractis, ut significemus eius simplicitatem. Quod ergo dicitur Deitas vel vita vel aliquid huiusmodi, esse in Deo, referendum est ad diversitatem, quae est in acceptione intellectus nostri et non ad aliquam diversitatem rei*[EN11] (*S. theol.* I, *qu.* 3, *art.* 3, *ad.* 1). *Deus in se consideratus est omnino unus et simplex: sed tamen intellectus noster secundum diversas conceptiones ipsum cognoscit, eo quod non potest ipsum ut in se ipso est, videre. Sed quamvis intelligat ipsum sub diversis conceptionibus, cognoscit tamen quod omnibus suis conceptionibus respondet una et eadem res simplex*[EN12] (*ibid., qu.* 13, *art.* 12 c). And even more positively: *Sicut diversae res uni simplici rei, quae Deus est, similantur per formas diversas, ita intellectus noster per diversas conceptiones ei aliqualiter similatur .... Et ideo de uno intellectus noster multa concipiens non est falsus neque vanus, quia illud simplex esse divinum hujusmodi est, ut ei secundum formas multiplices aliqualiter assimilari possint*[EN13] (*S. c. gent.* I, 35). Polanus put it this way: *Proprietates Dei essentiales ut non realiter, ita nec ex natura rei sed ratione distinguntur, aut modo potius, id est nostra conceptions et comprehensione seu nostro intelligendi modo*[EN14] (*Synt. theol. chr.*, 1609, *col.* 902). Quenstedt wrote: *Quia intellectus noster finitus infinitam et simplicissimam Dei essentiam uno conceptu adaequato adaequate concipere nequit, ideo distinctis et inadaequatis conceptibus essentiam divinam inadaequate repraesentantibus eandem apprehendit, qui conceptus inadaequati dicuntur affectiones et attributa Dei*[EN15] (*Theol. did. pol.*, 1685, I, *c.* 8, *sect.* I, *th.* 3). And it could be bluntly formulated by

---

[EN10] designations of those virtues which God invariably possesses, inasmuch as is possible and worthy for humans to speak of God

[EN11] Speaking of God, we use concrete nouns, in order to signify his subsistence, since for us only composite things subsist. And we use abstract nouns in order to signfy his simplicity. Thus, the fact that God's being is called 'deity' or 'life' or something of another kind, is to be attributed to the diversity which is in the reception in our intellect, and not to some diversity in the object

[EN12] God in himself has been considered to be altogether a simple unity. But on the other hand, our intellect knows him according to diverse concepts, such that it is not possible to see him as he is in himself. And although he understands himself in diverse concepts, he nevertheless knows how the same simple unity corresponds to all his concepts

[EN13] Just as diverse things are likened in diverse forms to the one simple thing which is God, so also our intellect is likened to him in its difference. And thus our intellect conceives many things with respect to the one and is not false or vain (in doing so), since that divine simplicity is of such a kind that they be able in their difference to be likened to him according to multiple forms

[EN14] The essential properties of God are distinguished neither in reality nor by their nature, but by reason. Or rather, only by our reasoning and comprehension, or by our way of understanding

[EN15] Since our finite intellect cannot adequately conceive of the infinite and utterly simple essence of God in one sufficient concept, therefore distinct and inadequate concepts represent inadequately the divine essence. In this way the intellect apprehends that essence. These concepts are inadequately called the affections and attributes of God

Wegscheider as follows: *Cognitio attributorum Dei ... ob mentis nostrae imbecillitatem ita comparata est, ut ... anthropopathiam plus minusve redoleat, nec nisi analogice, symbolice atque imperfecte esse possit*[EN16] (*Inst. Theol.*, 1815, § 60). The emphasis could also be laid on the fact that, in becoming known to us in this multiplicity of attributes, God Himself has condescended to adjust Himself to our capacities of understanding. This was the opinion of John of Damascus: "God is nameless, but in His mercy allows Himself to be named, as befits our need" (*Ekd.* I, 12). Calvin took the same view: "The attributes of God express *non quis sit apud se, sed qualis erga nos: ut ista eius agnitio vivo magis sensu quam vacua et meteorica speculatione constet*[EN17] (*Inst.* I, 10, 2). So, too, did Wolleb: *Proprietates divinae sunt attributa Dei, quibus se nobis infirmis cognoscendum praebet et a creaturis distinguit*[EN18] (*Chr. Theol. comp.*, 1626, I, 1, 2). And so the attributes of God according to C. I. Nitzsch are conceptual expressions of the real relation of God to the world:" The idea of God discloses its quality only as the movements and changes of self- and world-consciousness give occasion " (*Syst. d. chr. Lehre*[6], 1851, 149). The nominalistic background and tendency of all these opinions is unmistakable. It is clear that on this basis there is no desire simply to abandon and deny the attributes of God, but actually to assert them, as is in fact done. Even Schleiermacher does this, and more so Thomas Aquinas, and especially Protestant orthodoxy which stood foursquare on this ground. The thesis could even be advanced as in Quenstedt: *Attributa divina ante omnem intellectus nostri operationem revera et proprie sunt in Deo*[EN19] (*Theol. did. pol.*, 1685, I, *c.* 8, *sect.* 2, *qu.* 2), in which the basic nominalism was apparently—but only apparently—transcended. Even Polanus realised: *Proprietates essentiales Dei sunt in Deo ab aeterno in aeternum ... non sunt posteriores essentia Dei quia reipsa sunt idem .... Sine proprietatibus divinis essentialibus Deus esse non potest, ne sine seipso sit*[EN20] (*ibid., col.* 903 f.). And also Petrus van Mastricht: *Omnia attributa vere Deo competere. Est enim, non per cogitationem tantum nostrum, sed ex naturae suae conditione bonus, sapiens, Justus, etc.*[EN21] (*Theor.-pract. Theol.*, 1698, II, *cap.* 5, 7). But immediately afterwards [329]
Polanus continues: *Non sunt proprie loquendo multae proprietates in Deo sed una tantum, quae nihil aliud est quam ipsa divina essentia ... sed respectu nostri quasi multae proprietates dicuntur, quia in nobis sunt multae*[EN22]. And Quenstedt, too, qualifies what he had said: *Si enim proprie et accurate loqui velimus, Deus nullas habet proprietates sed mera et simplicissima est essentia quae nec realem differentiam, nec ullam vel rerum vel modorum admittit compositionem .... Quia vero simplicissimam Dei essentiam uno adaequato conceptu adaequate concipere non possumus, ideo inadaequatis et distinctis conceptibus inadaequate essentiam divinam repraesentantibus eum apprehendimus, quos ...*

[EN16] The knowledge of the attributes of God, on account of the weakness of our minds, has been gained such that it seems more or less like anthropopathy, and can only be possible analogically, symbolically, or imperfectly

[EN17] not who he is on his own terms, but as he is toward us: so that knowledge of him consists more in living awareness than in useless heavenly speculation

[EN18] Divine properties are attributes of God, by which he offers himself to be known to us in our weakness and distinguishes himself from his creatures

[EN19] Divine attributes in fact exist strictly speaking in God himself, even before the all the operation of our intellects

[EN20] The essential properties of God are in God from eternity to eternity ... They are not subsequent to the essence of God, since they are identical with it ... God cannot be, without the essential divine properties, otherwise he would be without himself

[EN21] All attributes truly come together in God. For he is by virtue of his own nature good, wise and just, etc, not merely by virtue of our reflection

[EN22] Strictly speaking, there are not many properties in God, but only one, which is nothing other than the very divine essence. But as far as we are concerned, many properties are spoken of, since for us there are many

attributa vocamus. Et sic intellectus noster distinguit, quae ex parte rei distincta non sunt[EN23] (*ibid., ekth.* 3). So, too, does Petrus van Mastricht: *Attributa Deo competere quasi in esse quodam secundo, quatenus prius essentiam Dei concipimus velut radicem a qua attributa oriuntur. Concipimus enim, Deum esse, antequam concipere possumus, eum misericordem, sapientem, justum esse*[EN24] (*loc. cit.*). It was gladly conceded that this *modus concipiendi*[EN25] was *non destitutus omni fundamento in re*[EN26] (Quenstedt, *ibid., font. sol.*, 5), and on this was based the justification and necessity of speaking *vere et proprie*[EN27], not merely anthropopathically, of God's attributes. Even in Catholic dogmatics, which follow St. Thomas, there is much talk of this *fundamentum in re*[EN28]. But an explanation of what is to be understood by this *fundamentum* has never been vouchsafed. Nor could it properly be investigated. For the presupposition stood firm that by the being of God must be meant His *essentia*[EN29] as such, i.e., at bottom His *nuda essentia*[EN30], whose simplicity must be conceptually the first and last and real thing, the *proprium*[EN31], with which we are here concerned, and in comparison with which every other statement can have no further value than that of a concession, a purely secondary truth. It is very plain in Polanus, Quenstedt and van Mastricht that they are making efforts to do justice to the emphasis with which the Bible speaks of the being of God as having specific attributes. The statement that the *proprietates Dei*[EN32] are not *qualitates aut accidentia*[EN33] of His being but this being itself, may be defined as the kernel of the older doctrine of the divine attributes. But it was invariably interpreted unfavourably to the *proprietates*[EN34], so that in the last resort the latter necessarily lose their reality in favour of the *essentia*[EN35]. For they were conceived as rooted, not in the *essentia*[EN36] as such, but—in spite of occasional reservations and occasional happy assertions to the contrary—only in its relation to us and our relations to it. The fact that the life of God was identified with the notion of pure being, the fact that the idea of God was not determined by the doctrine of the Trinity, but that the latter was shaped by a general conception of God (that of ancient Stoicism and Neo-Platonism), was now avenged at the most sensitive spot. Starting from the generalised notion of God, the idea of the divine simplicity was necessarily exalted to the all-controlling principle, the idol, which, devouring everything concrete, stands behind all these formulae. As a result it was impossible to make proper use of what Augustine had so happily indicated with his phrase *multiplex simplicitas*[EN37] or *simplex*

[EN23] For if we were wanting to speak strictly and accurately, God has no properties, but is pure and utterly simple essence, which admits no real differentiation, and no composition of items or modes. But since we cannot adequately conceive of the utterly simple essence of God with one adequate conception, therefore we represent the divine essence inadequately with inadequate and distinct concepts, and apprehend him in this way. These concepts we call attributes. And thus our intellects distinguish what are not distinct parts

[EN24] The attributes meet in God almost in a second being, inasfar as we conceive of the essence of God as a root from which the attributes arise. For we conceive that God exists before we can conceive that he is merciful, wise, just etc.

[EN25] mode of conceiving

[EN26] not destitute of any basis in fact

[EN27] truly and properly

[EN28] basis in fact

[EN29] basis

[EN30] bare essence

[EN31] proper

[EN32] properties of God

[EN33] qualities or accidents

[EN34] properties

[EN35] essence

[EN36] essence

[EN37] multiple simplicity

multiplicitas[EN38]: the triumphant unity in God of the Lord with glory and of glory with the Lord. From this starting-point we can speak only hesitantly about the reality of the divine perfections. On this basis, when we speak of God, we must mean essentially only the simplicity and not the richness, at best the simplicity of the richness, but at bottom only the simplicity. We may try to specify, but in the last resort we can intend and demonstrate only the barrenness of *nuda essentia*[EN39]. This was done only in the last resort. There was at least a hesitation. The themes suggested by the Bible were not simply abandoned. In spite of the alien presupposition, and within the conditions which it imposed, they were adopted and an attempt was made to exploit them. This was the best feature of all these systems. But there was in fact a hesitation between the reality and unreality, between an objective and a purely [330] subjective discrimination of the divine attributes. As D. F. Strauss (*Die chr. Glaubenslehre*) ridiculed, they were placed in an "unhappy midway position." This is indisputable. It was indeed an unhappy position because the attributes of God had to be affirmed *proprie*[EN40] and yet they could not be; because the *proprie*[EN41] uttered by the lips could be interpreted only as an *improprie*[EN42]; because in this position what had to be affirmed had already been denied by the whole approach.

It is to the credit of certain German theologians of the 19th century that in this matter they broke utterly, not only with the total, but also with the partial nominalism of the Thomistic and orthodox Protestant tradition. "Christian faith lives in the countenance of the eternal and omnipresent, the holy and gracious God, and for it these specific attributes belong so little to the purely subjective sphere of a mere perception of God which does not correspond to anything really existing in God that for it God would cease to be the living and true God without such attributes and would become a lifeless shadowy abstraction. That the many, the manifold, the diverse, is thus attributed to God in His self-existence does not embarrass faith or lead it astray as regards God's absoluteness and unity. On the contrary, it would not recognise God as the real, the absolute, the One, if it were not permitted to ascribe to Him also the attributes of eternity, omnipotence and holiness as objectively belonging to Him." "The dogmatic formulation of these attributes can correspond to faith-consciousness only when both aspects—the objective reality of the attributes as manifold and distinct (in accordance with their meaning), and also the unbroken unity of God on which these attributes ultimately rest, and which alone in fact confers on them their reality—stand out clearly and complete each other without contradiction" (F. H. R. Frank, *Syst. d. chr. Wahrh.*[2], 1885, I, 222 f.). The statement that the attributes of God are nothing other than His being is correct, as is also the further statement that in them the relationship of God to the other, to the created world, is made known. But it is not right to oppose these statements "as though, because God's relation to the other is expressed in them, these attributes are so much the less or not at all the being of God, or as though, because the attributes actually are and express the being of God, this somehow precludes them from expressing it in its relationship to the other. For they must belong to the divine being, they must constitute and characterise the divine being, if they are at all divine attributes, and if that which is divine cannot come to God from that which He is not" (*op. cit.*, p. 226). "If God exists only in a relationship to the world, then all His attributes are only relations, revelations and effects in the world—and such a view imperils God's independence of the world; for in that case He becomes what He is only through His relationship to the world .... But there is a relationship

EN38 simple multiplicity
EN39 bare essence
EN40 properly
EN41 properly
EN42 improperly

of God to Himself ... and in this is grounded the justification for affirming immanent or essential attributes in God" (G. Thomasius, *Christi Person und Werk*[3], 1886, I, 38). J. A. Dorner argued on the same correct lines: "If God refuses to allow us any knowledge of His being in itself, but only of His being in its relation to the world, then He reveals to the world, because not Himself, necessarily some other than Himself" (*System der chr. Glaubenslehre*[3], Vol. I, 1886, 191). "Since God cannot wish to appear other than He is, and since no dualistic power checks His will to reveal Himself, then it must be that in God's self-revelations we see revelations of what and how He is (not simply what and how He is not), and therefore the revelation of objective attributes" (*op. cit.*, p. 186). This is the line of thought which we must develop.

We shall develop the truth of the multiplicity, individuality and diversity of God's perfections—in view of the nominalistic contesting and the semi-nominalistic weakening of them and in answer to both—in three explanatory propositions.

[331] 1. The multiplicity, individuality and diversity of the divine perfections are those of the one divine being and therefore not those of another divine nature allied to it. In regard to the realistic understanding of the divine perfections, the question has been asked whether it does not imply the existence of a second, alien divinity in God. To such a question our answer must be a flat negative. In so far as God is almighty, eternal, wise and merciful, it does not add anything new or strange or half-divine to His being as the One who loves in freedom. On the contrary, the divine being as the One who loves in freedom is the divine being in the multiplicity, individuality and diversity of these perfections. He does not possess this wealth. He Himself is this wealth. He is not what He is in a height or depth beyond these His perfections in their multiplicity, individuality and diversity. But He is Himself the perfect One in the abundance and variety of these His perfections. Every question: Of what nature is God? can be understood only as a repetition of the question: Who is God? and any attempt to answer the former question can be only a repetition of the answer which is given us by God Himself to the latter question—an answer which makes possible and necessary both the question: Who is God? and the question: Of what nature is God? In describing God as almighty, eternal, wise, or merciful, we are only repeating this answer; we are only naming Him again and yet again as the One who loves in freedom. But by reason of the fact that it comes from the living One who loves in freedom this answer is so framed that we must continually repeat it, not speaking of any other but God's one being, but in continual recognition and confirmation of the plenitude and richness of this one being of God. God is in essence all that He is. But He is in essence not only one, but multiple, individual and diverse. And these are His perfections.

The maxim opposed to the realistic understanding of these perfections: *In Deum non cadit accidens*[EN43], is therefore correct in itself. But just because it is so true it must be applied from

[EN43] Nothing comes to God as an accident

both points of view. When Gilbert de la Porrée (d. 1154) taught that the Godhead as the fulness of the divine attributes was really distinct from God, that God was God through His Godhead, just as man is man through his humanity, Bernard of Clairvaux and the Synod of Reims (1148) in the presence of Pope Eugenius III rightly brought against him the proposition: *non aliquo sensu catholico posse negari, quin divinitas sit Deus et Deus divinitas. Si vero dicitur: Deum sapientia sapientem, magnitudine magnum, aeternitate aeternum, unitate unum, divinitate deum esse et alia huiusmodi—credimus nonnisi ea sapientia, quae est ipse Deus, sapientem esse, nonnisi ea magnitudine, quae est ipse Deus, magnum esse, nonnisi ea aeternitate, quae est ipse Deus, aeternum esse, nonnisi ea unitate, quae est ipse Deus, unum esse, nonnisi ea divinitate, Deum, quae est ipse, id est se ipso sapientem, magnum, aeternum, unum Deum*[EN44] (Denz. No. 389). Two centuries later the same problem occupied the Greek Church, unfortunately with just the opposite result. It was the monks of the mountain of Athos who under the leadership of Gregorius Palamas expounded the doctrine of an eternal and uncreated light which could yet be communicated to the creature, and had shone among other places on the mount of transfiguration, and had also appeared to them. In the discussion arising from the opposition by the [332]
monk Barlaam, these so-called "Hesychasts" (so-called because their real aim was a theological foundation for mysticism) worked out the view that although this light is *ἄκτιστον*[EN45], unearthly, and divine, as comprehending all the divine effects, influences and exercises of power in its relation to the world, it must be distinguished from the true being of God, and represents as it were a halfway stage of the divine, on which it becomes capable of a link with the creature and can communicate to it a higher nature. "It is a question of divine influences (*θεότητες*) proceeding from God and indissolubly bound up with Him, of emanations from the Trinity which is complete in itself" (*P.R.E.*[3], Vol. 8, art. *Hesychasten*). To this the unfortunately ineffective answer was given, especially by Nicepnorus Gregoras, that such a distinction between the being and the effective reality of God must lead either to the affirmation of a further divine hypostasis and therefore to a quaternity in God, or else to the supposition of a divine power in the world without subject, to a doctrine of two gods, an *ὑπερκείμενος*[EN46] and an *ὑφείμενος*[EN47]. God's being in itself is not without effect, and God's effects are those of His being: God not only has but is *αὐτοενέργεια*[EN48], and it is in Him that there is to be sought and found whatever twofoldness and manifoldness He evinces in His relation to the world. But the abstract conception of the simplicity of the divine being on the one hand, and on the other hand the imperious desire to have a direct mystical experience of the power of God, have always been too strong in the Greek Church and theology for it to be possible to make a halt here. A synod of Constantinople in 1351—without attaining conceptual clarity—ranged itself on the side of the Hesychasts, and Eastern Orthodoxy is committed to their doctrine up to the present day. The Western Church rightly took the part of Barlaam and his defeated supporters: for the Hesychastic doctrine separates what must not be separated if the being and attributes of God are not to become in

---

EN44 In any catholic meaning, it cannot be denied that divinity is God and God divinity. If it is said truly, God is wise by virtue of his wisdom, great by virtue of his greatness, eternal by virtue of his eternity, one by virtue of his unity, God by virtue of his divinity and other such things – then we believe that he is wise only by virtue of that wisdom which is itself God, that he is great only by that greatness which is itself God, that he is eternal only by virtue of that eternity which is itself God, that he is one only by virtue of that unity which is itself God, and that he is God only by virtue of his divinity which is the very thing that is itself the wise, great, eternal and one God

EN45 uncreated

EN46 a superior

EN47 a subordinate

EN48 self-motivation, spontaneity

fact two distinct divine spheres; if the being of God is not to become completely formless and the form of God completely lacking in being. At the same time it must be asked whether Western orthodoxy, in so far as it transferred itself to the semi-nominalistic line and therefore sought to limit the attributes of God to His relation to the world, is not itself on the path which leads to the errors of Gilbert de la Porrée and Gregorius Palamas (note for instance the above-quoted sentence of Petrus van Mastricht about the *esse quodam secundo*[EN49] in which the attributes of God have their reality). If it is desired to avoid these errors, we have not only to challenge the separation of the attributes from the being of God, but also to note and emphasise the positive aspect of our proposition—that the perfections of God in their multiplicity and variety do not arise simply from His relation to the world, but are those of His own being as He who loves in freedom.

2. The multiplicity, individuality and diversity of the perfections of God are those of His simple being, which is not therefore divided and then put together again. In God multiplicity, individuality and diversity do not stand in any contradiction to unity. Rather the very unity of His being consists in the multiplicity, individuality and diversity of His perfections, which since they are His are not capable of any dissolution or separation or non-identity, and which again since they are His are capable of genuine multiplicity, individuality and diversity. The plurality which is to be predicated of God can therefore, even in its multiplicity, because it is the multiplicity of God, signify only the unity. The unity which is to be predicated of God must with equal necessity, because it is in reference to God, signify the plurality. Every individual trait which is to be
[333] affirmed of God can signify only the one, but the one which is to be affirmed of Him must of necessity signify also every individual trait and the totality of all individual traits. Every distinction in God can be affirmed only in such a way as implies at the same time His unity and therefore the lack of essential discrepancy in what is distinguished. But again, it would not really be the unity of God if no distinctions were recognised and confessed. Our doctrine therefore means that every individual perfection in God is nothing but God Himself and therefore nothing but every other divine perfection. It means equally strictly on the other hand that God Himself is nothing other than each one of His perfections in its individuality, and that each individual perfection is identical with every other and with the fulness of them all.

Totus ipse sibimet ipsi similis et aequalis est; totus quum sit sensus et totus spiritus et totus sensualitas et totus ennoia et totus ratio et totus auditus et totus oculus et totus lumen et totus fons omnium bonorum[EN50] (Irenaeus, *Adv. o.h.* II, 13, 3). *Καθ' ὅλον γὰρ οὐδὲν ἐφ' ἑαυτοῦ τῶν ὑψηλῶν τοῦτων ὀνομάτων διεζευγμένων τῶν ἄλλων ἀρετὴ κατὰ μόνας ἐστίν*[EN51]. Apart from its unity with all the others, no one of the divine perfections will be good and hence divine

[EN49] 'second being'

[EN50] His whole self is alike and the same as itself, even though the whole is sense and the whole is spirit and the whole is sensuality and the whole is thought and the whole is reason and the whole is hearing and the whole is an eye and the whole is light and the whole is the fount of every good

[EN51] For, viewing the whole, none of these exalted names for God divorced from the others is good by itself

(Gregory of Nyssa, *Or. cat.* 20). *Proprietates in Deo non sunt ... res ab essentia aut a se invicem diversae*[EN52] (Wolleb, *Comp. theol. chr.*, 1626, I, 1, 2, c. 1). *Proprietates Dei non sunt partes essentiae divinae, sed quaelibet proprietas essentialis est ipsamet Dei essentia tota et integra, ita ut essentia Dei et essentialis Dei proprietas non sunt aliud et aliud, sed unum et idem. ... Quicquid Deus est aut in sese agit, uno et eodem actu, qui est ipsius essentia, id est in sese agit; ideo uno et eodem actu simplex, infinitus, immutabilis est, uno et eodem actu vivit, intelligit, vult, amat*[EN53], etc. (Polanus, *op. cit., col.* 902 f.). But as against this we must also emphasise another statement of Polanus: *Proprietates essentiales Dei sunt in Deo ab aeterno in aeternum ... non sunt posteriores essentia Dei, qua reipsa sunt idem ... Sine proprietatibus divinis essentialibus Deus esse non potest, ne sine seipso sit: ipse enim ipsissima sapientia, bonitas, potentia est*[EN54]. We must reject out of hand the semi-nominalistic reservation that in the last resort we can speak of the *proprietates Dei*[EN55] only *improprie*[EN56], that the most characteristic inner being of God is a *simplicitas*[EN57] which is to be understood undialectically. If we refuse to do this and to recognise that God's being transcends the contrast of *simplicitas*[EN58] and *multiplicitas*[EN59], including and reconciling both, it is hard to see how we can escape the view of a God who is extremely lofty in His pure simplicity but also quite empty and unreal. It is also hard to see with what justification and emphasis, in consideration of God's relation to the world, we can still speak of His various perfections as those of the one true God. If God is the God who is rich in Himself, and if He is the one true God even in His works *ad extra*[EN60], we cannot emphasise either His *simplicitas*[EN61] or His *multiplicitas*[EN62] as though the one or the other *in abstracto*[EN63] were the very being of God, as though the one inevitably precluded the other. We can only accept and interpret God's *simplicitas*[EN64] and *multiplicitas*[EN65] in such a way as to imply that they are not mutually exclusive but inclusive, or rather that they are both included in God Himself.

3. The multiplicity, individuality and diversity of God's perfections are rooted in His own being and not in His participation in the character of other beings. The recognition of divine attributes cannot be taken to mean that for us God is subsumed under general notions, under the loftiest ideas of our knowledge of creaturely reality, and that He participates in its perfections. It is

---

EN52 The properties in God are not things distinct from his being or his self

EN53 The properties of God are not parts of the divine essence, but any essential property at all is itself the whole and undivided essence of God. Thus as the essence of God and the essential property of God are not one thing and another, but one and the same ... However God is or acts in himself, in one and the same act, which is his very own essence, that is 'his action in himself'. Therefore in one and the same act, he is simple, infinite and immutable; in one and the same act, he lives, understands, wills, loves

EN54 The essential properties of God are in God from eternity to eternity ... They are not subsequent to the essence of God, since they are identical with it ... God cannot be, without the essential divine properties, otherwise he would be without himself. For he is the very self of wisdom, goodness and power

EN55 properties of God

EN56 improperly

EN57 simplicity

EN58 simplicity

EN59 multiplicity

EN60 outside himself

EN61 simplicity

EN62 multiplicity

EN63 in the abstract

EN64 simplicity

EN65 multiplicity

[334] not that we recognise and acknowledge the infinity, justice, wisdom, etc. of God because we already know from other sources what all this means and we apply it to God in an eminent sense, thus fashioning for ourselves an image of God after the pattern of our image of the world, i.e., in the last analysis after our own image. Even less in the ontic sphere is it that God shares in truths and realities distinct from Himself, that He is subordinated to certain general laws of being, so that He can be defined in accordance with this participation and subordination and therefore to have such and such qualities. God is subordinate to no idea in which He can be conceived as rooted or by which He can be properly measured. There are not first of all power, goodness, knowledge, will, etc. in general, and then in particular God also as one of the subjects to whom all these things accrue as a predicate. But everything that God is, and that is in God, is—as the origin of all that is distinct from God and that can be the predicate of other subjects too—first and properly in Him. Indeed, it is first and properly God Himself as the One who loves in freedom, He Himself in His own being. Therefore God does not borrow what He is from outside, from some other. On the contrary, it is the problem of everything that exists outside of Him that it can be what it is only in virtue of the truth and reality imparted to it by God. God is the being of all beings, the law of all laws, and therefore the nature of every nature. In Himself, then, He is rich, multiple, individual and diverse. He does not need to become this by entering into relation with the "golden outpouring of the world."

The older dogmatics expressed this logically by the declaration that God's attributes are not *formae accidentales seu accidentia*[EN66], and are not to be understood in the sense that God is subject to the categories of being or of our thought: *Nihil est in Deo non per se subsistens*[EN67], i.e. nothing which presupposes as general possibilities quantity, quality, movement, suffering, space, time and so on. But apart from all such presuppositions God is in Himself—as pure act without potentiality—the basis of all such presuppositions, and therefore is in His own being infinite, good, wise and merciful. *Proprietates Dei essentiales sunt actus, prout Deus actus purissimus est et simplicissimus*[EN68] (Polanus, *op. cit., col.* 904). All this would be excellent, so far as it goes, if it were not for the cloven hoof of semi-nominalism which at once appears and obviously compromises everything again with the explanation: *Proprie loquendo*[EN69] there is only one *proprietas Dei*[EN70], namely His *essentia—sed respectu nostri quasi multae proprietates dicuntur, quia in nobis sunt multae: in Deo autem sunt una reipsa; ratione tantum differunt, rationeque multae sunt, et quidem non ipsius Dei sed nostri ratione, nimirum magis ut intelligentiae nostrae accommodantur, quam ut revera sunt* (*quae enim creatura eas ut sunt, intelligeret?*) *inter se distinguntur, quoniam tam ὑπερούσιον καὶ ὑπερουράνιον φύσιν explicare aut intelligere non nisi nostris verbis et pro nostri captus ratione possumus. Intellectus noster non potest uno simplici actu, sed necesse habet multis distinctisque actibus, ut alia omnia, ita et Deum*

EN66 accidental forms or accidents
EN67 there is nothing in God which does not subsist through himself
EN68 The essential properties of God are acts, just as God is most pure and most simple act
EN69 Strictly speaking
EN70 property of God

cognoscere[EN71] (*op. cit., col.* 904). The fiction which is concealed behind this consideration consists in the fact that, owing to the dazzling effect of the Platonic-Aristotelian idea of being, in which men thought they had attained knowledge of God, it was felt necessary to ascribe a much higher dignity to the idea of the one as against that of the many—so much higher, in fact, that in the application of this idea of the one it was thought possible to speak [335] of God *proprie*[EN72], as though even in this case God is not spoken of *respectu nostri, pro nostri captus ratione*[EN73]; as though in view of God's (own) hiddenness in His revelation it does not have to be totally conceded that our ideas—including that of the one also—are in themselves unsuitable and inadequate for the comprehension of God; and as though on the fundamental assumption that God in His hiddenness has revealed Himself to us and has authorised us to apply our conceptual systems to Him, while realising their limitations, the multiplicity of His being is not to be taken just as seriously as its unity. Yielding to this fiction and on the basis of a philosophical prejudice introducing the distinction between *proprie*[EN74] and *improprie*[EN75] where everything is in itself to be understood and spoken *improprie*[EN76], but *proprie*[EN77] on the ground and after the pattern of the divine revelation, these thinkers did the very thing which they were trying to avoid. On the one hand, they falsely defined the being of God, which they were supposed to be defining *proprie*[EN78], in such a way that it did not transcend but was subject to this notion of unity. On the other hand, they made the multiplicity of the divine attributes, which they wanted to ascribe to God only *improprie*[EN79], dependent on the discursiveness of the human intellect and the manifoldness of the created world. In both cases—contrary enough to the original intention—they worked under the presupposition of an intrinsically fixed order of ideas within the framework of which they thought to do God the honour of including His being in the notion of the one but of excluding it from the supposedly less exalted notion of the many. But the whole point was that they should not have subsumed the idea of God at all in either case, but that they should have done justice conceptually to His revealed being as such. That is, they should have given the glory to God in His multiplicity just as seriously and truly as in His unity and confessed Him unreservedly in His multiplicity as such—God Himself as the One, but as the One who is also the Many.

The further fundamental question to which we must now turn, is this: To what extent do these many individual and various perfections of God exist? How do we come to recognise them as such, and to speak of them *proprie*[EN80],

---

EN71 essence – but as far as we are concerned, it is as if there are many properties, since to us there are many. Yet these are in fact a unity to God. They differ only in reason, and in reason they are many – that is, in our reason, not in that of God himself. They are distinguished, doubtless, more as they are accommodated to our intelligence that as they really are (for what creature could understand these properties as they are?) since we cannot speak of nor understand 'the super-essential and superheavenly nature' only in our words and by the reason of our understanding. Our intellect cannot know God in his one simple act, but has of necessity to know God (as well as everything else) in many distinct acts

EN72 properly

EN73 'as far as we are concerned', 'by the reason of our understanding'

EN74 correctly

EN75 incorrectly

EN76 incorrectly

EN77 correctly

EN78 correctly

EN79 incorrectly

EN80 correctly

i.e., on the basis of God's revelation, and in responsibility to this revelation, without reservation in respect of their truth?

In traditional theology this question is known as the problem of the derivation and distribution of the divine attributes. The apparent unsuitability of these ideas is obvious at once. We can see how close and tempting at this point is a total or partial nominalism. For what is there to derive and distribute when it is a question of the being of God and His perfections? Were we not compelled at the outset to declare that each of the divine perfections is materially identical with each of the others and with the fulness of them all, indeed with God Himself? that every statement about the divine attributes can only be a repetition of the statement about the divine being? How, then, can there be a derivation and a distribution? Well, we can and must put the question. One of the useful results of our previous considerations is that we can realise that this is not a meaningless but a necessary question. That God in all His multiplicity is the One and that all multiplicity in Him is He Himself, the One, is only one aspect of the matter, which we must certainly keep in view. But again, it is also
[336] written that God not only appears but is almighty, eternal, just, wise, merciful—not merely for us but in Himself. And although in all this He is concealed from us in so far as these words are our words and not His own Word about Himself, yet it remains true that we are invited and authorised by His revelation to name Him with these words of ours in the confidence that in this way we are moving in the sphere of truth and not of falsehood so long as we are always willing to allow Him to be Himself the interpreter of these human words which He has placed upon our lips. If this is the case, the question of understanding His being in detail, the question of the derivation and distribution of His attributes—however inappropriate such ideas may seem to be at first sight—cannot really be meaningless and void. If we are not to renounce altogether the task of saying who and in what mode God is—and in the Christian Church, at any rate in theology, particularly dogmatics, there can be no question of such a renunciation—we will not try to evade this very task, however strange it may appear. The knowledge of God is true knowledge and not vague surmise and sentiment. As knowledge it has to be expressed in words. It cannot spare itself the trouble of formulation. The objectivity of God in His revelation has to be taken seriously, so that in regard to God we cannot be content merely with a devout silence and a rapturous whisper. The humility of our knowledge of God does not consist in the laziness of the servant who took his pound and buried it (Mt. 25^{18}), but in the fact that, invited and authorised by revelation to do so, we give God the honour which belongs to Him, to the very best—no less—of our ability, i.e., of the ability which He Himself gives us. But this being the case, we not merely may but must ask in human words and concepts what God is and is not, and in what way He is what He is, and therefore in some sense what are the upper and lower aspects, the right and the left, the contours of His being. And that is the question of the derivation and distribution of His attributes. If we refuse to ask these questions, we must consider

whether we are not secretly of the opinion that it is preferable to renounce the attempt to know God, or to abandon ourselves in this matter to our own arbitrary opinion or to chance. We must consider how we can accept responsibility for either the one or the other in view of the fact of divine revelation, which takes from us the pretext of our incapacity, and in face of which we have therefore no excuse if—especially in view of the many attempts in this sphere already undertaken in the history of theology—we should wish to prefer laziness to industry or confusion to order.

No serious attempt to expound the Christian doctrine of God has in fact been able completely to evade the problem which confronts us, although obviously all or the majority of those who have occupied themselves with the subject have had to overcome at this point a certain difficulty. It is rather laughable to notice how again and again earlier attempts to say something appropriate in this connexion, and especially what is supposed to be the chaotic diversity of these attempts, have at once evoked the astonishment, the pity and the rather [337]
sceptical amusement of those who came later. But although the latter would obviously have preferred to ignore the whole matter, they found it quite impossible to avoid coming to grips with the question on their own account, taking up some attitude to its problems and finally enriching the wealth of previous material with further possibilities.

If we look closely, the task will be found to be not so impossibly difficult as may at first sight appear. It is going too far to speak of chaos in face of the undeniable abundance of previous attempts to solve the problem. If we talk in this way we shall inevitably lose courage and drop the question as meaningless. Nor is it the case that every newcomer to this question has found a new solution, so that we ourselves will have to find a new answer on the assumption that everything so far accomplished is confused and unserviceable. The case is rather that there are a number of errors which we have to avoid and reject, but that they are relatively easy to discover, summarise and unmask. And on the other hand there is also a classical, and to some extent ecumenical line of theological reflection into which the previous course of our argument readily leads. We shall have to move along it in our own distinctive manner (if we can convince ourselves of its rightness). But from the presence of many companions to the right and left, we may conclude that it does not need any special depth of intelligence to find our bearings correctly in the whole matter.

In this connexion we may consider as obvious errors all those types of a doctrine of attributes which attempt to define and order the perfections of God as though they were the various predicates of a kind of general being presupposed as known already, whereas in reality each of them is the characteristic being of God Himself as He discloses Himself in His revelation. The right way, on the contrary, will consist in understanding the attributes of God as those of this His special being itself and therefore of His life, of His love in freedom.

It is noteworthy that although these errors are ultimately rooted in the mistakes which constantly beset the doctrine of the early Church, they have become palpably manifest only in more recent types of theology. Orthodoxy, on the other hand, in spite of the doubtful nature of its approach, displayed sure instinct in moving into the right way, at least as regards fundamentals, and in remaining in it. We will now indicate the various principal attempts from which we must dissociate ourselves in view of our previous considerations. They fall into three categories.

1. The attempt has been made to bring the attributes of God as it were within a psychological framework. This has its occasion and its relative justification in the fact that Holy Scripture undoubtedly characterises God as a person and therefore as a thinking or knowing and a willing subject. Rightly, therefore, the dogmatics of the early Church did not omit to speak of the *intellectus*[EN81] and *voluntas Dei*[EN82], nor can we omit to do so in so far as we interpret God as the One who loves in freedom. In the theology of the 18th and 19th centuries it was thought necessary to broaden this very simple psychology by speaking of a feeling in God
[338] (as, for example, A. E. Biedermann, *Dogmatik*, 1869, 635, and R. Seeberg, *Chr. Dogm.*, I, 1925, 334, 428 f.). The ontological aspect of the Godhead in its freedom or absoluteness or aseity, which appears to recede into the background in such an attempt, is understood by its exponents as a framework which fashions and embraces all these psychological categories. In Biedermann's essay, as we have seen, this framework is in fact understood in such a way that it absorbs these categories. The psychological expression of the idea of God is, therefore, a mere form of the inherently impersonal and absolute process of spirit. It is not true in itself, but it has conceptual value. When put in this logical way, the doubtfulness of the whole approach becomes apparent. Orthodoxy did not press it to this logical conclusion. It was willing to allow truth to the psychological attributes of God, although with regrettable nominalistic reservations. And it spoke with equal definiteness of the other attributes of God which cannot be brought under any psychological category because they are the attributes of divine freedom, absoluteness or aseity, and yet as such they are no less (though no more) but with equal truth the attributes of the one divine being. The psychological category must be duly taken into account as a principle of derivation and distribution, seeing that God is the One who does actually love in freedom. But it must not be given the position of a supreme governing principle in the whole doctrine of attributes, because there can be no such overriding principle where God Himself is all. Nor must it subsequently be assigned a position of inferiority as is apparent in Biedermann. The freedom of God is not merely the form of His love nor is His love only the form of His freedom. It is only the arbitrariness of an attempt to make the being of God correspond definitely with the being of man, to find in God the absolute expression of man, which can give rise to this psychological approach. And this arbitrariness betrays itself in its empty formalism, for in the definition of knowing, willing and feeling generally, what after all is said about God? What happens here to the presupposition that in regard to the attributes of God it cannot be a question of neutral descriptions, but only of divine perfections? For instance, is the wisdom of God only a specific mode of His knowledge, or the justice, holiness or mercy of God only a specific mode of His will? Where is the beneficence and the absolute authority of a God who is defined in so human and at bottom so neutral a way?

2. A further principle of derivation and distribution that has been proposed is the religiogenetic. This second and, in its way, very interesting type is represented by Schleiermacher and his most authentic pupil Alexander Schweizer. We have seen how Schleiermacher tried to interpret the attributes of God as an objectification of the individual aspects of the religious self-consciousness. According to him there results from this consciousness itself (apart from the antithesis of sin and grace) God's eternity, omnipresence, omnipotence and omniscience. From the religious consciousness in antithesis (i.e., the consciousness of sin)

EN81 intellect
EN82 will of God

there results God's holiness and justice. And from the religious consciousness of a resolution of this disharmony (the consciousness of grace) there results God's love and wisdom. In A. Schweizer (*Chr. Glaubenslehre*², Vol. I, 1877) pious feeling finds God in the world of nature as omnipotence, omniscience, eternity and omnipresence, in the world of ethics as goodness, holiness, wisdom and justice, and in the specifically Christian life of sanctification as love and grace, fatherly wisdom and mercy. We must at once concede to this attempt that in its way—here too within the limits of the nominalistic presupposition—it has aimed with obvious sincerity at getting beyond a purely formal idea of God and at bringing out the beneficence and authority of God. But what justification is there for attributing to the actual successive stages in the religious consciousness something specially corresponding in the being of God? With what right can it be said of the consciousness of sin, for example, that in it is implied the realisation of the holiness and justice of God, or of pious feeling towards the world of nature that it necessarily leads to the knowledge of God's omnipotence and omnis- [339]
cience? What place does this leave for the insight so carefully and rightly preserved in orthodoxy that the divine being cannot be torn asunder into a series of attributes each real and true in itself? Is there at Schweizer's first stage a real knowledge of God's eternity without the knowledge of God's holiness and mercy, which is presumably not reached until the second and third stages? And is the recognition of God's justice, which is possible at the second stage, really the justice of God without the grace of God, which is presumably not recognisable until the third stage? Is not the criterion that we are really confronted by an attribute of God the fact that it must be an attribute of the one God Himself and therefore must include in itself every other and the totality of all others? Do we recognise the being of God otherwise than by recognising God Himself in His absoluteness, and therefore in each distinct attribute every other attribute and the totality of them all? The creative role which in this approach is assigned to the subject of religious experience, and in particular the naturalistic theology which lies at the basis of it, works itself out in the shape of an utterly catastrophic dissolution and destruction of the whole conception of God. Schleiermacher and Schweizer certainly did not desire such a dissolution. But if it is insisted that the various stages—and this was Schleiermacher's express meaning—are simultaneous strata or aspects of one and the same religious consciousness, why is there this concern for their independence, their value as special sources of knowledge? If, on the other hand, we take seriously the genetic character of these various stages—as Schweizer did in contradistinction to Schleiermacher—this derivation and distribution leads not so much to the attributes of the one being of God as to a hierarchy of general and particular, superior and subordinate, divine or rather religious ideas and hypostases hanging lifelessly in the air. The whole wrongheadedness of the nominalistic treatment of the doctrine of attributes becomes apparent in this attempt of Schleiermacher and Schweizer. What is found is just what is sought, but only what is sought, viz., the gigantic reflections or projections of the human religious consciousness. What is found is man himself and as such on his supposed way to God which in reality is only the way to his own inner self. And it is only with difficulty that he can be persuaded that in this way he has found God. "This dissolution, according to which God the Creator does not really possess for the disciples of Schleiermacher the attributes of justice, wisdom, mercy, etc., follows quite naturally from the fact that man insists on constructing the idea of God from the human understanding and consciousness, and so utters things about God which have no solidity and reality in themselves, but only formal validity" (J. Wichelhaus, *Die Lehre der hl. Schrift*³, 1892, 333).

3. The third type is perhaps best defined as the historico-intuitive, and it is the one which calls forth the strongest disapproval. For, although it has for some time been very pressingly recommended on account of its supposed great simplification and religious deepening of the problem (F. Nitzsch, *Lehrb. d. ev. Dogm.*, 3rd edn. by H. Stephan, 1912, 452), it treats the

whole matter in a truncated and innocuous way which completely fails to do justice to its full seriousness, in spite of the many true and important things which are noted. An illustration of the argument used may be taken from the dogmatics of Julius Kaftan (3rd–4th edn., 1901, §§ 13–18). First it is explained that what has usually been characterised as the freedom of the divine being ("the absolute") really entered Christian theology only as a result of the world-renouncing nature of early piety and the philosophical tradition of antiquity. It was unfortunately retained by Protestant orthodoxy, which was dependent on Scholasticism, and, most regrettably, by Luther himself in *De servo arbitrio*[EN83]. In face of this tradition we must get back to the divine self-revelation attested in Scripture and to be received in faith, especially as it is rooted and breaks forth in the innermost consciousness of the personal life of Jesus. While the absolute is only a theological framework in every religion of the spirit, we [340] must infer from revelation that God is an other-worldly personal Spirit. In this connexion other-worldly means only that the divine being and life are distinct from those of the world (i.e., the material world) and that the attributes of this spirit are love, holiness and omnipotence. Holiness is to be understood as the predicate of love, and again omnipotence as the predicate of holy love. What does this involve? The Neo-Platonism of orthodox tradition has been completely jettisoned and with it the arbitrary speculations of its liberally minded heirs. And God's revelation attested in Scripture seems now to have gained expression. But is this really the case? Only to the extent that the spirit which is now described as love, distinguished as holy love and finally equipped with almighty power (it differs from the spirit of the Hegelians by reason of its strongly moralistic character), the spirit which constitutes the secret of the personal life of Jesus, is proclaimed as the divine being, and God is subjected to these metaphysical categories, and to this conceptual schema. But this spirit is not really, or in any sense, the divine Spirit. It is a particular interpretation of the human spirit. This is shown by the directness with which, by dint of historical intuitions, its reality is read off from the personal life of Jesus as from a blackboard. There is read out of revelation that which has previously been read into it as an already known universal. In this way there can be constructed the being of a God who is only too familiar apart from all revelation. If the serious defect of the orthodox tradition had really been overcome in this scheme, if the revelation of God had really been allowed to speak, it would have been impossible simply to ignore the problem of the aseity (the freedom) of God to which the orthodox tradition and even the speculative Liberals rightly draw attention even though they handle it with unfortunate results. But this is what inevitably happens when it is thought to avoid the Scylla of speculation by taking refuge in the Charybdis of historical intuition. To what extent are the love, holiness and omnipotence in question really *divine* love, holiness and omnipotence? This is the question to which the Ritschlians return as unsatisfactory an answer as do the orthodox and their liberal heirs to the question to what extent the infinite simple being (which for them is God) really deserves to be called *divine* being? If love is lacking to the freedom which the latter rightly stress, freedom is lacking to the love which the Ritschlians again rightly stress. What happens in both cases may be called "a strong simplification" and even, if we like, "a religious deepening". Obviously, however, it is not a Christian simplification and deepening in either case, but from the Christian aspect the procedure adopted on both sides involves what we can only describe as an over-simplification.

Besides these, there is, however, another and better way. It has all kinds of variations, but the theme remains unmistakable. It was followed by the older theology, and in its track many of the more recent theologians. Briefly this way was and is characterised by the fact that serious attention is paid to the twofold question answered in the preceding section: Who and what is God? in respect of the diversity as well as the unity of its two parts, with the result

---

[EN83] On the Freedom of the Will

that a doctrine of attributes is strictly to be understood and expounded as that which alone it can be—a repetition and development of the doctrine of the being of God. On this path—which for us will mean that we shall have to enquire into the perfections of the divine loving and those of the divine freedom—the orthodox Lutheran theologians of the 17th century distinguished more or less happily and exactly—not without a dangerous admixture of their dangerous basic ideas, but in substance with obvious consistency and accuracy—between *attributa negativa*[EN84] and *positiva*[EN85], or *quiescentia*[EN86] and *operativa*[EN87], or *interna*[EN88] and *externa*[EN89], or *absoluta*[EN90] and *relativa*[EN91], or *immanentia*[EN92] and *transeuntia*[EN93], or *primitiva*[EN94] and *derivata*[EN95], or *metaphysica*[EN96] and *moralia*[EN97]. In the older Reformed schools the distinction was almost invariably between *attributa incommunicabilia*[EN98] and *communicabilia*[EN99]. Among the later theologians Wegscheider (*Instit. Theol.*, 1815, §§ 62 and 64) distinguished between attributes of the *substantia perfectissima infinita per se spectata*[EN100] [341]
and attributes of the *substantia perfectissima spiritualis*[EN101]. Martensen (*Chr. Dogm.*, 1856, 85) enquired about the relationship between the unity of God and the opposition in which He finds Himself towards the world. Frank (*Syst. d. chr. Wahrheit*², 1885, I, 232 f.) tried to interpret the attributes first as attributes of the absolute God and then as such of the personal triune God, but with not the slightest suggestion "that the attributes which first referred to the absolute God are not at the same time those of the personal being and those connected primarily with the personal God are not also proper to His absolute Godhead." R. A. Lipsius (*Lehr. d. ev. prot. Dogm.*², 1879, 224) distinguished between the metaphysical and psychological attributes of God, while Wichelhaus (*Die Lehre der hl. Schrift*³, 1892, 333 and E. Böhl, *Dogmatik*, 1887, 45 f.) tried to follow out the same distinction in the light of the distinction between the biblical names for God, Elohim and *Yahweh*, *θεός*[EN102] and *κύριος*[EN103]. Even among the Ritschlians, in spite of their quite different point of view, traces of this classical distinction can be detected. O. Kirn (*Grundriss d. ev. Dogm.*, 1930, 55) distinguishes between "formal (metaphysical) attributes which express God's transcendence over the world," and "material (ethical) attributes which express the content and direction of the divine will and action." T. Haering (*Der chr. Glaube*, 1906, 320) distinguishes attributes of God's holy love and attributes of His absolute being. And finally even for E. Troeltsch (*Glaubensl.*, 1925, 183 f. and 212 f.) and H. Stephan (*Glaubensl.*², 1928, §§ 12 and 13) the divine attributes have been grouped under the categories of the holiness and the love or the "nearness" of God. It is worth noting that even H. Cremer (*Die chr. Lehre v. den Eigenschaften Gottes*², 1917), who in

EN 84 negative
EN 85 positive attributes
EN 86 dormant
EN 87 active
EN 88 internal
EN 89 external
EN 90 absolute
EN 91 relative
EN 92 immanent
EN 93 transcendent
EN 94 primary
EN 95 derivative
EN 96 metaphysical
EN 97 moral
EN 98 incommunicable
EN 99 communicable attributes
EN100 most perfect infinite substance, regarded of itself
EN101 most perfect spiritual substance
EN102 God
EN103 Lord

this matter goes his own way, has in fact reached no other method of classification. The same twofold division—attributes of the divine being and attributes of the divine activity—also governs the exposition of Roman Catholic doctrine (J. M. Scheeben, *Handb. der kath. Dogmatik*, Vol. I, 1925, 513 and 616; H. Hurter, *Theol. dogm. comp.*[12], 1907, II, 23 and 52; B. Bartmann, *Lehrb. d. Dogm.*[7], 1928, I, 116 and 132; F. Diekamp, *Kath. Dogm.*[4], 1930, 150 and 184). In spite of all the differences of nomenclature, basis and arrangement in this classification, and in spite of all the doubts which we can and must feel almost everywhere in matters of detail, it is impossible to overlook or deny the fact that in the last resort it is the same thing which is here perceived and meant with greater or lesser acuteness, so that we have a certain broad consensus of Christian theological opinion at this not unimportant point. On the one hand it is a question of the moment of God's aseity, absoluteness or freedom: of God in the exaltation proper to Him in Himself, as against all that is not Himself. And on the other hand it is a question of the moment of the love of God, of the activity of His personal being. In this matter the chaos of opinion is not as great as perhaps at first sight appears, and it should be clear that in accordance with the presuppositions previously discussed we have no real need to look around for a radically new solution. Indeed, we have absolutely no other choice but to adopt basically—reserving the right of more detailed elucidation and purification—this fourth and, as we may call it, classical line of approach.

A fully restrained and fully alive doctrine of God's attributes will take as its fundamental point of departure the truth that God is for us fully revealed and fully concealed in His self-disclosure. We cannot say partly revealed and partly concealed, but we must actually say wholly revealed and wholly concealed at one and the same time. We must say wholly revealed because by the grace of revelation our human views and concepts are invited and exalted to share in the truth of God and therefore in a marvellous way made instruments of a real
[342] knowledge of God (in His being for us and as He is in Himself). We must say wholly concealed because our human views and concepts (the only ones at our disposal for the knowledge of God, and claimed by God Himself as a means to this end) have not in themselves the smallest capacity to apprehend God. A true doctrine of the divine attributes must in all circumstances attest and take into account both factors—God's self-disclosure and His self-concealment. The knowledge of God must not be swallowed up in the ignorance. Nor, again, must the ignorance be swallowed up by the knowledge. Both demands are laid upon us by God Himself in His revelation: the obedience of knowledge and the humility of ignorance. And in laying down both requirements God is equally the one true God. The one grace of His self-revelation is at the root of both, and, because His self-revelation is His truth, we must add: He Himself, His own most proper reality. And in both ways, through His self-disclosure and His concealment, He is at one and the same time knowable and unknowable to us. In other words, in His self-revelation and concealment He has become for us an object of our human knowledge while remaining completely unknowable to us in both aspects (even in that of revelation). The relation between the two is not such that in His self-unveiling we have grounds for knowing Him, and in His self-concealment for not knowing Him; in the former case for speaking, in the latter for being silent. We have to know Him integrally and

therefore in both these aspects. At every point, therefore, we have to be silent, but we have also to speak. The honour which we give Him is in both cases alike problematical. But we are summoned to both alike. We can evade neither. We have thus to recognise Him both in His hiddenness and in His self-disclosure. It will certainly be true that in both cases He remains completely unknowable to us even as we may and must know Him. In all our thinking and speaking about Him we never become His masters. We are always and must always be His servants, and indeed quite unprofitable servants. But it is also true—and this must be stated just as vigorously—that in both cases He becomes completely recognisable by us, not because of our capacity, thinking and speaking, but because of the grace of His revelation, which we cannot refuse to receive, however little we may be able to control it. In order to do justice to this whole state of affairs it is obviously incumbent upon a doctrine of divine attributes to say two things. We cannot confess simultaneously both our knowing and our not knowing. Nor should we try to do so. For it is in such a way that the two things do not exist simultaneously, but only alongside of each other and in succession, that God has revealed Himself in Jesus Christ. Nor does a temporal simultaneity, if we are to trust His revelation, correspond to God's own reality. But, again, we may not and should not wish to confess the one to the exclusion of the other, thus allowing our knowledge to be swallowed up in a presumed absolute and final ignorance, or on the other hand our ignorance to be dis- [343]
solved in a presumed absolute and final knowledge. For in God's self-revelation and therefore in God's reality there is no such merging of the one in the other. God's reality is of such a character that the one exists with the other, in the other, alongside of and after the other, an eternal simultaneity and successiveness. So, then, we are not compelled to retire within the limitations of our capacity for knowledge, but speak directly in view of the reality of the object itself, when we say that in any doctrine of divine attributes both factors must be particularly emphasised, alongside each other and therefore successively—God's self-disclosure and also His concealment.

This unity and this distinction corresponds to the unity and distinction in God's own being between His love and His freedom. God loves us. And because we can trust His revelation as the revelation of His own being He is in Himself the One who loves. As such He is completely knowable to us. But He loves us in His freedom. And because here too we can trust His revelation as a self-revelation, He is in Himself sovereignly free. He is therefore completely unknowable to us. That He loves us and that He does so in His freedom are both true in the grace of His revelation. If His revelation is His truth, He is truly both in unity and difference: the One who loves in freedom. It is His very being to be both, not in separation but in unity, yet not in the dissolution but in the distinctiveness of this duality. And this duality as the being of the one God necessarily forms the content of the doctrine of His perfection. The doctrine must consequently treat of the perfections of His love and also of the perfections of His freedom. According to all that we have said, this cannot mean that we shall now begin to speak of two different subjects. The unity of self-disclosure and concealment, of the knowability and unknowability of God, constitutes the biblical idea of the revelation of God, just as the unity of love and freedom constitutes the biblical idea of the being of God. In both cases therefore—and in respect of each individual characterisation—we shall have to speak of the one God integrally. Therefore, explicitly or implicitly, when we speak of the love of God we shall have to speak also of His freedom, when we speak of His freedom we shall have to speak also of His love, and when we speak of one individual aspect we shall have to speak also of all the others. But if we do not wish to deviate from Scripture, the unity of God must be understood as this unity of His love and freedom which is dynamic and, to that extent, diverse. What we have here is, then, a complete reciprocity in the characterisation of the one Subject. Always in this reciprocity each of the opposing ideas not only augments but absolutely fulfils the other, yet it does not render it superfluous or supplant it. On the contrary, it is only in conjunction with the other—and together with it affirming the same thing—that each can describe the Subject, God.

[344] Apart from Frank, T. Haering is the modern theologian who has shown a particularly felicitous touch in these matters, and he evinces a fine understanding of this reciprocity. He expresses it by speaking of "the absolute personality" of God on the one hand and His "holy love" on the other. The emphasis in the former case is on the adjective and in the latter on the substantive. In this way, we are continually reminded of the counterbalancing second concept which is so indispensable for a true understanding: in the one case, that the attributes of the personal God are those of the Self-existent; and in the other, that whichever name we may give we can speak only of one and the same God. But we cannot speak rightly of this one God except in the mutual characterisation and limitation of these two names—of His love by His freedom, and of His freedom by His love.

For us too, then, there arises the necessity of speaking of God's attributes in a twofold series. The unity and distinction of the complete trust and the complete humility in which the Christian knowledge of God is attained (in view of the complete disclosure and the complete concealment of the one God in His revelation), and the unity and difference in which God loves as the One who is free, and is free as the One who loves, make any other way but this impossible to us. Therefore the two fundamental features of the being of God—His love and His freedom in their unity and diversity—necessarily indicate the two directions in which we shall have to think, now that it can no longer be a question of analysing our knowledge of God as such, but of presenting the One already known. In the following sections, then, we shall have to treat of the perfections of divine love and the perfections of divine freedom.

But before we adopt this line of approach which we know to be basically and generally that of a whole theological tradition, we must come to an understanding with regard to the question how far we may or may not associate ourselves with this tradition. What has previously been attempted on this generally and basically acceptable path is not so consistent, unambiguous and secure that even in regard to the question as a whole, quite apart from any details, we do not have to avoid certain misunderstandings and make certain corrections. Three decisive points are at stake.

1. It is in the nature of the case that when we speak of God's love we have occasion to think chiefly of God in His fellowship with the other, or, to be more specific, with the world which He has created. And on the other hand, when we speak of God in His freedom, it would appear to be chiefly a question of His transcendence over against all that is not Himself and therefore over against the created world. But this cannot be a true and basic distinction. For it is also a question of God's transcendence over everything that is not Himself even in His fellowship with the world which He has created. And again, this transcendence is itself no other than that which He discloses and exercises in His fellowship with the world. God is not first the One who loves, and then somewhere and somehow, in contradistinction to that, the One who is also free. And when [345]
He loves He does not surrender His freedom, but exercises it in a supreme degree. The principle of division which we recognise at this point cannot mean that out of the distinction suggested but also overcome in revelation we have to establish a separation between a God in Himself and a God for us, in which the essential being of God will probably be decisively sought in His sovereign freedom and the perfections proper to it, eternity, omnipotence and so on, while the love of God and its perfections, holiness, justice, mercy and so on, are treated nominalistically or semi-nominalistically as a question of mere economy, as non-essential, as perhaps purely noetic determinations, so that the final and decisive word in our doctrine of God is the affirmation of God as the impersonal absolute.

It is not to be denied (it would be surprising if it were otherwise) that the various bases of distinction suggested by the Lutheran Orthodox theologians point more or less plainly in this direction. Therefore, if we do not repudiate the principles as such, we must add by way of elucidation that there are no *attributa absoluta*[EN104] which are not also *relativa*[EN105], no *quiescentia*[EN106] which are not also *operativa*[EN107], no *metaphysica*[EN108] which are not also *moralia*[EN109], and on the other hand, no *externa*[EN110] which are not also *interna*[EN111], no *transeuntia*[EN112] which are not also *immanentia*[EN113], no *derivata*[EN114] which are not also *primitiva*[EN115]. Even the distinction favoured by the Reformed between *attributa*

EN104 absolute attributes
EN105 relative
EN106 dormant attributes
EN107 active
EN108 metaphysical attributes
EN109 moral
EN110 external attributes
EN111 internal
EN112 transcendent attributes
EN113 immanent
EN114 derivative attributes
EN115 primary

incommunicabilia[EN116] and *communicabilia*[EN117] can be admitted only as a distinction, but in no sense as a separation. For which of the attributes of God, in which as Creator, Reconciler and Redeemer He allows His creatures to share, is not, as His own, utterly incommunicable from the creaturely point of view, i.e., communicable only by the miracle of grace? And again, which of these incommunicable attributes has not God nevertheless communicated to the creature in that His Word was made flesh? Is not God's mercy completely unfathomable and inaccessible to us? And has He not implanted His eternity utterly in our hearts? In His Son God has opened up to us and given us all, His own inmost self. How then can His sovereign freedom be understood as a limitation of His love? How can it be sought elsewhere than in this love itself? Again, the very fact that we know Him and possess Him only because He has revealed Himself and given Himself to us in the miracle of His grace means inevitably that He stands over against us in all the austerity of His majesty and difference from us, and that we ill recognise His love if we do not see in it His freedom. The knowledge of the majesty of God must not be misused to set up that idol of the one and absolute which is "properly" without motion, utterance, or action. Nor must the knowledge of God's condescension be so misused that finally we seek Him only in certain relations in which we must stand and which have to be interpreted as such. But as in the former aspect God must be recognised as eternal love, so in the latter He must be understood as the freedom personally entering our world of time. What He is there in the height for us and for our sakes, here in the depths He is also in Himself. And we are speaking of God only when we know that He is both—and both in this reciprocal relation, and differentiated unity.

We cannot, then, attribute to this whole distinction between God in Himself and God in His relation to the world an essential, but only a heuristic, significance. It does, of course, have this significance. That God is both knowable and unknowable to us, the One who loves and the One who is free, becomes
[346] actually clear to us in this distinction. Neither of the two aspects is self-explanatory. Neither can be simply assumed. Both must become clear to us. The truth of both becomes manifest in the event of revelation in which God makes the transition from there to here, from His being in Himself to His being in fellowship with us, thus disclosing the truth of both these aspects, not in the form of a separation but of a distinction, as the same thing in distinguishable forms. By this distinction in God of His being in Himself and for us, as it is brought out in the event of revelation, the distinction between His love and His freedom can and must become clear to us; His love in that God as He is in Himself wills also to be God for us, His freedom in that He will and can be for us no other than as He is in Himself. We recognise the latter distinction through the former, and with it the division of the divine attributes. But we cannot allow it an essential significance if we wish to avoid the well-known traps into which the orthodox doctrine of God has fallen.

2. The division of the divine perfections according to this twofold principle can involve the temptation of attempted epistemological deduction. If, for example, the distinction between God in Himself and God for us is interpreted at this point as primary, it is only a step to the consideration that if the

---

EN116 incommunicable attributes
EN117 communicable

freedom of God is identical with God's being in Himself in its transcendence over all that is distinct from it, its perfections obviously cannot be described by the aid of concepts whose proper objects can be sought only in the realm of realities distinct from God. This being the case, it is necessary in describing them to transcend these realities. But how is this possible since our ideas are indissolubly bound up with these realities of quite a different order? Obviously there is only one answer—which is thought to be the true one—that we have to employ negative concepts, i.e., those which express the negation of the realities which are properly denoted by human ideas, but which through this negation point beyond these realities and therefore—so it is supposed—to God as the One who in sovereign freedom stands over against this realm of earthly reality. And if, on the other hand, the love of God is identical with His being for us, in His fellowship with the world which He has created, the perfections of this divine love cannot be characterised by concepts which have as their content the being and nature of the created world as such, but we can attempt to render these ideas transcendental by expanding, elevating and enriching them, by using them in the superlative, so that they receive a form in which they can no longer denote the world but—so it is supposed—only the love of God turned to the world and manifested in the world. The two possibilities may then be completed, or rather grounded and comprehended, in a third possibility, according to which God in Himself and God for us is seen to confront the world as its basis, and the world is therefore a negative and positive witness to the perfection of its divine basis. Thus human concepts properly denoting the realities of this world may be employed to denote the being of [347]
God and its perfections.

This is the doctrine of the *via triplex* which is well known in dogmatic history in association with the name of Pseudo-Dionysius Areopagita (*De div. nom.* VII, 3)—the *via negationis* (ἐφαιρέσεως)[EN118], *eminentiae* (ὑπεροχῆς)[EN119] and *causalitatis* (αἰτίας[EN120]). The establishment of this doctrine need not necessarily be regarded as the establishment of a rationalistic proof of God's existence and therefore as a substitute for the knowledge of God by revelation. At a pinch it can be interpreted as a proposed method for the formation of theological concepts in complete independence of the question of our knowledge of God. Now obviously it must have been very tempting (and many of the orthodox succumbed to the temptation) to divide the attributes of God summarily into negative and positive, i.e., those falling under the heads of *via negationis*[EN121] and *via eminentiae*[EN122], whilst the third, the *via causalitatis*[EN123] was (probably rightly) interpreted by Schleiermacher and A. Schweizer as the common presupposition and crown of both, and was not actually used as a third method co-ordinated with the first two.

[EN118] way of negation
[EN119] way of transcendence
[EN120] way of causality
[EN121] way of negation
[EN122] way of transcendence
[EN123] way of causality

Even at best, and supposing that we have here to do, not with an attempt at natural theology, but only with a method for the formation of concepts, it must still be pointed out that the division into these two categories ought certainly not to be dependent on an epistemological distinction. As far as the *via negationis*[EN124] is concerned, it is not the case that if our concepts negate earthly realities, by this their antithesis to that which is not God they automatically imply an approximation to God's being in Himself. How can our negation be a trustworthy transcending of the created world and as such a trustworthy description of God? And even if it is the case that by reason of their negativity negative conceptions are fitted to express God's being in Himself, this method is suspicious by the fact that, as we have seen, God's freedom is not in any way identical with God's being over against the world, but is just as operative in His relation to the world as in His being in Himself, and therefore is by no means to be exhaustively described in negative concepts—not even if we can rightly attribute to the latter a special appropriateness to describe the transcendent God. God is the One who is free even in His being for us, in which He is certainly not to be apprehended only by means of negative concepts. Again, so far as the *via eminentiae*[EN125] is concerned, it is not true that as our concepts try to surpass earthly realities in the form of superlatives they necessarily move towards the love of God turned to the world and manifested in the world. This kind of transcending of the created world can be extremely unreliable in itself, and in any event it is an extremely unreliable description of God. But even supposing a reliable transcendence is attainable by this means, even supposing our concepts in this form are in some sense adapted to describe God's being for us—and on the basis of divine grace it may well be that as regards both the *via eminentiae*[EN126] and the *via negationis*[EN127] they are so adapted—we have still to remember that God's love is in no way coincident
[348] with His being for us. He is the One who loves in Himself quite apart from His relation to the existence of another. Therefore the concepts by which, superlatively, we attempt to transcend this other, make shipwreck on the rock of this eternal self-existence of God. The *via negationis*[EN128] and the *via eminentiae*[EN129] may, indeed, perform their specific though limited services in the formation of concepts to describe the divine perfections. But, however that may be, the distinction between the two categories of divine attributes certainly cannot be made coincident with these two methods in the formation of theological concepts, which in any case are not the only ones.

What remains as a secure body of truth in the doctrine of the *via triplex*[EN130] does not

[EN124] way of negation
[EN125] way of transcendence
[EN126] way of transcendence
[EN127] way of negation
[EN128] way of negation
[EN129] way of transcendence
[EN130] threefold way

belong to our present argument. It is that which—neutral as regards this fundamental distinction—may be legitimately meant by the *via causalitatis*[EN131] (assuming that the method of natural theology is not implied). We have already said earlier that our views and concepts, necessarily referring as such to earthly realities, can and may and must—not in virtue of any immanent capacity, which they inevitably lack in this respect, but in virtue of the divine command and blessing—become descriptions of God as the Lord of the world, and therefore theological views and concepts. Why should not the *via negationis*[EN132] and the *via eminentiae*[EN133] be considered in this connexion? At the proper place there is a necessity and freedom to use even these logical possibilities. But these two possibilities cannot possibly form the framework of the Christian knowledge of God and the division of the divine perfections.

3. The order in which these two series of divine attributes are formulated is not a matter of indifference. It is, of course, true that in both cases, whether we are speaking of the love or of the freedom of God, we are concerned with the one God, with the glory of the Lord in its fulness, in which there can be no more or less and therefore no before and after. At a first glance, then, it may well appear that we can begin and end at either point without deriving any particular advantage and without incurring any particular danger. But this conclusion is overhasty. The logical rigour of the dialectic which occupies us must not conceal from us the fact that we are not concerned with any sort of dialectic but with the very special dialectic of the revelation and being of God, in the apprehension of which we are not left to chance or caprice but must adjust ourselves to the order intrinsic to the theme, or realised in it. It is important not to miss this order if we are not to miss the thing itself. But it is undeniable that this order, and to a great extent also the thing itself, has been fairly generally missed in the tradition to which in essentials we have adhered. For instance, theologians have nearly always treated first of the *attributa absoluta, quiescentia, incommunicabilia*[EN134], etc., i.e., of the perfections of the divine majesty, or, as we would term it, the divine freedom, and only then have they been willing to discuss the *attributa relativa, operativa, communicabilia*[EN135], etc., i.e., the perfections of the divine love. The fundamental error of the whole earlier doctrine of God is reflected in this arrangement: first God's being in general, then His triune nature—with all the ambiguities and sources of error which must result from this sequence. Its nominalism or [349]
semi-nominalism is also reflected in it, for the order undoubtedly implies that it is a question first of what the being of God is properly in itself, and only then of what it is improperly in its relationship *ad extra*[EN136]. And finally there is reflected what is actually the most doubtful feature of its conception of God: that God is first and properly the impersonal absolute, and only secondarily,

EN131 way of causality
EN132 way of negation
EN133 way of transcendence
EN134 absolute, dormant, incommunicable attributes
EN135 relative, operable, communicative attributes
EN136 to that outside of itself

inessentially and in His relationship *ad extra*[EN137] the personal God of love with the attributes of wisdom, justice, mercy, etc. But this sequence corresponds neither to the order of revelation nor to the nature of the being of God as known in His revelation. In God's revelation the disclosure of God is in fact the first and the last, the origin and the end, of the ways of God. God's revelation is first and last a Gospel, glad tidings, the word and deed of divine grace. Not without concealment, for in His revelation God shews Himself to be the secret of all secrets; not without the revelation of His omnipotence and eternity, of His hidden majesty; not without the Gospel becoming for us Law and judgment; not without exposing our sin and helplessness, our distance from God and therefore the transcendence of God over all that He Himself is not. Nor is all this involved only provisionally or apparently or incidentally, in such a way that this aspect of the divine speaking and action can be ignored. It is involved in such a way that this second aspect is seen as complementary to the first, as included in it, and manifesting itself truly only in the light of it. Only now that the mystery of God is disclosed is it seen to be a mystery: for what do we know of the mystery of God without revelation? Only as God reveals Himself does He also conceal Himself. Only as God speaks and acts do His omnipotence and eternity become real to us. Only as He gives Himself to us as the One who loves does He withdraw from us also in His holy freedom. Only through the power of the Gospel does there arise for us a divinely binding and authoritative Law, and a knowledge of our sin, and therefore of our creatureliness, our distance from God, and therefore the recognition of God's transcendence in Himself and over against all that He is not. It is not that God in His revelation is the second of these aspects to a lesser degree than He is the first. The truth is that He is it differently. He is it Himself in this relationship of the second with the first. He is it in this sequence. And a knowledge of His being and attributes which is to be faithful to the intrinsic character of His revelation must adhere to this sequence. The same point results from a consideration of the being of God as knowable in His revelation. We have seen that the essence of the divine being is to be the One who loves us and who loves in Himself, the One who is active in founding and maintaining fellowship. But He is this as the One who is free, in His freedom, and therefore as the self-existent One, unconditioned by anything else, Himself conditioning everything else. He is it, therefore, in His
[350] majesty, omnipotence and eternity. He is it in His aseity. Nor again is He all this provisionally, apparently or incidentally, in such a way that this aspect of His being can be ignored. Even in His freedom He is the One who loves. Therefore His Godhead, in so far as it is to be understood as His freedom, is the Godhead of His love. It is as the personal triune God that He is self-existent. And although the converse is certainly true, it is only because we must first say that it is as the personal triune God that He is self-existent; as the One who loves that He is the One who is free. If there is full reciprocity, as we have seen,

---

[EN137] to that outside of himself

this order obtains even in the full reciprocity, not signifying a difference of value between the two aspects of divinity, but the movement of life in which God is God, corresponding exactly to His revelation of Himself as God. And in our apprehension and exposition of the perfections of God we must adhere to this order and sequence.

It is clear that the older scholastic doctrine, to whose basic thoughts we formally adhere, will be given a greatly changed appearance by these three modifications and especially by the third—the reversal in the order of the two categories. But it is surely the appearance corresponding to the compulsion of the subject.

[351] § 30

THE PERFECTIONS OF THE DIVINE LOVING

The divinity of the love of God consists and confirms itself in the fact that in Himself and in all His works God is gracious, merciful and patient, and at the same time holy, righteous and wise.

1. THE GRACE AND HOLINESS OF GOD

God is He who in His Son Jesus Christ loves all His children, in His children all men, and in men His whole creation. God's being is His loving. He is all that He is as the One who loves. All His perfections are the perfections of His love. Since our knowledge of God is grounded in His revelation in Jesus Christ and remains bound up with it, we cannot begin elsewhere—if we are now to consider and state in detail and in order who and what God is—than with the consideration of His love. In the Gospel of Israel's Messiah and His fulfilment of the Law, of the Word that was made flesh and dwelt among us, of Him who died for our sins and rose again for our justification—in this Gospel the love of God is the first word. If then, as is proper, we are to be told by the Gospel who and what God is, we must allow this primary word to be spoken to us—that God is love. We must recognise and understand all His perfections as the perfections of His love. This is in spite of the fact that at a first glance we might suppose that we ought to seek the divinity of the divine being much rather in the freedom of God, i.e., in His unity, constancy and eternity, in His omnipresence, omnipotence and glory. This freedom of God will be our theme in the next section. God's freedom is in fact no less divine than His love. And God's love is in fact divine only in so far as it is exercised in His freedom. But again, God's love, too, is no less divine than His freedom. And again, God's freedom is divine only in so far as it is the freedom in which He loves. And not according to value and dignity, not in the sense of any hierarchy, but in the sense of the intrinsic manner in which God is God (as was shown at the end of the preceding section), according to the intrinsic order of the divine life, He is first of all the One who loves and then and as such the One who is free. The recognition of this does not mean that first of all, provisionally setting aside God's freedom, we can and will turn exclusively to the love of God as such, and afterwards equally exclusively to His freedom. In a static systematisation of that type
[352] we do not do justice to the intrinsic mode of God's being. There is no love of God in itself and as such, just as there is no freedom of God in itself and as

such. God's being consists in His being as the One who loves in freedom. Thus in thinking of His love we have constantly to bear in mind His freedom (and later, in thinking of His freedom, we must not forget His love). It can involve only a change of emphasis or key if we now tread a way demanded by the peculiar characteristic of God's being itself. This way can consist only in our thinking first of the love of God as it really exists in His freedom and then of His freedom as it really exists in His loving. But the "first" and "then," the sequence, can be reversed only arbitrarily and at the cost of great artificiality and misapprehension. We cannot allow ourselves such caprice. Therefore we begin with the perfections of the divine love: with the intention and in the confidence that in this way, even if indirectly, we are beginning also with the divine freedom. God is gracious, merciful and patient both in Himself and in all His works. This is His loving. But He is gracious, merciful and patient in such a way—because He loves in His freedom—that He is also holy, righteous and wise—again both in Himself and in all His works. For this is the freedom in which He loves. Thus the divinity of His love consists and confirms itself in the fact that it is grace, mercy and patience and in that way and for that reason it is also holiness, righteousness and wisdom. These are the perfections of His love. In this its divinity consists and is confirmed.

Why precisely in these attributes? Every doctrine of God's perfections has to come down, in detail, to a certain choice and grouping of concepts—a choice and summary which as such will not be able to appeal to any direct intimation of Holy Scripture nor to the voice of any sort of relative authority. Both Church creeds and the older and more recent dogmatic systems have shewn in regard to the enumeration of individual attributes, as also in regard to their grouping, great differences as well as certain agreements, and in this matter Holy Scripture itself does not anywhere give us authoritative directions. We have here the specific form of a problem which has already arisen in regard to the order of dogmatics as a whole. *Methodus est arbitraria*[EN1] was our conclusion then, and we repeat it now. The kind of choice and grouping which we must now attempt can always have the basic character only of a trial and proposal. But it must not on that account be arbitrary, i.e., unreasonable or perverse. Our own attempt and proposal rests first upon a consideration of the question by what specific determinations does the love of God—not love according to a general conception, but the love of God in Jesus Christ, as attested in Holy Scripture—become for us an event and reality so that we may and must infer in consequence that these are determinations of the divine being. The first series, grace, mercy and patience, furnishes an answer to this question. Secondly, it rests upon a consideration of the question in what determinations does the freedom of God stand—again not a universal idea of freedom but the freedom of God in Jesus Christ as attested in Holy Scripture—when His love is actualised for us. The second series provides the answer to this question—holiness, righteousness and wisdom. Whether these two answers are correct, satisfying and compelling, and whether consequently our proposal is serviceable, can be seen only from our exposition itself, or from the relationship to the biblical witness to revelation. It is to be noted that what appears to be an unavoidable systematisation is only a means to an end. The end is the most fully concrete answer to the [353]
question: Who and what is God?, i.e., the answer which most faithfully follows and corresponds to the self-manifestation of the living God. The means is an exposition of ideas

[EN1] Method is a matter of choice

ordered and controlled as far as possible by this object in its self-manifestation. Our proposal relates to this means. A confused essay committing itself impetuously to concepts of any sort, a meaningless or self-willed choice and arrangement, will obviously be a bad means unworthy of the honour of God, who is not a God of confusion but of order (1 Cor. 14^{33}). A certain degree of systematisation need not then mean a usurpation if it is an unpretentious attempt to think and speak worthily, or at any rate not unworthily, of this object.

We begin our consideration of divine love with a study of the concept of divine grace as it stands directly confronted with and controlled and purified by the concept of divine holiness.

When God loves, revealing His inmost being in the fact that He loves and therefore seeks and creates fellowship, this being and doing is divine and distinct from all other loving to the extent that the love of God is grace. Grace is the distinctive mode of God's being in so far as it seeks and creates fellowship by its own free inclination and favour, unconditioned by any merit or claim in the beloved, but also unhindered by any unworthiness or opposition in the latter—able, on the contrary, to overcome all unworthiness and opposition. It is in this distinctive characteristic that we recognise the divinity of God's love.

Gratia in Deo residens est essentialis proprietas eius nimirum benignissima voluntas Dei et favor, per quem vere et proprie est gratiosus, quo favet et gratis benefacit creaturae suae (Polanus, *Synt. Theol. chr.*, 1609, *col.* 1040). *Gratia Dei est favor eius gratuitus, quo creaturae rationali ac inprimis hominibus credentibus benefacit, vel est benignissima Dei voluntas qua sine merito omni favet et benefacere gaudet*[EN2] (Quenstedt, *Theol. did. pol.*, 1685, I, *c.* 8, *sect* I, *th.* 31). The formula of Polanus is to be preferred to that of Quenstedt as the more comprehensive.

Above all, we maintain that according to the dominant meaning of the terms *chen, chesed,* χάρις[EN3] in the linguistic usage of the Bible, grace is an inner mode of being in God Himself.

"I will have mercy on whom I will have mercy" (Ex. 33^{19}). To promise to show, to give grace, to make grace prevail, to fill or crown with grace, is all God's work, taking place in consequence of the fact that He is gracious in Himself and therefore gives Himself to be known as gracious and acts graciously. Whosoever finds grace, finds it in His eyes, and therefore in His presence. It is the grace of Him who dwells in the burning bush (Deut. 33^{16}), and therefore of the author of the covenant with Israel, and as such it is everlasting mercy (Is. 54^{8}; Ps. 89^{3}), reaching unto the heavens (Ps. 108^{5}; cf. Ps. 103^{11}). According to the recurrent formula of Paul, it is the grace of our Lord Jesus Christ, i.e., the grace which dwells and is manifest, knowable, effectual and imparted in the person of Jesus Christ. We must not follow Roman Catholic dogma (cf., e.g., Bartmann, *Lehr. d. Dogm.*[7], Vol. II, 1929, 3 f.), in making an *a priori*[EN4] and decisive definition of grace as a supernatural gift, and then proceeding to characterise it as a third element mediatorial between God and His creatures. Grace is certainly a gift—and indeed a very supernatural gift. In fact it epitomises all the gifts of God—

[EN2] The grace residing in God is his essential property, without doubt the most benign will and favour of God, through which he is truly and properly gracious, by which he favours and freely bestows his benefits upon creation

[EN3] grace

[EN4] axiomatic

not merely revelation, reconciliation and redemption, but also creation. But it is a gift—and [354]
this must be our *a priori*[EN5] definitive description—in so far as the Giver, i.e., God Himself, makes Himself the gift, offering Himself to fellowship with the other, and thus showing Himself in relation to the other to be the One who loves. And the supernatural element arising from the fact that God is gracious does not constitute a third factor. On the contrary, divine grace consists in the fact that God as the First founds and maintains direct fellowship between Himself and the second, His creature. The archetypal form of God's gift of grace lies in the incarnation of His Word, the unity of God and man in Jesus Christ. And in this there was no third mediating element between God and man. The secret essence of grace manifested in the fact that out of two beings—entirely by the will and power of the primal being—there has now been made one; that between God and man there has been instituted the direct peace which Paul is accustomed to mention in connexion with the word grace and clearly as its determining content. Between the gracious God and him to whom He is gracious there must not be intruded the gnosticising conception of grace as a mediatorial sphere. Everything depends here on the immediacy of the relation and on the fact that the being and action of God, of which we are thinking, is really God's *essentialis proprietas*[EN6] and is understood as God Himself who, as He is Himself and acting according to His nature, is gracious. That is why the Old and New Testaments speak so emphatically with reference to God of "My" or "Thy" or "His" grace. That is why biblical man not only prays: "Help me according to thy grace" (Ps. 109^{26}), "Think upon me in thy grace" (Ps. 106^{4}), "Quicken me by thy grace" (Ps. 119^{88}), "Cause me to hear thy grace" (Ps. 143^{8}), and so on, but in most places directly and simply: "Be gracious unto me." On the other hand it is never said: "Give me, lend me grace!" or anything of that sort. For this reason, too, all that the apostles wish to their congregations can be summed up in the familiar formula of greeting: "Grace be with you." For the same reason the word of God—Ac. 14^{3}, 20^{32}—can quite simply be called the word of grace. And with Paul, grace, his own conversion, his apostolic office and its exercise, and the preaching of the Gospel constitute a single integral whole: "But by the grace of God I am what I am: and His grace which was bestowed upon me was not in vain; but I laboured more abundantly than they all: yet not I, but the grace of God which was with me" (1 Cor. 15^{10}; cf. Rom. 1^{5}). Grace denotes, comprehensively, the manner in which God, in His essential being, turns towards us. This turning, which is that of a superior to an inferior, and takes place in the form of a condescension, is contained even in the meaning of the word χάρις, the Latin *gratia*, our English grace, and most strongly of all the German *Gnade*. Especially the Old Testament contexts in which the word appears make it clear that in His turning everything which God confers on man as a benefit is implied: His truth, His faithfulness, His law, His mercy, His covenant (Dan. 9^{4}), or, according to the apostolic formula of greeting, His peace. All this is primarily and fundamentally His grace also.

But grace means a turning, not in equality, but in condescension. The fact that God is gracious means that He condescends, He, the only One who is really in a position to condescend, because He alone is truly transcendent, and stands on an equality with nothing outside Himself. His inmost being in grace is that He wills not to remain in this position. His transcendence stands out as the presupposition of His condescension fulfilled in the saving turning—which includes every conceivable benefit—to that which is not on an equality with Himself. Not on an equality! Now this means that grace is a being and

---

[EN5] axiomatic
[EN6] essential property

action of God upon which no one and nothing has any claim. What this [355] implies positively we shall have to show when we come to speak of God's mercy. In the idea of grace as such, to which we are confining ourselves here, there is included from our present point of view only the negative aspect that God's turning is not the answer and correspondence to something meritoriously performed by the partner to whom He turns. If there is such a partner deserving of such a response and possessing a claim to God's notice, able to condition His grace, we shall obviously have to speak of an equality, even if only partial, between this partner and God. But such an equality does not come into consideration with regard to God. In the grace of God, His transcendence over against every counterpart is thrown into sharp relief. The mere fact that God is gracious implies that He Himself owes nothing to any counterpart. His condescension is free, i.e., unconditioned, i.e., conditioned only by His own will. His inclination, good will and favour which He turns towards His partner in this act of condescension is a sheer gift which something necessarily called forth by it can neither precede nor follow, for, whatever follows it has its ground in this prevenient cause. It is thus a gift in this strictest sense of the term.

Δωρεὰν ἐλάβετε[EN7] (Mt. 10[8]). It is from a gracious election (*κατ' ἐκλογὴν χάριτος*[EN8]) that the remnant of Israel and the Church of Jesus Christ derives: *εἰ δὲ χάριτι, οὐκέτι ἐξ ἔργων, ἐπεὶ ἡ χάρις οὐκέτι γίνεται χάρις*[EN9] (Rom. 11[5f.]). Grace means redemption : *καὶ τοῦτο οὐκ ἐξ ὑμῶν, θεοῦ τὸ δῶρον. οὐκ ἐξ ἔργων, ἵνα μή τις καυχήσηται. αὐτοῦ γάρ ἐσμεν ποίημα, κτισθέντες ἐν Χριστῷ Ἰησοῦ ἐπὶ ἔργοις ἀγαθοῖς*[EN10] (Eph. 2[5], [7–10], cf. 2 Tim. 1[9]). "According to the good pleasure of his will, to the praise of the glory of his grace, God hath made us accepted in the beloved" (Eph. 1[5f.]).

The biblical conception of grace involves further that the counterpart which receives it from God is not only not worthy of it but utterly unworthy, that God is gracious to sinners, that His being gracious is an inclination, good will and favour which remains unimpeded even by sin, by the resistance with which the creature faces Him. Again, the positive element to be discussed here will fall for special consideration under the heading of God's mercy. Grace in itself means primarily that the sin of the creature, the resistance which it opposes to God, cannot check, weaken or render impossible the operation of divine grace. On the contrary, grace shows its power over and against sin. Grace, in fact, presupposes the existence of this opposition. It reckons with it, but does not fear it. It is not limited by it. It overcomes it, triumphing in this opposition and the overcoming of it.

The grace of Jesus Christ is related to the sin of Adam in such pure superiority and preponderance that more often than not Paul can express it simply by a *πολλῷ μᾶλλον*[EN11]

EN 7 You have freely received

EN 8 'according to the election of grace'

EN 9 and if it is by grace, then it is no longer by works, or grace would no longer be grace

EN10 and this is not from yourselves; it is the gift of God; not by works, so that no-one may boast. For we are God's workmanship, created in Christ Jesus for god works

EN11 how much more

which he does not need to argue further (Rom. $5^{15, 17}$), but which appears to him so decisive and thoroughgoing that he can finally say: *οὗ δὲ ἐπλεόνασεν ἡ ἁμαρτία ὑπερεπερίσσευσεν ἡ χάρις*[EN12] (Rom. 5^{20}). The fact that God is gracious—this is how the superiority is shown—implies that He forgives the sinner his sin (Ex. 34^{9}, Num. 14^{19}). That is, He Himself with His inclination, good will and favour intervenes on behalf of the one who has sinned against Him. His own good free will is to Him truer and more significant—infin-
itely more so—than the evil will of the sinner. He does not regard and treat the latter as he [356]
would have to be regarded and treated on the basis of his evil human will, but as he must be regarded and treated on the basis of the good will of God now turned towards him: because He is God, because this covering and wiping out of sin, because this unmerited, kind, and utterly different view and treatment of His creature is not merely in His power but is His right and therefore His majestic will. "The Lord is merciful and gracious, slow to anger, and plenteous in mercy .... He hath not dealt with us after our sins; nor rewarded us according to our iniquities. For as the heaven is high above the earth, so great is his mercy toward them that fear him. As far as the east is from the west, so far hath he removed our transgressions from us" (Ps. $103^{8f.}$). That this should happen and be true for us is the prayer of biblical man when he cries out: "Be gracious unto me." This is what God's inclination, good will and favour means for God Himself and for us. It is always God's turning to those who not only do not deserve this favour, but have deserved its opposite.

It is to be noted how important it is for this supreme meaning of the concept that in understanding its root we maintain against the Roman Catholic conception of divine grace the thesis that grace is not merely a gift of God which He might give or not give, or an attribute which might be imputed to Him or not be imputed. No, grace is the very essence of the being of God. Grace is itself properly and essentially divine. This is, of course, the secret of the forgiveness of sins. For this reason the latter does not imply merely a noteworthy episode the scope of which is open to doubt. Forgiveness cannot be an object of uncertainty. It cannot be accepted and treated lightly. It meets us, not in spite of, but in and with all the holiness, righteousness and wisdom of God. It claims us, cleansing, judging and redeeming us. It is also our true and final consolation. For God Himself is in it. He reveals His very essence in this streaming forth of grace. There is no higher divine being than that of the gracious God, there is no higher divine holiness than that which He shows in being merciful and forgiving sins. For in this action He interposes no less and no other than Himself for us. With His good will He takes up our cause and responsibility for us in spite of our bad will. In this action He is manifested in the whole majesty of His being. As we sin against God Himself, God Himself takes action to reconcile us by being gracious to us. If we find and recognise and receive His grace, we find and recognise and receive no less and no other than Himself. Thus there takes place by grace the only thing that is effective against sin. By grace sin is attacked and wiped out at its root. Therefore there is no more fear and no more self-will where grace is found and recognised and received. Where grace is revealed and operative, God Himself is always revealed and operative. It is not necessary for us to strive after a higher, better,

---

EN12 Where sin abounded, grace abounded all the more

more helpful revelation. God's promise and also His command, God's truth and also His power, God's judgment and also His restoration cannot fail where God is gracious. Again, where God is revealed and operative, He is always the
[357] gracious God. God is *vere et proprie gratiosus*[EN13]. He is so even when He is for us the unknown and hidden God. He is so even when He is the God who is denied and hated by us and therefore provoked against us. He is so even as the God against whom we sin and who therefore judges and punishes us. We know and rightly understand our sin only when we have realised it to be enmity against the grace of God. And we turn from our sin only when we return to the grace of God. Any other idea of God, in which He is not yet gracious, or not yet essentially decisively and comprehensively known as gracious, is really, whether it is affirmed or denied, a theology of the gods and idols of this world, not of the living and true God. And to it will correspond the faith that we bring to its object, the confession of sin by which we stand over against it, the conversion to it which we suppose we must experience or have already experienced. All this religious experience will lack real seriousness and power because the true God, in face of whom alone there is real seriousness and from whom alone flows real power, is the gracious God: He alone, for He alone is the living and true God. Fundamentally and decisively God distinguishes Himself from the creature by His grace. Fundamentally and decisively His divinity consists and confirms itself in His grace. Therefore it is not simply that we may, but we must establish as a criterion whether we have found and are worshipping a God or an idol, the following: whether we have found grace—not grace in general or in any arbitrary sense—but grace before Him and in His very presence; whether it is grace which we have learnt to venerate and worship as God.

This is how God loves. This is how He seeks and creates fellowship between Himself and us. By this distinctive mark we recognise the divinity of His love. For it is in this way, graciously, that God not only acts outwardly towards His creature, but is in Himself from eternity to eternity.

One might object that in His own being there cannot be a creature standing over against Him, still less any opposition from this other, and therefore that there cannot take place any special turning, or condescension, or overcoming of the resistance of the other, and consequently that there cannot be any scope for grace. Our reply is that there is not in fact any scope for the form which grace takes in its manifestations to us. The form in which grace exists in God Himself and is actual as God is in point of fact hidden from us and incomprehensible to us. For this very reason even in its manifestation and effectiveness for our sakes and towards us it is for us always the mystery which can thus be appropriated only as such and in faith. For this very reason grace can be revealed and imparted to us only by grace. But in this mystery it is actually revealed and operative as God's being and action in our midst. How then can

EN13 truly and properly gracious

it be denied that primarily it is real in God Himself in a form which is concealed from us and incomprehensible to us—in Him who as Father, Son and Holy Spirit is One, who is utterly at one in Himself, in whom therefore there is [358] neither the need nor the capacity for any turning and condescension, in whom there is no strife and therefore no reconciliation? Must we not say, then, that just because this is so, just because He who is Father, Son and Holy Spirit is from eternity to eternity the centre and source of all unity and all peace, therefore He must be the origin and essence of that which we know as grace in such a very different form? How can it have divine reality in the form known to us if it does not have reality in the unfathomable life of God Himself? From the sphere and source alone where it is not yet a special turning, not yet condescension, not yet an overcoming of opposition, where it is manifest in the pure love and grace which binds the Father with the Son and the Son with the Father by the Holy Spirit—from this sphere and source alone can it become what in our experience we know it to be: a turning towards the creature, a condescension, an overcoming of resistance. And from this divine source it will be this in so far as it has divine reality in the form known to us.

We now place this concept of the grace of God alongside that of His holiness. This cannot mean that we imply a need either to qualify or to expand what is denoted by the concept of grace. In grace we have characterised God Himself, the one God in all His fulness. We are not wrong, we do not overlook or neglect anything, if we affirm that His love and therefore His whole being, in all the heights and depths of the Godhead, is simply grace. But in our heart and on our lips, in our mode of knowledge, this thing grace is in no sense so fully and unambiguously clear, or above all so rich and deep, as it is in the truth of God which by this concept we apprehend—yet apprehend as we men apprehend God by faith, i.e., in such a way that our knowledge must needs expand and grow and increase. For this reason the idea of grace, not in itself, not in God, but in our mode of knowledge, requires qualification and expansion. Our notion of grace is not able to grasp in its clarity and richness all that grace is in God Himself. If we are concerned about the truth of the God who is wholly grace, we cannot and must not cling to our idea of grace as though our understanding of God had no need to grow, as though this idea of ours enabled us to acquire control over God. In our understanding of the being of God it can be a question only of our continually making clear to ourselves how God gains control over us. For this reason we must not cling to any of our ideas. For this reason we must constantly be prepared to allow our ideas to be qualified and expanded. We have already recognised this in presupposing the great reciprocal qualification and expansion of the two leading ideas of the love and freedom of God. In doing this we did not postulate a cleavage and dualism in God, but were obliged and wished to respect the unity of God in the clearness and fulness of His revelation and being. We must adopt the same [359] procedure at every point in the details as well. We will therefore make the kind of distinction which does not imply a second factor alongside a first, but simply wishes to recognise the one according to the clearness and fulness with which it is a unity in God. We are not, then, making any crucial change of theme when we go on to speak of God's holiness. We are merely continuing to speak of God's grace. In the case of all the other concepts which will engage our attention in this and the following sections, we shall still continue to speak only of the grace of God. But if we are to go on to speak of the one rich grace of God, we must in fact develop further concepts. We shall do so always from the point of view that God is utterly and wholly grace, yet not by clinging stubbornly to our idea of grace as the focal point, but by realising that that one focal point may bear other names and thus by allowing the one focus to express other ideas and in that way to control what we think and say.

God's loving is a divine being and action distinct from every other loving in the fact that it is holy. As holy, it is characterised by the fact that God, as He seeks and creates fellowship, is always the Lord. He therefore distinguishes and maintains His own will as against every other will. He condemns, excludes and annihilates all contradiction and resistance to it. He gives it validity and actuality in this fellowship as His own and therefore as good. In this distinctiveness alone is the love of God truly His own divine love.

Sanctitas Dei est proprietas eius essentialis, per quam intelligitur naturam eius esse universe et perfectissime iustam, in qua prorsus nihil iniqui, nihil mali, nihil labis inest ac perinde esse etiam summe puram et castam amantemque et causam puritatis et castitatis in creaturis rationalibus, contra autem summe abhorrentem ab omni impuritate et immunditie sive interna sive externa eamque severissime detestantem et punientem[EN14] (Polanus, *Synt. Theol. chr.*, 1609, *col.* 1185). *Sanctitas Dei est summa omnino labis aut vicii expers in Deo puritas, munditiem et puritatem debitam exigens a creaturis—sive qua Deus summe purus mundus et sanctus est omnisque puritatis et sanctitatis in creaturis autor*[EN15] (Quenstedt, *Theol. did. pol.*, 1685, I, *c.* 8, *sect.* 1, *th.* 34). If we can cite the definitions of grace given by these two authors without essential objection, we must observe concerning their formulation of the idea of divine holiness that in spite of its correctness in detail it makes the fatal mistake, precisely in regard to the grace of God, of not realising clearly the unity of the divine being, and of allowing holiness to appear as a second or third factor in God alongside the primary one. This is also true of the penetrating exposition of Petrus van Mastricht (*Theor. Pract. Theol.*, 1698, II, 19, 5 f.), who in the concept of the *sanctitas Dei*[EN16] wishes to distinguish between: 1. the *segregatio*[EN17] (in which God is marked off from everything general and as such "profane"; 2. the *dedicatio*[EN18] (in which God does what He does for His own sake, *sibi addictus, seipsum quaerens*[EN19]); 3. the *repraesentatio*[EN20] (in

[EN14] The holiness of God is his essential property through which it is understood that his nature is everywhere most perfectly just, in which there is absolutely nothing wicked, nothing evil, and nothing disgraceful, and similarly that he is also utterly pure and chaste and loving, the cause of purity and chastity in his rational creatures, and by contrast utterly hateful impurity and contamination, whether internal or external, most severely detesting and punishing it

[EN15] The holiness of God is the utmost purity in God, which has no part of any kind in disgrace or vice, requiring the required spotlessness and purity from his creatures. Thus God is utterly pure, spotless and holy, and is the author of all purity and holiness in his creatures

[EN16] grace of God

[EN17] separateness

[EN18] dedication

[EN19] concerned with himself, seeking himself

[EN20] representation

which He is the author and also the fulfiller of His law); 4. the *detestatio*[EN21] (His utter aloofness from the evil repudiated and characterised by Him as such). This analysis is noteworthy in that it makes holiness an aspect of divine freedom. So much the more deplorable is its failure to note the connexion on the other side. From the outset, however, the problem is to show the fact and extent that God as gracious is also holy, and again that as holy He is also gracious. If we allow ourselves to be guided by Scripture in this matter, we shall not make a [360] distinction here, and therefore we shall not differentiate a second from a first without revealing the connexions and thus remaining within a unified knowledge of the one God.

The common factor linking the biblical concepts of the grace and the holiness of God is seen in the fact that they both in characteristic though differing fashion point to the transcendence of God over all that is not Himself. When we speak of grace, we think of the freedom in which God turns His inclination, good will and favour towards another. When we speak of holiness, we think of this same freedom which God proves by the fact that in this turning towards the other He remains true to Himself and makes His own will prevail. How can we properly separate these two aspects? The freedom with which God remains true to Himself cannot shine more gloriously than in the freedom with which He turns towards the creature without regard to the latter's merit and worthiness. And again, this freedom cannot be manifested and understood except as the freedom with which He remains true to Himself. The bond between the concepts of grace and holiness consists further in the fact that both point to God's transcendence over the resistance which His being and action encounters from the opposite side. When we speak of grace, we think of the fact that His favourable inclination towards the creature does not allow itself to be soured and frustrated by the resistance of the latter. When we speak of holiness, we think, on the other hand, of the fact that His favourable inclination overcomes and destroys this resistance. To say grace is to say the forgiveness of sins; to say holiness, judgment upon sins. But since both reflect the love of God, how can there be the one without the other, forgiveness without judgment or judgment without forgiveness? Only where God's love is not yet revealed, not yet or no longer believed, can there be here a separation instead of a distinction. In this case forgiveness would be inferred *in abstracto*[EN22] from sin, and judgment from condemnation. It would not be God's judgment in the one case or God's forgiveness in the other. If we speak in faith, and therefore in the light of God and His love, and therefore of God's forgiveness and judgment, as our insight grows we shall distinguish, but we shall certainly not separate, between God's grace and God's holiness. The link between the two is decisively summed up in the fact that both characterise and distinguish His love and therefore Himself in His action in the covenant, as the Lord of the covenant between Himself and His creature.

[EN21] detestation
[EN22] in the abstract

The holy God of Scripture is certainly not "the holy" of R. Otto, that numinous element which, in its aspect as *tremendum*[EN23], is in itself and as such the divine. But the holy God of Scripture is the Holy One of Israel. That is the primary and fundamental thing to be said about Him. But this does not mean first of all and decisively the God who is exalted over Israel, separated from it and confronting it, to be feared by it as the One to whom it has obligations. The holiness of God does mean all this too, but only because it means primarily
[361] and decisively this—that God has adopted and chosen Israel as His child, has given it His promise, and has already conferred upon it His gracious help. Note that the saying in Exod. 15[11]: "Who is like Thee, O Lord, among the gods? who is like thee, glorious in holiness, fearful in praises, doing wonders?" belongs to the hymn of praise uttered because of the deliverance at the Red Sea; that the saying in 1 Sam. 2[2]: "There is none holy as the Lord, for there is none beside thee; neither is there any rock like our God" belongs to the song of Hannah after the hearing of her prayer; and that the saying in Ps. 77[13]: "Thy way, O God, is holy!" comes from a song summarising the acts of God performed for His people. According to Is. 41[14], 43[3 14], 47[4], 48[17], 49[7] and 54[5] the Holy One of Israel is the Redeemer (*goel*). The Israelites will hold His name holy because they will see what His hands have done for them (Is. 29[23]). In all these and similar passages holiness could obviously stand for grace, since it characterises God as Him who is and acts for Israel. And the same applies precisely to the most important use of the notion in the New Testament, viz., to the description of the application of the grace of Jesus Christ to the Church and its members by the presence and gift of the Holy Spirit. To be sure, in this case too, and especially, "holy" means separate, that which confronts, arousing awe and the sense of obligation. But it clearly means primarily and fundamentally that which singles out, blesses, helps and restores, and only in this positive connexion does it have that other significance.

It is, then, only as God affirms His victorious good will, as the concept of grace implies, that what holiness specially denotes is true and actual—the aloofness with which God stands over against the resistance He encounters, His judgment upon sin. He exercises this judgment, His judgment, in such a way that it can be manifest and truly appreciated and experienced as divine judgment only in this way, the way of grace. But of course it must also be said that this way leads necessarily and unavoidably to the truth and reality of judgment, and therefore to the holiness of divine grace.

We are thinking here of the solemn warnings of Paul in Rom. 6[1 15]: Is it possible to continue in sin that grace may abound? Can we sin because we do not stand under the law but under grace? The answer is: μὴ γένοιτο[EN24]. We are dead to sin, and therefore cannot live to it any longer (v. 2); μὴ γένοιτο[EN25]. Freed from sin, we have become the servants of righteousness (v. 18). This is the holiness of the grace of God.

That God is gracious does not mean that He surrenders Himself to the one to whom He is gracious. He neither compromises with his resistance, nor ignores it, still less calls it good. But as the gracious God He affirms Himself over against the one to whom He is gracious by opposing and breaking down his resistance, and in some way causing His own good will to exert its effect

---

[EN23] the terrible
[EN24] by no means!
[EN25] by no means!

upon him. Therefore the one to whom He is gracious comes to experience God's opposition to him.

"For whom the Lord loveth He correcteth; even as a father the son in whom he delighteth (Prov. 3^{12}). This text is cited emphatically in two places in the New Testament: Heb. 12^{6} and Rev. 3^{19}. And in Titus $2^{11f.}$ we read: "The grace of God that bringeth salvation to all men hath appeared, teaching (or correcting) us." This is the holiness of God's grace. Just because God is gracious we must fear Him. For: "If we sin wilfully after that we have received the knowledge of the truth, there remaineth no more sacrifice for sins, but a certain fearful looking [362]
for of judgment and fiery indignation, which shall devour the adversaries. He that despised Moses' law died without mercy under two or three witnesses: of how much sorer punishment, suppose ye, shall he be thought worthy, who hath trodden under foot the Son of God, and hath counted the blood of the covenant, wherewith he was sanctified, an unholy thing, and hath done despite unto the Spirit of grace? For we know him that hath said, Vengeance belongeth unto me, I will recompense, saith the Lord. And again, The Lord shall judge his people. It is a fearful thing to fall into the hands of the living God" (Heb. 10^{26-31}). Note the context of this text (which is perhaps the most emphatic in the whole Bible on the theme of God's holiness). It is a fearful thing to fall into the hands of the God who has sent us His Son, who is the Lord of the covenant sanctified by the blood of Jesus Christ, who is the Spirit of grace. In the last resort this is the only thing to be feared. But it really is fearful. For here there is a conflict between God and the creature, a conflict in which the creature can be only the threatened party. The revelation of God, just because it is a revelation of His love and grace, means the revelation of His opposition to man, i.e., of His opposition to the opposition in which man exists over against Him.

Only in this opposition is God known in His being as love and grace. For only in this relationship of opposition does He actually create and maintain fellowship between Himself and us, and turn towards us. Only in this tension, as we experience and recognise it as such, and subject ourselves to it, do we truly believe in Him and yield to Him the right which He has against us and over us: the right in which we can then place our confidence. If He is not present to us in this tension, He is not present to us at all. If we refuse to recognise and, as is right, to suffer this His opposition to us, we are also repudiating His grace. To believe in God means that we bow to this His opposition to us, accepting, and—despairing of ourselves but not of Him—allowing His good will towards us to be our ground of confidence and hope.

We cannot do this if that which we encounter in God is sheer abstract opposition, and not the opposition of His good but also gracious, beneficent and saving will towards us; if His opposition is not, so to speak, implicated in the marvellous work of His election and favour: just as the tables of the Law with their annihilating commands and threats were hidden in the ark of the covenant and so placed under the throne of grace besprinkled with the blood of atoning sacrifices. But again this covenant cannot stand without the revelation of the Law of God in all its holiness, and therefore not without the revelation of the divine opposition and judgment, of the wrath of God from heaven against all the ungodliness and unrighteousness of men (Rom. 1^{18}). There can, therefore, be no real faith in God which in the presence of the marvellous work of divine election and favour does not feel compelled to utter the cry of Peter in Luke 5^{8}: "Depart from me; for I am a sinful man, O Lord." Rightly understood, it is the believer and the believer alone who speaks in this way. For from grace and only from grace does the judgment proceed which compels a man to speak in this way.

The man without grace and faith will not speak in this way. Rather he will attempt to evade the judgment and hide it from himself. In fact, he will not be able to appreciate it. He will merely be judged in fact, and fall an eternal victim to judgment, without realising it. He will suffer without surrendering himself to that which encounters him, without repentance and without knowledge, and therefore without help and without hope. It is a well-known fact that [363] Luther usually referred the consciousness of sin, the fear of God's wrath and penitence, to a special revelation of divine Law, holiness and wrath, separate from the revelation of divine grace; to a special aspect of God's being, its majesty and hiddenness. In this respect we do not follow Luther because this scheme cannot honestly be maintained in face of the apparently more complicated but in truth far simpler testimony of Scripture. In Scripture we do not find the Law alongside the Gospel but in the Gospel, and therefore the holiness of God is not side by side with but in His grace, and His wrath is not separate from but in His love. But Luther seems fortunately to have contradicted Himself many times. That the Holy Spirit, the One who convicts the world in respect of righteousness (i.e., in the resurrection of Jesus Christ) and of judgment (upon the prince of this world), also convicts the world in respect of sin (Jn. $16^{8f.}$), was after all written effectively in his Bible too. And so Luther could express himself in the following terms in a sermon about Peter's draught of fishes (Lk. 5^{4-11}): "Yea, what more serious and terrible indication of God's anger over sin could there be than the suffering and death of Christ His Son? The consequence of it is that when the passion of Christ really moves a man's heart, he must spontaneously see and feel therein the unendurable anger of God over sin, and be terrified that the world is too narrow for him, as St. Bernard also witnesses was his experience; when he rightly considers the passion of Christ he exclaims: Ah! I thought I was safe, and I did not know about the judgment and wrath which had gone forth upon me, until I realised that the only Son of God had to die for my sake. For this spectacle is so terrible that even the damned in hell will have no greater pain and consciousness of God's reprobation than what springs from the sight of the death of the Son of God, the effect of which they have allowed to be lost upon them; just as Judas the traitor, since he refused to heed the friendly warning of the Master or to consider what he was doing to Him, was finally driven to such terror by this realisation that He pronounced his own condemnation when he said: 'I have betrayed the innocent blood' (Mt. 27^{4}). Therefore St. Peter also preaches to him here the law of his sin and of God's wrath from this great benefit of Christ" (1538, *E.A.*, 13, 116 f.). And on another occasion Luther referred to the "sad, piteous, tragic, moving, blood-stained spectacle which is put before us on Good Friday, that Christ hangs there between murderers and dies in great agony. We ought to consider such a spectacle, as we have already said, in such wise that we conclude therefrom that all this has happened because of our sin, that He, the righteous and eternal high priest, has been willing to give Himself as a sacrifice for our sin, and to pay for it with His death. For every man should realise that his sins have wounded Christ and done Him to death in this terrible way, and that the sufferings of Christ are nothing but the bearing of your sins and mine. Therefore as often as we think of such a sad blood-stained spectacle we must think only that we see there our sins and their provocation of God's terrible wrath, into which we fall with our sins, which is so great that no creature can carry it nor effect atonement except the Son of God alone through His own sacrifice and death (*Pred. über Matth.* 28^{1-10}, 1531, acc. to Dietrich, *E.A.*, 3, 299).

The holiness of God consists in the unity of His judgment with His grace. God is holy because His grace judges and His judgment is gracious.

In this sense Jesus Christ Himself is the Holy One of God (Mk. 1^{24}; cf. Ac. 3^{14}, Rev. 3^{7}). The unity of the Old and New Testament is at this point unmistakable and indisputable. The Holy One of Israel in Deutero-Isaiah is the most exact description of the name of *Yahweh* which determines the whole history of Israel. It sums up the promise given to Israel and Israel's hope and expectation. God deals with Israel from the days of the patriarchs, through Moses and David up to the restoration from Exile, in such a way that He reveals and confirms Himself once and for all as the Holy One of Israel, i.e., the One who in Israel maintains and [364] fulfils His own will. We certainly cannot say that the idea of holiness as contrasted with the thought of revelation signifies the inaccessibility of God over against His people and as such points to an older stratum in Old Testament theology which was later "rejected" in the New Testament community in favour of the idea of the love and mercy of God (thus A. Ritschl, *Rechtf. und Versöhnung*, Vol. 2, 1900, 89–102). The revelation and hiddenness of God are indeed to be distinguished in the Old Testament, but not separated, and the same applies to God's grace and God's holiness. In revealing Himself, God reveals Himself as the hidden God, but the hidden God reveals Himself. And just because He is gracious God shows His holiness, and as the Holy God He manifests His grace. It is in this unity that God speaks and acts according to the witness of the New Testament. According to 1 Pet. $1^{15f.}$ the God is holy who has called the Christian community as those who are redeemed by the blood of the Lamb without blemish and without spot, and who as such must place their hope entirely in grace. Jesus invokes as holy Father (Jn. 17^{11}) the One who will keep the disciples in the name in which He has given them to Him, that they may be one even as the Father and the Son are one. The holy God according to 1 Jn. 2^{20} is He from whom Christians receive their anointing and have their being in Christ. As we have already indicated, He is the Holy Spirit, who epitomises all perfected fellowship between God and man, and who according to 1 Cor. 2^{10} is also the epitome of the "deep things" of God. And the very fact that specific allusions to the holiness of God in the New Testament are often brought into connexion with Old Testament passages only goes to show that the New Testament witnesses in this matter desired to speak and did in fact speak in conscious unity with the Old Testament. But quite apart from the linguistic aspect, it is puzzling how the heart of the New Testament message, viz., the passion narrative and the indissoluble connexion between Christ's death and resurrection as directly or indirectly attested in so many apostolic texts, can be so disregarded that even momentarily we can lose sight of the necessity of seeing the grace of God in His judgment and therefore His judgment in His grace.

Because, in virtue of what God does to Israel, God and Israel belong together, and because God continues to have dealings with Israel in this partnership and as its Creator, God is holy. That the idea is to be understood in this sense is shown by the fact that the holiness required of Israel—Ye shall be holy; for I am holy (Lev. 11^{44}; 1 Pet. 1^{16})—has essentially the character of cultic holiness. The holiness of man and of human actions, of things and places, is constituted, so to speak, by their serviceableness in the fellowship founded and initiated by God between Himself and man. Unholiness is therefore unserviceableness to this end. The holiness of God describes the form of His attitude in this fellowship. Sin is whatever disturbs and makes this fellowship impossible. For this reason God's attitude in this fellowship is characterised by holiness, exclusiveness, the condemnation and annihilation of sin. The holiness of God thus involves peril to the man with whom He has fellowship. Since his sin disturbs this fellowship and makes it impossible, man himself becomes impossible. As a sinful man he cannot stand before God. He must perish. That he should himself be holy is not, therefore, a command by which God urges him to secure for himself a status or merit in His presence. But as God's command it is quite simply the command to cleave to His grace. And again, this command to be holy is not a command which man might or might not fulfil. But as a divine command it is simply the command of self-preservation. In the presence of God man stands or falls as he becomes holy. But he becomes holy in virtue of the holiness of the God who graciously takes action on his behalf. The whole concrete content of the Holiness Code simply illustrates—as is necessary in the economy of revelation in expectation of Jesus

Christ—this complete, all-embracing divine action for man. It reminds man—and therefore
[365] all these commands must be kept—that all along the line God's own holy will is dealing with him, and that he, intrinsically unholy man, is saved by it, not because he sanctifies himself, but because in obedience to these commands he submits himself to the holiness of God. Because the good will of God is His own free will, therefore the content of the Holiness Code cannot be assimilated to a general system of the ethico-teleological type. We are continually astonished that this or that command is grounded in the affirmation: "For I am the Lord." In unending variations—and the multiplicity is not superfluous because it makes clear the point at issue—it is always a question of the same thing, that in the realm of contingent reality, acting personally, inscribing His name as it were with His own independent curves and lines in personal, everyday, popular life, and again with the same independence cutting out of this life what He destines for His service or has declared to be contrary to it, God binds Himself to this people, giving it His presence and self, being the One who makes it holy and its holiness. And so the keeping of the Holiness Code cannot even remotely signify anything which might be construed as a meritorious righteousness of works. The keeping of it can mean only that Israel accepts this contingent reality of its God, that He may dwell with it in His glory, that He may be its holiness, so that Israel itself may not be consumed by the divine holiness. In so far as it consists inwardly and essentially in adoration of divine grace, in gratitude for the gift of the covenant, obedience simply means dread of the destruction which must at once and at every point overtake Israel if it "transgresses," i.e., oversteps the line marking out the contingent reality of God's self-manifestation in its midst, thus falling a victim to the mortal opposition of God to human sin. There is sin only where man transgresses the commandments of God, i.e., enters the sphere of this opposition. It is just because God is so gracious to Israel that it must so basically and totally fear Him. It is only as God sanctifies Himself in its midst, and therefore requires holiness from it, i.e., the respecting of His own holiness, that He makes it possible for Israel to have fellowship with Him—a fellowship in which as the chosen people it is the redeemed people. We are not exaggerating, but simply noting the plain unmistakable meaning of the text itself viewed in its context, if we declare that the divinity of the love of God is in few other passages of the Bible so distinctly manifest as in that Book which is so often misunderstood and regarded as obscure, useless and imprisoned within the limitations of its period, the Book of Leviticus, and in those parts of the Pentateuch which are related to it—in this connexion we may also think of the Book of the prophet Ezekiel which is viewed with similar disapproval. What is the meaning of Messianic expectation and promise if they are not present here? here where nature and grace, reason and revelation are so irreconcilably juxtaposed because the Law which slays and the Gospel of God which makes alive are interwoven in the most astonishing way. J. Wichelhaus was certainly right when (long before R. Otto) he wrote on this point: "Man cannot and will not understand that it is just because God is good that He is holy and just because He loves that He is angry and chides and hurts and casts into the flames. The holiness of God is terrible to man. In His holiness God has for man the appearance of a Moloch, a Saturn, a consuming fire. God is in His holiness a consuming fire, and therefore, if man is to be brought back again to God, He must be supremely praised and loved by man in His holiness" (*Die Lehre der hl. Schrift*[3], 1892, 343). It was A. Ritschl who in contradistinction to this insight tried to reduce everything that the Old Testament says about the wrath of God to the idea of occasional outbursts of God's passion and destructiveness against the enemies of Israel and those who broke the covenant in Israel itself, by which the righteous in Israel were not affected, but to which they subjected themselves out of sympathy "with the people." As he saw it, this idea, like that of divine holiness generally, recedes more and more in the New Testament behind the thought of divine love and grace. That is to say, it becomes an expres-

sion, to be understood "only eschatologically," of the ultimate victory of God against His [366]
adversaries. "From what religious point of view can we Christians be interested in applying the concept of the wrath of God to our present-day experiences? ... Whoever invokes God as His God is not far from God, nor is God far from him: such a one, therefore, is not exposed at that moment to the divine wrath" (*Rechtf. und Versöhnung*[4], Vol. 2, 1900, 119–156). Quite apart from the exegetical violence done by his thesis, Ritschl failed to see that with the present experience of the divine wrath he was also eliminating its eschatological reality, and that with the elimination of the idea of divine wrath in general he was eliminating that of divine grace and love, converting it into an idea which has scarcely anything in common with the contingent reality in which, according to the witness of the Old and New Testament, God in His own person encounters man. If God does not meet us in His jealous zeal and wrath—exactly as He meets Israel according to the witness of the Old Testament, exactly as He meets it later in the crucifixion of His own Son—then He does not meet us at all, and in spite of all our asseverations about divine love, man is in actual fact left to himself. That man is not abandoned in this way, that God is really gracious to him, is shown in the fact that God confronts him in holiness. It is in this way that God is present with him, taking over and conducting the cause which sinful man is impotent to conduct himself. It is in this way that God reconciles man to Himself. The fact that God does not permit Israel, the righteous, or the Church to perish means that he cannot allow them to go their own way, unaccused, uncondemned and unpunished, when they are and behave as if they were people who do not participate in this salvation and protection. The burning bush of Exod. 3^{2} cannot be consumed. But the unconsumed bush must burn. This bush is Israel. And the flame which burns it but does not consume it is the God of Israel, the holy God. When God spake: Let there be light, and there was light, and God saw that it was good, God separated the light from the darkness and the light He called day and the darkness night (Gen. $1^{3f.}$). This separation could only have been avoided if God had not spoken: Let there be light, and there had not been light, and God had not seen that the light was good. Because this is true and actual, it must also be true and actual: "And the light of Israel shall be for a fire, and his Holy One for a flame: and it shall burn and devour his thorns and his briers in one day; and shall consume the glory of his forest, and of his fruitful field, both soul and body: and they shall be as when a standard-bearer fainteth. And the rest of the trees of his forest shall be few, that a child may write them" (Is. $10^{17f.}$). And at this point how can we help thinking of Is. $6^{1f.}$ where the prophet sees the Lord sitting on a throne high and lifted up, and his train filled the temple? Above it stood the seraphims, and one cried to another: "Holy, holy, holy, is the Lord of hosts: the whole earth is full of his glory. And the posts of the door moved at the voice of him that cried, and the house was filled with smoke." Then the prophet exclaims (exactly like Peter in Lk. 5): "Woe is me! for I am undone; because I am a man of unclean lips, and I dwell in the midst of a people of unclean lips: for mine eyes have seen the King, the Lord of Hosts." And accordingly there follows the terrible touching of his lips with a live coal from the altar, but also the explanation : "Lo, this hath touched thy lips; and thine iniquity is taken away, and thy sin purged." Consider this point. It is not after but in the manifestation of wrath and judgment that there comes the pardon, reconciliation, calling and commissioning of the prophet, in short, the grace, which was obviously from the very outset the secret meaning of this whole revelation of God's holiness. In this sense we clearly have to understand the preaching of judgment to the people with which Isaiah is at once entrusted, and in fact the prophetic preaching of judgment generally, even when it is not completed and qualified by any specific prophecy of salvation. How can it be ignored as the immediate inevitable consequence of the revelation of holiness and the Law of holiness? It is where the name, the people, the city, the house of God is, that judgment must begin (Jer. [367]
25^{29}; 1 Pet. 4^{17}). Binding Himself to Israel, God binds Israel to Himself, and binding Israel to

Himself, He becomes to it the inextinguishable fire whose flame is nothing else but the flame of His love. Making Himself its God, He subjects it to His Law, His threats and His punishments in order to confer on it His blessings by this subjection. Separating it from among the peoples, in all the things in which its native way of life is the same as that of the heathen, He must deal with it just as He does with the latter, and indeed incomparably more strictly. To this day He must heap misfortunes upon Israel as compared with other peoples in order to accomplish supremely its separation and therefore its promise, and therefore His own gracious election and turning to this people. The *freedom* of grace is revealed in the fact that it is always manifest in judgment. But it is the freedom of *grace* which is revealed in this way. If it is God who enters into fellowship with man, and if this happening spells grace and election, is it not inevitable that the opposition, indeed the consuming opposition, between God and sinful man should be made manifest? And conversely, if God did not make known His consuming opposition to sin and therefore to sinful man, how could He really hold fellowship with man, seeing He can do so only on the basis of grace and election? To accept God's grace necessarily means, therefore, to respect God's holiness, and therefore to accept, heed and keep His laws, to fear His threats, to experience His wrath and to suffer His punishment. Otherwise acceptance of grace is indistinguishable from heathen quietism. But again, respect for God's holiness, if it is not a vain heathen religion of fear, can only mean directly to accept God's grace in thankfulness, to be contentedly replenished by it. "Wherefore we receiving a kingdom which cannot be moved, let us hold fast thankfulness, whereby we may serve God acceptably with reverence and godly fear. For our God is a consuming fire" (Heb. $12^{28f.}$). Again, if anywhere the unity of Old and New Testaments is visible, if anywhere we not only can but must speak of the Old Testament witness to Christ and of Christ as the fulfilment of the Old Testament, it is precisely in this connexion where the too fashionable exegesis of both Testaments has always tried to divorce Moses and Christ, the Law and the Gospel. For it is the witness of the Old Testament and its fulfilment that God made to be sin (2 Cor. 5^{21}) His own beloved Son in whom He was well pleased (Mk. 1^{11}), that He condemned sin in Him (Rom. 8^{3}), and that because He thus humbled Himself unto the death of the cross, He gave Him the name which is above every name (Phil. 2^{9}), and that in all this, in confirmation of what had always been His revelation of holiness, He made His own business the sanctification of His people, the expiation of its sin, the embodiment of His will in the life of His people, thus giving this people the opportunity of receiving and accepting by faith the divine judgment, but also of finding in it the forgiveness of sins and the promise of eternal life and therefore of fleeing sin as surely as it cannot wish to flee from divine grace. "And for their sakes I sanctify myself, that they also might be sanctified through the truth" (Jn. 17^{19}) When we look at Jesus Christ we cannot fail to see how the apparently varied threads in the Old Testament witness of God all intertwine, His election and His wrath, His forgiveness of sins and His commandments, His graciousness and His holiness; and that according to the Old Testament witness the Lord who deals with Israel is the one God in all this diversity. Again, the Old Testament attests and affirms that Jesus Christ, in whom God turns to man while remaining completely true to Himself, discloses a life which in the Old Testament sense can be adequately described only by the appellation God. If God's love is what is revealed to us in Jesus Christ, if Jesus Christ Himself is the revealed love of God, there is an end of the divorce between God's grace and holiness, and there remains to us only the recognition and adoration of Him who is both gracious and holy: gracious as He is holy and holy as He is gracious.

[368] We may now say again, with richer insight, that in this way God *loves.* By this mark, that it is holy love, we recognise the divinity of His action and being. For again we must add that God not only acts as the Holy One, but that as He acts

He is, from everlasting to everlasting. In Him, of course, there is no sin which He has first to resist. But in Him there is more. There is the purity, indeed He is Himself the purity, which as such contradicts and will resist everything which is unlike itself, yet which does not evade this opposing factor, but, because it is the purity of the life of the Father, Son and Holy Spirit, eternally reacts against it, resisting and judging it in its encounter with it, but in so doing receiving and adopting it, and thus entering into the fellowship with it which redeems it.

2. THE MERCY AND RIGHTEOUSNESS OF GOD

The fact that among the biblical attributes of God we select two further divine perfections, both individually and in their interconnexion, does not mean that we are leaving behind what we have already said of the divine being, i.e., the perfections of His grace and holiness, in order to turn our attention as it were to another aspect of deity. In this whole enquiry and exposition we must never forget that there exists "another" in God only in so far as it is still one and the same thing. But in God Himself, and therefore also for us, there is a fulness of the divine perfections, not in poverty, but in richness, and therefore continually different, and to be viewed and conceived in its development. We continue our consideration and discussion of the love of God and therefore of God Himself as the One who loves in freedom. But continuing to study this one object we come necessarily, if we follow the testimony of Holy Scripture, from the first to the second proposition, that God is merciful and righteous. Continuing! The first assertion, that God is gracious and holy, is not therefore exhausted and abandoned. On the contrary, we can regard the task which now faces us, and indeed all possible tasks in this sphere, simply as a further analysis and elucidation of this first affirmation. In fact we shall have to repeat and understand again that God is gracious and holy. We shall have to repeat it with ever-growing insight. Our second affirmation and all further affirmations can thus be regarded simply as variations of this first theme. But as the being of God in itself is really one in real plenitude and not in poverty, our knowledge of God can be coherently developed yet still be more than the mere logical unfolding of a single principle and proposition. We not only can but must place alongside our first affirmation a second and a third: not with the idea of adding something new, but with the idea of continually saying the one thing, on the presupposition of what has already been said, in ever new forms. In this [369]
sense, we now learn and repeat that the one thing which God is, is also mercy and righteousness.

We begin with the perfection of the divine mercy. The word itself in its Latin and German, but especially its biblical usage, teaches us that in this notion we are not merely in the proximity but in fact at the very centre of the concept of divine love and its specific determination as grace. In a general idea of love, the thought of mercy is not necessarily included—any more than that of grace.

Love in itself and in general can also fall under quite other descriptions. But the love of God as the Creator's will for fellowship with His creature bears necessarily the character of grace, i.e., the free inclination of an unconditionally superior towards one who is unconditionally subordinate. If this is true, with the absoluteness with which it must be true of the two partners we are now considering, we must consider these two partners more precisely, the One who loves and the object of His love, and go on at once to say that divine love bears necessarily the character of mercy. The word "necessarily" can and must be understood literally in this connexion. In the relationship between this love and its object, and therefore in the grace of God, we have to do with the "turning" of a "need" (*Not-Wende*). The free inclination of God to His creature, denoted in the biblical witness by grace, takes place under the presupposition that the creature is in distress and that God's intention is to espouse his cause and to grant him assistance in his extremity. Because grace, the gracious love of God, consists in this inclination, it is, and therefore God Himself is, merciful; God's very being is mercy. The mercy of God lies in His readiness to share in sympathy the distress of another, a readiness which springs from His inmost nature and stamps all His being and doing. It lies, therefore, in His will, springing from the depths of His nature and characterising it, to take the initiative Himself for the removal of this distress. For the fact that God participates in it by sympathy implies that He is really present in its midst, and this means again that He wills that it should not be, that He wills therefore to remove it. We can see at once that the idea of the mercy of God is not evolved logically from a merely general notion of grace. Understood in quite general terms, as the free condescension of a superior to an inferior, it does not necessarily include the superior's participation in, and determination speedily to relieve, the distress of the inferior. Grace in itself and in general might equally well mean an unsympathetic and ineffectual inclination on the part of the superior. But we are speaking of the grace of God and therefore of the concrete relationship in which it becomes actual, of His grace towards the one to whom He is gracious. In this relation mercy is included in grace; grace itself is mercy. And by this
[370] mark and this alone we recognise the divinity of the love and grace of God: by the fact that it is merciful.

Misericordia Dei est gratiosissima voluntatis divinae propensio, qua Deo cordi est miseria hominis, eandemque benevole sublevatam cupit[EN26] (Quenstedt, *Theol. did. pol.*, 1685, I, *c.* 8, *sect.* 1, *th.* 32). It is a peculiarity of the LXX that the normal translation for the Old Testament *chesed* (where we would expect χάρις[EN27])) is ἔλεος[EN28], of which the Old Testament equivalents are properly *chanan* and *racham.* But in this way there is correctly suggested the affective aspect of love, peculiar, in fact, to the biblical conception of grace. The concept is, therefore, pre-

[EN26] The mercy of God is that most gracious inclination of the divine will, by which the misery of man reaches God's heart, and by which he kindly desires that misery to have been consoled.

[EN27] grace

[EN28] mercy

sented immediately and unmistakably in the concrete content which the biblical background implies. It is well known how often grace and mercy appear side by side in the Old Testament, the one clearly determining and elucidating the other. The New Testament terms **ἔλεος**[EN29] and **οἰκτιρμοί**[EN30] do not suggest, of course, only a feeling but an action, yet the kind of action which is determined by a feeling. Quenstedt was right exegetically and substantially not to fear the anthropomorphic character of the expression: *qua Deo cordi est miseria*[EN31]. The main point is, as the Latin and German words make very clear, that God's love and grace are not just mathematical or mechanical relations, but have their true seat and origin in the movement of the heart of God. It is here that we can appreciate the meaning of the idea of personality in God, and what has to be defended by its maintenance against the conception of God as an impersonal absolute. In any other relation between God and creature except that attested in the Bible, in any relation which, if need be, can be described in mathematical or mechanical terms, the idea of personality in God is perhaps dispensable. But in the relation between the merciful God and the "miserable" creature (i.e., in need of mercy) it emerges—and here at last it must emerge—that it is indispensable, and expresses the truth. It was quite natural that Schleiermacher should consider it impossible to ascribe to God a state of feeling specially awakened by the suffering of others and going out to assist them, and therefore that he should try to eject the idea of the mercy of God from the language of dogmatics to that of homiletics and poetry (*Der chr. Glaube*, § 85). The source of the feeling of sheer dependence has no heart. But the personal God has a heart. He can feel, and be affected. He is not impassible. He cannot be moved from outside by an extraneous power. But this does not mean that He is not capable of moving Himself. No, God is moved and stirred, yet not like ourselves in powerlessness, but in His own free power, in His innermost being: moved and touched by Himself, i.e., open, ready, inclined (*propensus*) to compassion with another's suffering and therefore to assistance, impelled to take the initiative to relieve this distress. It can be only a question of compassion, free sympathy, with another's suffering. God finds no suffering in Himself. And no cause outside God can cause Him suffering if He does not will it so. But it is, in fact, a question of sympathy with the suffering of another in the full scope of God's own personal freedom. This is the essential point if we are really thinking of the God attested by Scripture, and speaking only of Him. Everything that God is and does is determined and characterised by the fact that there is rooted in Him, that He Himself is, this original free powerful compassion, that from the outset He is open and ready and inclined to the need and distress and torment of another, that His compassionate words and deeds are not grounded in a subsequent change, in a mere approximation to certain conditions in the creature which is distinct from Himself, but are rooted in His heart, in His very life and being as God. When, therefore, Polanus says: *Deus est misericors sua aeterna et simplici essentia, non autem qualitate aliqua, non affectu, non passione*[EN32] (*Synt. Theol. chr.*, 1609, *col.* 1119), he is right to the extent that by this negation he wishes to avoid the conception of a God who can be moved and stirred from without. The "affection" of God is different from all creaturely affections in that it originates in Himself. But in this sense it cannot [371]
be denied. In this sense it is God's mercy as it can also be God's wrath. We recall that in Lk. 1[78] it is expressly a question of the **σπλάγχνα**[EN33]—the bowels of God's mercy. Phil. 1[8] speaks in the same sense of the **σπλάγχνα Χριστοῦ Ἰησοῦ**[EN34]. In Phil. 2[1] and Col. 3[12]

EN29 mercy
EN30 mercies
EN31 by which the misery reaches God's heart
EN32 God is merciful in his eternal and simple essence, and not in some quality, affection or passion
EN33 mercy
EN34 mercy of Jesus Christ

these σπλάγχνα[EN35] are linked with οἰκτιρμοί[EN36], and in a whole series of Synoptic passages the verb σπλαγχνίζεσθαι is used for "have mercy," and always denotes the compassion of Jesus. In view of all this we shall have to take the positive part of Polanus' sentence as seriously as the negative. The mercy of God really means His σπλάγχνα[EN37], and no less than all His other attributes denotes His *aeterna et simplex essentia*[EN38]. The God whom Jesus Christ calls Father is merciful (Lk. 6[36]), rich in mercy (Eph. 2[4]), the Father of mercies and therefore the "God of all comfort" (2 Cor. 1[3]). All that He does gains both its power and its character from this source. Grace is rightly received and understood as such, free and unmerited grace, but in the effectual reality of the turning of God denoted by it, if we note the actual context: "I will be gracious to whom I will be gracious, and will shew mercy on whom I will shew mercy" (Ex. 33[19]). The impassibility of God cannot in any case mean that it is impossible for Him really to feel compassion. Where grace is manifest and effectual, it is always a question of the misery of man. In this fact its freedom is implied. It is really a gift made to one who is poor and in misery. But, on the other hand, it is always a question, no more and no less, of the heart, the innermost being of God. This is not closed but open to feel the distress of man. God cannot be moved from outside, but from inside His own being He shares it in sympathetic communion. It is here that we see the power of grace. This means, of course, that in fact it is not merely a gift of God, but God Himself the Giver who gives Himself as the gift. In this connexion we may also think of the passages where the mercy of God at first sight seems to be related "only" to the physical need of man (e.g., Phil. 2[27]). "His tender mercies are over all his works" (Ps. 145[9]). Measured by the Lord's holiness the whole creation as such lies in need and misery and is dependent on the fact that God's mercy is new every morning (Lam. 3[23]). And God does not refuse to give Himself to it. He maintains it as He has created it. He takes into account its frailty and need, giving Himself anew to it every morning. That all this is true becomes especially clear when the work of God assumes the form of His self-revelation, reconciliation and sanctification, the form of His covenant with Israel, the form of Jesus Christ.

We have seen how grace in Jesus Christ stands in victorious opposition to the resistance set up by the creature to God. The mercy of God, too, expresses this opposition. The point is, however, that not merely in regard to its consequences and punishment, not merely in view of the judgment which it brings down upon itself, but in itself this resistance has in the light of the merciful grace of God the appearance of man's distress and suffering and misery. Arrogance is seen as pitiable folly, the usurpation of freedom as rigorous bondage, evil lust as bitter torment. It is again true that man by his own fault has plunged himself and is continually plunging himself into these ills, and in view of this we shall have to speak later of the righteousness of God. But it is also true that this resistance of the creature, this sinfulness of man, has in itself and as such the simple meaning of folly, bondage and torment. And as such it is the object of God's compassion. In concrete the mercy of God means therefore His compassion at the sight of the suffering which man brings upon himself, His con-
[372] cern to remove it, His will to console man in this pain and to help him to overcome it. The freedom of God is such that His grace and condescension to

EN35 mercy
EN36 mercies
EN37 mercy
EN38 eternal and simple essence

man can, may and must have the meaning and effect of making man's sin and guilt an object of divine compassion, so that He can hate sin and for this very reason love the sinner, pitying sinful and guilty man even as He opposes him, and in this pity entering into dealings with him. And this pity is no mere sentiment, but power and deed. We are assured of this by the fact that it is not too light a thing for God to turn favourably to man in this way, and indeed to be open to man in this way, to be for Him the One who is merciful, even prior to his creation and any turning to him, from all eternity.

God grieveth in eternity
My misery beyond measure,
He called to mind His mercy mild,
To help me was His pleasure.
He turned to me His Father's heart,
'Twas not for Him the trifler's part,
He gave His costliest treasure.

For mercy now the time has come,
To His own Son confiding,
Away, heart's crown, from heaven's throne,
Salvation now providing.
To help poor man from sinful loss,
Endure for him the bitter cross,
And be his life abiding.

(Luther: "*Nun frewt euch lieben Christen gmeyn* ... " 1523? *W.A.* 35, 424, 4.) Note that God is merciful, i.e., the time can come for Him to be merciful, because He pities in eternity, because He has only to call to mind His mercy. The sovereign freedom and power of His mercy are not, then, merely (as H. Cremer still asserts in his *Lexikon*, Art. ἔλεος) those of an attitude in the economy of salvation, but genuinely and truly the freedom and power of His Godhead. God the Father, Son and Holy Spirit is merciful in Himself. In this essential freedom and power He speaks and acts mercifully in His revelation, reconciliation and sanctification, in His covenant with Israel, in the epiphany and parousia of Jesus Christ.

We read in Rom. 9^{16}, in direct connexion with the quotation from Ex. 33^{19}: "So then it is not of him that willeth, nor of him that runneth, but of God that sheweth mercy"; and immediately after, in Rom. 9^{18}: "Therefore hath he mercy on whom he will have mercy." Rom. 11^{32} is also to be understood in this sense: "For God hath concluded them all in disobedience, that he might have mercy upon all." God's mercy is God's freedom. Hence it is impossible to understand this "all" mathematically and mechanically, as the sum of all mankind, to whom God owes His grace as such. On the contrary, according to the passages in Rom. 9 they are undoubtedly the elect people which once was no people, but has now become His people, the people of those who were once without grace but have now found grace (1 Pet. 2^{10}). As God's mercy it is necessarily a grace which chooses, and it is manifest and effectual as such to those who love Him (Ex. 20^{6}) and fear Him (Ps. 103^{13}; Lk. 1^{50}). But in this way and to them it is powerfully, incontestably and irresistibly manifest and effectual, that no human sin or guilt can suspend its working, but it is just human sin and guilt which are the occasion of the powerful divine compassion. Again it is of the freedom and the power of "the tender mercy of our God" that it is said in Lk. $1^{78f.}$ that by it "the dayspring [373]
from on high hath visited us, to give light to them that sit in darkness, and in the shadow of death, to guide our steps into the way of peace." Again it is of the freedom and power of the

divine mercy that it is said in 1 Pet. 1^{3} that by it God "hath begotten us again unto a lively hope by the resurrection of Jesus Christ from the dead," or in Tit. 3^{5} that by it—not on account of any righteous works which we have done—God has "saved us, by the washing of regeneration, and renewing of the Holy Ghost." And, again, when it is a question of the God who is rich in mercy in Eph. $2^{4f.}$, it is through mercy that we who were dead in our trespasses—have been made alive with Christ. Again it is mercy in Ps. $78^{37f.}$: "Their heart was not right with him, neither were they steadfast in his covenant. But he, being full of compassion, forgave their iniquity, and destroyed them not." And again in Is. 54^{7-10}: "For a small moment have I forsaken thee, but with great mercies will I gather thee. In a little wrath I hid my face from thee for a moment; but with everlasting kindness will I have mercy on thee, saith the Lord thy Redeemer ... for the mountains shall depart, and the hills be removed, but my kindness shall not depart from thee, neither shall the covenant of my peace be removed, saith the Lord that hath mercy on thee." In all these and similar statements we must understand the predicates in the light of the subject and then interpret the subject in its predicates. That God who is provoked to anger is not only angry, but for the sake of that which provokes Him sets bounds to His anger and is compassionate, and that this compassion is His and is therefore active, where His wrath slays, to make alive and renew and enlighten—that is the secret and at the same time the simple and manifest reality of His mercy.

It is to be noted that when we confess God to be merciful it is not even remotely possible to demonstrate this as a logically deducible truth. All that we can do is to acknowledge the actual reality of God. What else can we produce as a proof of this confession except the fact that God has given Himself to be known by us as merciful in the name of Jesus Christ? How can we try to recognise the reality of the mercy of God except in this name?

The revelation of this name as the epitome of the expectation of Israel and the recollection of the Church is also in Holy Scripture the epitome of the reality of God's mercy. We cannot get behind this name to learn why God is merciful. But we can infer from this name with unshakable certainty that He is. In this recognition and confession everything depends on the fact that by the Word and Spirit of God we are linked to this name, that in and with this revelation, attested to us by the Word and Spirit, the revelation of the mercy of God stands immediately before us, that by this name we are divinely and therefore incontestably and irresistibly comforted. We are comforted by an acceptance that not merely our creatureliness, not merely the need and the misery of our existence in its sheer dependence, but the very heart of this misery, our revolt against Him on whom we are utterly dependent, is in fact the object of His own participation, His care, His suffering, and therefore also His assistance and intervention. Before we are touched or can be touched by any pain which we have brought on ourselves by our sin and guilt, before we are sorry for or can be sorry for our sin, before death and hell can frighten us, and before we feel the greater terror that we are such sinners as have deserved death and hell, already in the One against whom we sin and are guilty and whose punishment threatens us we have to do with the God who Himself suffers pain because of our sin and guilt, for whom it is not an alien thing but His own intimate concern. And as God is far greater than we His creatures, so much greater is His sorrow on our behalf than any sorrow which we can feel for ourselves. If we recognise God's
[374] mercy in Jesus Christ, this means necessarily that we can no longer try to experience and bear in the sorrow which we have to experience and bear for ourselves an, as it were, divine, eternal, irremovable weight of sorrow. Because God is merciful, a divine pain of this kind is not only taken away from us, but forbidden to us as something presumptuous—a tragic consciousness to which we may not pretend. The height and depth, the inwardness and

outwardness of our sorrow is really God's concern—and ours only as it is seen and borne by God. What is our suffering when we recollect that God has Himself felt it so keenly as to give His only begotten Son in order to remove it? Our suffering for sin has not touched us, and cannot touch us, as it touches Him. So we can never take it to our hearts in this way. When we realise the full depth of our sorrow as it is seen and borne and suffered by God Himself, any complaint of ours as to the form in which it confronts and affects us is silenced. Our lamenting comes too late and is always relatively too weak. Indeed, it is always ineffective and in the end untrue. For what is the use of our lamenting when the heart of our misery is that we are sinners and debtors to God, in face of whom we cannot do anything to make good? Who can complain when God has to complain, when the right to complain is His right alone? It is His heart, not ours, which is suffering when we think that we are the sufferers and that we have a right or obligation to lament. His heart is wounded, and wounded through our heart. How can we reverse the relationship and behave as though we have to suffer, as it were, in the void, divinely, eternally, or on our own account? In the recognition and confession of the mercy of God, what we are accustomed to take so seriously as the tragedy of human existence is dissolved. There is something far more serious and tragic, viz., the fact that our distress—the anguish of our sin and guilt—is freely accepted by God, and that in Him, and only in Him, it becomes real agony. That this is the case is due to the mercy of God. In the face of this mercy we must be silent. In the bearing of our pain, we must be modest and unassuming, as also in our lamentation and protests against it. We not only must, but may. For it is the third and crucial factor in our misery that we think that we ourselves must bear our agony, the agony of our sin and guilt, that we must accuse and judge and cleanse ourselves, and then take pity on ourselves for the consequences of our sin. Sin attains its true form as opposition to the grace of God. It becomes hopeless as such, and its consequences are hopelessly painful. But at this point the grace of God intervenes as the mercy of God. Jesus Christ enters human existence as the great joy which shall be to all people. He breaks down this resistance to grace by Himself appearing as grace triumphant, as the royal removal of our sin and guilt by the action of God Himself. Because our sin and guilt are now in the heart of God, they are no longer exclusively ours. Because He bears them, the suffering and punishment for them are lifted from us, and our own suffering can be only a reminiscence of His. As He takes to Himself our sin and guilt in His Son, we are freed from the necessity of seeing and suffering and lamenting except as His and by faith in Him, i.e., except as a burden of sin and guilt which is lifted from us by Him. It remains for us only to be the sinners whose place He has taken and who must therefore really have their life in Him.

The merciful God has taken action on our behalf both in freedom and in power. In freedom: for our sin and guilt were not His and did not have to become so. Because this is so, faith believes in God's grace and election in virtue of which we receive what we have not deserved. But also in power: for He has really taken to Himself and removed from us our sin and guilt. Therefore faith is joy and gratitude, an assurance which can no longer look back, only forwards. In freedom and power, awakening a humble but assured and unshakable faith, He took our place because He was God's eternal Son, [375]
because it was manifest in Him that God's eternal being is mercy, because there is nothing more real and true behind and beyond this substitution, because this substitution is the very essence of God's own being, of His divinity, for which we must glorify Him in joy and gratitude if we are not to sin wantonly against Him, if we are to let God be God.

That we both must and may is seen again at this point, in the light of God's mercy, to be an inseparable unity. Must or may the heathen praise God for the mercy that has come to them (Rom. 15^{9})? The question is obviously pointless. The Law of God commands and the Gospel permits us to answer love with love. But is not the converse equally true?

This, then, is how God loves. His love is merciful love. In the nature of the case, we do not need to emphasise the point that God is as merciful in Himself as He is merciful in His action. For the idea of mercy itself refers back from God's attitude and act to the depths of God's being, to His heart, His mind, Himself. All misunderstanding in regard to the idea of grace, as if it were not eternal in God Himself, becomes quite impossible when we have understood it as merciful grace. For it is then understood, not simply as God's turning towards us, but as His free, effectual compassion. Looking backwards, therefore, it is seen, not simply as an appearance, but as the disposition of the heart and being of God. Viewed as merciful grace the love of God descends to earth more deeply, and climbs higher to heaven, than the idea of grace in itself would permit us to suppose. It is in this sense that we must use it in all our future deliberations.

We now turn to the concept of the righteousness of God, which is specially significant in Scripture and has been so much disputed in the history of the Christian confession. As we do so we must keep well in view a consideration which concerned us when we passed from the idea of the grace to that of the holiness of God, and which subsequently controlled our whole explanation and exposition of the idea of holiness. This is, that we are not concerned with a second thing side by side with a first; but that in both cases we have to do with one and the same thing. Is it not, then, a question of the second thing? Of course it is, and absolutely. Indeed, we can even say that it is only a question of the second thing because this second thing is so utterly identical with the first. In this one thing, in God Himself, in the plenitude of His being, there is no division and therefore no mutual qualification and augmentation of His attributes. But this does apply to the concepts by which we are allowed to recognise God on the basis of His revelation and in the truth of His unity and plenitude, i.e., when this process takes place in due humility, and no one of our concepts tries to usurp authority and form a system, and therefore we allow these concepts to qualify and augment each other, and, recognising and attesting the One in His unity and fulness, we pass from one idea to the other. But we can-
[376] not do as we like. We must proceed in order, in the order determined by the object, by the revelation of God in Jesus Christ, and therefore by His being. According to this order, the mercy of God must precede His righteousness, just as His grace had to precede His holiness. It is not that God is less holy and righteous than merciful and gracious. God is altogether everything that He is. In everything that He is, He is Himself. And everything that He Himself is, He is in unsurpassable, unchallengeable perfection. But He is so in His own perfection, not in one which is arbitrarily determined, as, for example, the perfection of a circle or a ball. In the multiplicity of His perfections He is not

comparable to the multiplicity of the points on the periphery or surface of an object of this kind, which are all equally near to the centre, and equidistant from it. God cannot be compared to anyone or anything. He is only like Himself. And who and what He is cannot be constructed mathematically or logically or ethically or psychologically. We have simply to listen to Himself on the point. If we do this, if we adhere to His revelation in Jesus Christ, specific relations gradually emerge between His perfections, not in spite of the fact that in each of them He is no less wholly Himself than in all the others, but just because of it. We have seen that there exists a relationship between God's grace and holiness, a relationship of mutual penetration and consummation determined by grace, which necessarily precedes. The relationship between God's mercy and righteousness is similar. We shall have to emphasise the righteousness of God no less than His mercy. If possible, we shall have to emphasise it even more. But we cannot do this, we cannot speak at all of the righteousness of God which is so much emphasised in the Bible, if we do not proceed from a consideration of God's mercy. The relationship between God's mercy and righteousness will also present itself to us as a relationship of mutual penetration and consummation, but here again it will receive its characteristic stamp from the fact that divine mercy necessarily precedes. For only in this way does it correspond to the economy of the revelation and therefore the being of God, which must always be respected and never replaced by any arbitrarily introduced symmetry.

The loving of God is a divine action and being distinct from every other loving in the fact that it is righteous. Our point of departure must be that the righteousness of God is a determination of the love, and therefore of the grace and mercy, of God. And the love and grace and mercy of God have the determination of righteousness necessarily, as they have that of holiness. Necessarily, because if this love were not holy and righteous it would not be the love of God. The characterisation and determination of this love as righteousness and therefore divine springs from the fact that when God wills and creates the possibility of fellowship with man He does that which is worthy of Himself, and therefore in this fellowship He asserts His worth in spite of all contradiction [377]
and resistance, and therefore in this fellowship He causes only His own worth to prevail and rule. It is only in this characterisation and determination that the love of God is truly His divine love.

The definition must be framed on these lines if there is not to take place here a cleavage in the being of God, if the righteousness of God is to be seen in its unity with His mercy and also with a backward reference in its unity with His holiness. In its unity with His mercy: we defined the latter as a determination of the love and grace of God manifested in time as God's effectual participation in the misery of another, a participation prompted by His inmost being. From this it follows, not logically of course, that God is righteous, that, founding and maintaining in this way fellowship with another, He wills and expresses and establishes what corresponds to His own worth. But if it is in fact true that

God is righteous in this sense, and on the basis of His revelation we presuppose that it is true, it cannot be asserted of this definition of His righteousness that it is in logical contradiction to the definition of His mercy. God does not have to, but He can, take to Himself the suffering of another in such a way that in doing so, in founding and accomplishing this fellowship, He does what corresponds to His worth. Our definition of the righteousness of God can co-exist with that of His mercy and together with it make manifest the unity of God. The same applies in regard to the unity of God's righteousness and holiness. We defined the latter as the self-affirmation of the will of God which takes place in His founding and accomplishment of fellowship with another. Again, it does not follow logically that God is righteous, that what He wills and does and realises in this fellowship is what corresponds to His worth. That there is a divine worth which is maintained, defended and realised in this self-assertion of the divine will is something which is not included in it by any necessity of logic. But if in point of fact it is included, because in virtue of God's self-revelation it is clear that God's holiness is His righteousness, there does not exist any contradiction between God's holiness and righteousness according to the definition here given. They can co-exist and equally denote one being of God.

We have seen that the weakness of the definitions of Protestant orthodoxy in respect of the relationship between God's grace and holiness was that they did not make clear the unity of the divine being. The same is true in this connexion.

We read in Quenstedt: *Iustitia Dei est summa et immutabilis voluntatis divinae rectitude a creatura rationale quod rectum et iustum est exigens. Estque vel remuneratrix, qua bonos praemiis, vel vindicatrix, qua malos suppliciis afficit*[EN39] (*Theol. did. pol.*, 1685, I, *c.* 8, *sect*, 1, *th.* 35). This definition fits in only too well with the same author's definition of the holiness of God, in which the divine *exigere*[EN40] plays so decisive a part. Later Schleiermacher defined the righteousness of God on the same lines as "the divine causality in virtue of which, in the condition of universal sinfulness, there is ordained a nexus between evil and real sin" (*Der chr. Glaube*,
[378] § 84). But if it is defined in this way, what happens to what even Quenstedt calls the *gratiosissima voluntatis divinae propensio, qua Deo cordi est miseria hominis*[EN41]? If God in His righteousness is simply exacting, i.e., rewarding the fulfilment of His demands and punishing their non-fulfilment, how in His mercy can He take to heart the suffering of man? And if He does the latter, how can He give play to His righteousness, supposing that it is to be understood only as demanding and distributive? To illustrate its doubtful content we will at once contrast with the thesis of this Lutheran author the words of Luther himself, whose insights were strangely lost during the course of the 16th and 17th centuries. Luther expressed himself as follows in his exposition (1532) of Ps. 51 (on v. 1: *Miserere met, Deus, secundum magnam misericordiam tuam*)*: Sancti patres, qui in psalmos scripserunt, fere exposuerunt "iustus Deus" pro eo, quod iuste vindicat ac punit, non pro eo, quod iustificat. Inde mihi accidit iuveni,*

[EN39] The justice of God is the highest and immutable righteousness of the divine will, requiring what is righteous and just from his rational creatures. And it is either remunerative, by which he visits the good with rewards, or retributive, by which he visits the wicked with punishments

[EN40] requirement

[EN41] most gracious inclination of the divine will, in which there is mercy toward man in the heart of God

ut hanc appellationem Dei odissem et ex illa hexei seu habitu adhuc hodie quasi cohorresco, cum audio Deum iustum dici. Tanta est vis impiae doctrinae, si ea animi in prima aetate imbuantur, et tamen veteres doctores fere omnes sic exponunt. Sed si Deus sic iustus est, ut puniat iuste seu pro merito, quis potest subsistere in huius iusti Dei conspectu? Si quidem omnes sumus peccatores et afferimus ad Deum iustam poenarum infligendarum causam. Procul hinc cum tali iustitia et tali iusto Deo, quia nos omnes sicut "ignis consumens" vorabit. Quia autem Christum salvatorem Deus misit, profecto non hoc modo iustus vult esse, ut puniat pro merito, sed vult iustus esse et dici, ut agnoscentes peccata iustificet et eorum misereatur[EN42] .... And on v. 14 (*Exultabit lingua mea iustitiam tuam*[EN43]): *Hoc vocabulum Iustitiae magno sudore mihi constitit; sic enim fere exponebant, iustitiam esse veritatem, qua Deus pro merito damnat seu iudicat male meritos. Et opponebant iustitiae misericordiam, qua salvantur credentes. Haec expositio periculosissima est, praeterquam quod vana est, concitat enim occultum odium contra Deum et eius iustitiam. Quis enim eunt potest amare, qui secundum iustitiam cum peccatoribus vult agere? Quare memineritis, iustitiam Dei esse, qua iustificamur seu donum remissionis peccatorum. Haec iustitia in Deo grata est, facit enim ex Deo non iustum iudicem, sed ignoscentem patrem, qui iustitia sua vult uti non ad iudicandos, sed iustificandos et absolvendos peccatores. Hanc tuam iustitiam, inquit, non iustitiam hominum aut Most, ego cum gaudio et laetitia praedicabo, etiam si mihi hostes capiendi sint omnes homines, modo tu hoc facias ut etiam coram ecclesia me absolvas*[EN44] (*W.A.* 40^{11}, 331, 25 and 444, 36). And in the preface to his Latin writings of 1545 Luther expressed the same point again in the well-known summary of his theological development: *Miro certe ardore captus fueram cognoscendi Pauli in Epistola ad Rom., sed obstiterat hactenus non frigidus circum praecordia sanguis sed unicum vocabulum, quod est Cap. 1: iustitia Dei revelatur in illo. Oderam enim vocabulum istud "iustitia Dei," quod usu et consuetudine omnium doctorum doctus eram philosophice intelligere de iustitia (ut vocant) formali seu activa, qua Deus est iustus et peccatores iniustosque punit. Ego autem, qui me, utcumque irreprehensibilis monachus vivebam, sentirem coram Deo esse peccatorem inquietissimae conscientiae nec mea satisfactione placatum confidere possem, non amabam, imo odiebam iustum et punientem peccatores Deum, tacitaque si non blasphemia, certe ingenti murmuratione indignabar Deo, dicens: quasi vero non satis sit, miseros peccatores et aeternaliter perditos peccato originali omni genere calamitatis oppressos esse per legem decalogi, nisi Deus per*

EN42 (Have mercy on me, O God, according to your great mercy). The holy fathers who wrote in the Psalms have almost explained 'the just God' by virtue of the fact that he vindicates and punishes justly, and not by virtue of the fact that he justifies. Thence it struck me as a young man such that I hated this designation of God, and shrank from it, just as today I still shudder out of habit when I hear God called 'just'. So great is the force of this ungodly doctrine, that if these things are absorbed in the mind in early life, however almost all elderly teachers explain it thus. But if God is thus just, such that he punishes justly, or according to deserts, who can stand in the sight of this just God? If indeed we are all sinners and bring to God just reason for the infliction of punishments. Let us flee from such justice and such a just God! For he will devour us all like a 'consuming fire'. But since God sent Christ the Saviour, he truly wills not to be just inasmuch as he punishes according to deserts, but he wishes to be just, being described as the one who justifies those who confess their sins, and who has mercy on them

EN43 My tongue will praise your justice

EN44 This word 'justice' caused me to break out in a great sweat. For thus they wrongly explained, that justice was the true judgment by which God condemns according to desert or judges unfavourably those who deserve it. They opposed to justice the mercy by which those who believe are saved. This explanation is most dangerous – besides the fact that it is wrong – for it arouses secret hatred against God and his justice. For who can love one who wills to deal with sinners according to his justice? Therefore, may you remember that the justice of God is that by which we are justified, or, the gift of the forgiveness of sins. This justice in God is pleasing, for it makes God not a just judge, but a forgiving father who wills to make use of his justice not to condemn, but to justify and acquit sinners. This is your justice, David says, not that of men or of Moses, which I will preach with joy and happiness, even if all men are to become enemies to me. Only, may you act that I be forgiven in the presence of the church

euangelium dolorem dolori adderet et etiam per euangelium nobis iustitiam et iram suam intentaret. Furebam ita saeva et perturbata conscientia, pulsabam tamen importunus eo loco Paulum, ardentissime sitiens scire, quid S. Paulus vellet. Donec miserente Deo meditabundus dies et noctes connexionem verborum attenderem, nempe: Iustitia Dei revelatur in illo, sicut scriptum est: Iustus ex fide vivit, ibi iustitiam Dei coepi intelligere eam, qua iustus dono Dei vivit, nempe ex fide, et esse hanc sententiam, revelari per euangelium iustitiam Dei, scilicet passivam, qua nos Deus misericors iustificat per fidem, sicut scriptum est: Iustus ex fide vivit. Hic me prorsus renatum esse sensi et apertis portis in ipsam
[379] *Paradisum intrasse. Ibi continuo alia mihi facies totius scripturae apparuit. Discurrebam deinde per scripturas, ut habebat memoria, et colligebam etiam in aliis vocabulis analogiam, ut opus Dei, id est, quod operatur in nobis Deus, virtus Dei, qua nos potentes facit, sapientia Dei, qua nos sapientes facit, fortitude Dei, salus Dei, gloria Dei. I am quanta odio vocabulum "iustitia Dei" oderam ante, tanto amore dulcissimum mihi vocabulum extollebam, ita mihi iste locus Pauli fuit vere porta Paradisi. Postea legebam Augustinum de spiritu et litera, ubi praeter spem offendi, quod et ipse iustitiam Dei similiter interpretatur: qua nos Deus induit, dum nos iustificat .... Istis cogitationibus armatior factus coepi Psalterium secundo interpretari ...* [EN45] (*W.A.* 54, 185, 14). If we consider the thesis of Quenstedt in this light, we will certainly be warned against taking up the problem in the way he suggests.

But we must also express at this point a reservation in regard to the Reformed theologian Polanus. He defines the righteousness of God as *voluntas eius per quam ipse iustus est et omnis iustitiae in creaturis autor*[EN46], and then continues: *Iustitiae divinae regula summa perfectissima et infallibilis est voluntas eius. Nam Deus sibi ipsi lex est. Quicquid Deus fieri vult, eo ipso quod vult,*

[EN45] I was utterly seized by a remarkable passion for understanding Paul in the Epistle to the Romans, but thus far there had stood in the way not the cold blood around my heart, but a single phrase in Romans 1: 'in it, the justice of God is revealed'. For I hated that phrase 'the justice of God', because I had been taught by the usual custom of all the teachers to understood the phase philosophically, to refer to formal (as they call it) or active justice, by which God is just and punishes unjust sinners. But even though I had lived as a blameless monk, I felt myself to be a sinner with a most wicked conscience before God. I could not be confident that God was pleased by my satisfaction. I did not love – no, rather I hated – this just God who punishes sinners. Even if not with tacit blasphemy, then certainly with huge grumbling, I railed against God, saying, 'As if it truly were not enough that miserable sinners eternally lost on account of account of original sin, were crushed by every kind of calamity by the law of the ten commandments, God added woe upon woe with the gospel, and even aimed his justice and wrath at us through the Gospel. Thus I railed with a savage and disturbed conscience, but I grappled importunately with Paul in that passage, most eagerly desiring to know what he meant. I meditated for days and nights until by God's mercy, I attended to the context of the words. 'In it, the justice of God is revealed, as it is written, "The righteous shall live by faith".' There I began to grasp the righteousness of God by which the just live by the gift of God, that is, by faith, and that this verse, that the justice of God is revealed through the Gospel, refers obviously to the passive justice, by which God in his mercy justifies us through faith, just as it is written, 'The just will live by faith'. Here I felt myself to have been utterly born again, as having entered into paradise itself by open gates. There straight away another meaning of the whole of Scripture became plain to me. I then searched throughout the Scriptures as I could recall them, and I also found an analogy in other phrases: the work of God, that is, how God works in us; the power of God, by which he makes us able; the wisdom of God, by which he makes us wise; the might of God; the salvation of God; the glory of God. Now I praised this phrase, most sweet to me, with love as abundant as the hatred with which I had previously hated it. Thus that verse of Paul was truly the gate of Paradise for me. Afterwards I read Augustine's On the Spirit and the Letter, where I found, unhoped for, that he also understood the righteousness of God in a similar way: as that with which God clothes us when he justifies us ... With these thoughts, I was better equipped to begin a second interpretation of the Psalter

[EN46] his will by which he is just and the author of justice in all his creatures

iustum est: Quicquid Deus facit, scit et vult[EN47] (*Synt. Theol. chr.*, 1609, *col.* 1157 f.). We certainly cannot say that this definition of the righteousness of God is in conflict with that of His mercy. We can expand it without fear of contradiction: God's mercy is His righteousness because it is His will, and because the will of God, God being a law to Himself, is necessarily a righteous will. But it is of serious consequence that this expansion has to be made; that this sequence in which the will of God is revealed as righteous *eo ipso*[EN48], and in which it is also righteous *eo ipso*[EN49] in God Himself, is as little adopted into the definition as it is in the case of Quenstedt. Because this sequence is lacking, the grounding of righteousness in the will of God as such (although it is correct in itself) assumes a certain arbitrary appearance which, contrary to what happens in Quenstedt, threatens to compromise the holiness of God. For if God is in Himself the law and therefore righteous, He is distinguished from a tyrant, who one day caresses and the next day strikes, by the fact that His will, which obeys His own law, shows itself to be a good will, worthy of Himself and therefore really righteous, and that it is such a will in itself. But this cannot be evinced in the abstraction in which Polanus too talks about the righteousness of God. It would have been evinced if he had defined the righteousness of God—on lines which he fortunately picked up again later in his discussion—in close relationship with the concepts of the love and grace and mercy of God as a determination of the manner in which God founds and maintains fellowship. If in Quenstedt it is not clear how the mercy of God can co-exist with His righteousness, it is not evident in Polanus either (at least according to his definition) how God can be both merciful and righteous. And as, in face of the separation of the righteousness of God from His mercy, we can be corrected by Luther, so, in face of the separation of the mercy of God from His righteousness, we can be corrected by Anselm of Canterbury, who usefully impels us to view the problem, as must be done, from this angle too. How can God be good both to the good and the evil? How then, can He have mercy on the wicked and yet at the same time and in this very way be righteous? This is how Anselm poses the problem in *Prosl.* 9–11. His answer is as follows. The stream of divine mercy flows from the hidden fundamental goodness of God (the *altissimum et secretissimum bonitatis tuae*[EN50] as the unfathomable source of His being). Therefore just because God is *totus et summe iustus*[EN51] He is good even to the wicked too—not simply to all the wicked, but to the wicked too. He is not perfectly good if He is not good both to the good and the bad, but only to the good; if He does not confront even the wicked as the One who judges and also the One who shows mercy. What flows from His goodness, is also, as such, righteous. *Si misericors es, quia es summe bonus, et summe bonus non es, nisi quia es summe iustus: vere idcirco es misericors quia summe iustus es*[EN52]. God's mercy—we see how here Anselm proceeds by a method directly opposed to that of Luther, only to arrive at the same result—is [380]
known by His righteousness: *misericordia tua nascitur ex iustitia tua*[EN53]. How is that? God's righteousness consists in the fact that He is righteous to Himself, i.e., that He is goodness than which no greater can be conceived. But this goodness is a goodness according to which He not only judges but also has mercy, creating good out of evil. *Hoc itaque modo iustum es, ut*

EN47 The highest, most perfect and infallible rule of divine justice is his will. For God is a law to himself. Whatever God wills to happen, by virtue of the fact that he wills it, it is just. Whatever God does, he knows and wills

EN48 by definition

EN49 by definition

EN50 the deepest and most secret part of his goodness

EN51 wholly and utterly just

EN52 If you are merciful, since you are utterly good, and you are not utterly good, except that you are utterly just; truly on that account you are merciful because you are utterly good

EN53 your mercy is born from your justice

parcas malis et ut facias bonos de malis[EN54]. If He has mercy on the evil, He does not do so in an unjust but in a just manner. He does not do so *quia illorum meritis* (this would be unjust), *sed quia bonitati suae condecens est .... Ita iustus es, non quia nobis reddas debitum, sed quia facts, quod decet te summe bonum .... Sic ergo nascitur de iustitia tua misericordia tua; quia iustum est, te sic esse bonum, ut et parcendo sis bonus*[EN55]. It is just because God wills it. And what God wills is just because He wills what is worthy of Himself. Anselm posed the same problem rather differently, i.e., concretely in relation to the historical action of God in the atonement, in *Cur Deus Homo* I, 12 and 24. Ought not God to be able to forgive sins *sola misericordia*[EN56] and thus without due reparation of the injury done to His honour? The answer is that in God's kingdom there is no disorder. If an injustice is left by this *sola misericordia*[EN57], if it is, therefore, divinely validated, if it is exposed to no divine punishment, if it needs no divinely just reparation, then this *iniustitia*[EN58] has, as it were, the character of a second Godhead in the face of God. By the fact that God commands us to forgive our debtors, He reminds us that we must not arrogate to ourselves what is His privilege—to judge. But it is His concern in the freedom of His goodness, in which He stands above all necessity, to preserve His *dignitas*[EN59] in all circumstances. *Libertas enim non est nisi ad hoc, quod expedit aut quod decet, nec benignitas dicenda est, quae aliquid Deo indecens operatur*[EN60]. God can will only what is worthy of Himself. But He does will this. Therefore the omission of a due restoration of the order of His kingdom disturbed by sin cannot be rooted in the freedom of His goodness. It is not merciful to mediate forgiveness to man and yet leave him in his unrighteousness. Injustice is not only unrighteousness but also weakness. It therefore means unhappiness. If God's mercy is concerned with man's blessedness, then it must assume the character of this just reparation and therefore of a triumph of God's righteousness.

From Luther on the one side and Anselm on the other we have to learn that there is no righteousness of God which is not also mercy and no mercy of God which is not also righteousness. If this is the case, it is clear that no progress is possible if there is a fluctuation between God's mercy and righteousness, a hesitant and alternating consideration and underlining now of the one and now of the other. Bernard of Clairvaux called righteousness and mercy the two feet of God: *curato, ut neutro frauderis illorum. Si dolore peccati et iudicii timore compungeris, veritatis iudiciique vestigio labia impressisti. Si timorem doloremque divinae intuitu bonitatis et spe consequendae indulgentiae temperas, etiam misericordiae pedem te amplecti noveris. Alioquin alterum sine altero osculari non expedit, quia et recordatio solius iudicii in barathrum desperationis praecipitat et misericordiae fallax assentatio pessimam generat securitatem*[EN61] (*In Cant.*

[EN54] Therefore in this way you are just, in that you spare the wicked to treat the wicked with goodness

[EN55] with reference to their desert, but since it is in keeping with his goodness ... Thus you are just, not because you give us our due, but because you do what is proper, as utterly good, to you ... So therefore your mercy is born from your justice; since it is just that you are good, in order that you might be good in mercy

[EN56] by sheer mercy

[EN57] by sheer mercy

[EN58] injustice

[EN59] majesty

[EN60] For freedom is not freedom unless it does what is good and worthy, and if it is in any way unworthy of God, is not to be described as goodness

[EN61] advisedly, so that you are not deceived by either of them. If you are stung by sorrow from sin, or by fear of judgment, you have kissed the footprints of truth and judgment. If you temper your fear and sadness in the knowledge of God's goodness and in the hope of forgiveness to follow, you have known that you are embracing the feet of his mercy. But it is not right to kiss one without the other, since the recollection of judgment alone plunges one into an abyss of desperation, and a false self-flattery about God's mercy produces the worst kind of security

serm. 6). But may it not be that this metaphor of the two feet contributes to the fatal idea that we can really "kiss" God 's righteousness in abstraction from His mercy and His mercy in abstraction from His righteousness. May it not be that it enhances the dangers of *desperatio* and *securitas*[EN62] which are rightly indicated? The unity to which both Luther and Anselm draw our attention seems to have been more acutely realised by Augustine than by Bernard: *intendite ipsam misericordiam et iudicium ... Ne putetis, quia ista a se possunt in Deo aliquo modo separari. Videntur enim sibi aliquando contraria: ut qui misericors est, non servet iudicium, et qui iudicii tenax est, obliviscatur misericordiam. Omnipotens est Deus, nec in misericordia amittit iudicium, nec in iudicio misericordiam*[EN63] (*Enarr. in* Ps. 32, on v. 5).

As regards the biblical basis, we can take as our point of departure the fact that in Holy [381]
Scripture the attestation of God's mercy frequently takes the form of an admonition: "Great are thy tender mercies, O Lord; quicken me according to Thy judgments" (Ps. 119^{156}); "Rend your hearts and not your garments ... " (Joel 2^{13}); "Therefore seeing that we have this ministry ... " (2 Cor. 4^{1}); "I beseech you, therefore, brethren, by the mercies of God ... (Rom. 12^{1}). Or with an even more direct application: "Be ye therefore merciful, as your Father also is merciful" (Lk. 6^{36}). And in the parable of the wicked servant: "Shouldest not thou also have had compassion on thy fellow servant, even as I had pity on thee" (Mt. 18^{33}). On the other hand, there are even in the Old Testament at least as many passages in which, conversely, the thought of God's righteousness and judgment takes the form of expressions of trust, gratitude and joy. We read in Is. 30^{18-21} (directly following a warning of judgment): " And therefore will the Lord wait, that he may be gracious unto you, and therefore will he be exalted, that he may have mercy upon you: for the Lord is a god of judgment: blessed are all they that wait for him. For the people shall dwell in Zion at Jerusalem: thou shalt weep no more: he will be very gracious unto thee at the voice of thy cry; when he shall hear it, he will answer thee. And though the Lord give you the bread of adversity, and the water of affliction, yet shall not thy teachers be removed into a corner any more, but thine eyes shall see thy teachers: and thine ears shall hear a word behind thee, saying, This is the way, walk ye in it, when ye turn to the right hand, and when ye turn to the left." The Lord in His righteousness guides the footsteps of the man who calls upon him because of his enemies (Ps. 5^{8}). He saves him in his righteousness and does not let him be ashamed (Ps. 31^{1}). so that God's righteousness and His laws and statutes and judgments, rightly considered, are just as much an object of desire (Ps. 119^{16}), joy (Ps. $48^{11f.}$) and thankfulness (Ps. 7^{17}), as they are of awe and fear. Thus when the Old Testament speaks of the Law of God as a revelation of righteousness, even when it is a question of its transgression and of divine threats, we find always (and not merely in Ps. 119) that it is God's great blessing to Israel—His love which remains even though it is misesteemed and despised and repelled, and therefore becomes a curse. This emerges continually even in Paul's polemic against the *nomos*[EN64] (Rom. $7^{7\ 12-14\ 16}$). According to Scripture it is as the merciful God that God is to be feared, and as the righteous that He is to be loved. If we try to separate, or to evade, the alternation of fear and love, we speak of a different God from Him who bears this name in Scripture.

Let us attempt a connected statement. He who in Holy Scripture is called God, is in truth—not only additionally or partially or in one special aspect or appearance of His being, but wholly and utterly—the Judge. His revelation is

[EN62] despair and security

[EN63] Attend to mercy and to judgment ... Do not think that they can be in any way separated from each other in God. For they seem at times in opposition to each other: he is merciful, and does not make use of his justice, or he clings to his justice, and forgets his mercy. God is omnipotent, and does not lose his judgment in his mercy, or his mercy in his judgment

[EN64] law

wholly and utterly the Law, manifesting His will as righteousness, and distinguishing it from all unrighteousness. His activity is wholly and utterly the execution of this Law.

In this respect the New Testament does not differ from the Old. The ministry of the New Testament is also the ministry of righteousness (2 Cor. 3^{9}). In the New Testament also there is invoked as Father He who without respect of persons judges every man according to his works (1 Pet. 1^{17}). The seat of Jesus Christ proclaimed in the New Testament is a seat of judgment from which every man receives, whether good or ill, according to his conduct in earthly life (2 Cor. 5^{10}; Rom. 14^{10}). In the New Testament, too, we are to work out our salvation in fear and trembling "because it is God which worketh in you both to will and to do" (Phil. 2^{12-13}), i.e., because we know that in Him who accomplishes this we are dealing
[382] with the Judge, and in the work itself with our judgment. In the New Testament, too, in faith in Jesus Christ we live in responsibility towards Him who has revealed Himself to this faith: "For whosoever hath, to him shall be given, and he shall have more abundance: but whosoever hath not, from him shall be taken away even that he hath" (Mt. 13^{12}). Neither in the Old Testament nor in the New can the conception of justice ever be interpreted in such a way that there is no longer any true or serious question of the Law, of the Judge and of His judgment. It must sometimes be objected to Luther that the fact that God in His righteousness is in truth the *ignoscens pater*[EN65] cannot mean that He ceases to be the *iustus iudex*[EN66]. This point is especially to be made against A. Ritschl. We have to recognise that in his polemic against the *iustitia distributiva*[EN67] of orthodox dogmatics he has perceived and expressed what is biblically correct and reminded us of the better insight of Luther. But he went too far in the opposite direction—as was only to be expected in view of his attitude to the problem of the holiness and wrath of God—once he dissolved the justice of God into the mere "consistency of the divine guidance of men to salvation which is partly demonstrated in the pious and upright adherents of the old covenant, and partly expected for the community in whose salvation the rule of God will be consummated," trying to interpret it merely as "the criterion of the distinctive operations by which the community of Christ is realised and conducted to its goal" and finally attempting a straightforward identification with grace (*Unter. in d. chr. Rel.*, 1875, § 16). Certainly the righteousness of God is identical with the grace of God, but it is so as righteousness, and we have to see and understand exactly to what extent it is so as righteousness. Thus the concept is weakened when F. Nitzsch tries to give to the righteousness of God the general significance of "clemency" (ἐπιείκεια)—according to Aristotle "the mildness of the judge who, while he does not violate the law or become partial, takes into account individual circumstances." According to Nitzsch God as the King and Saviour of the covenant people handles the norm which governs it, and which springs from His own holiness, in such a way that in consideration of the people's special need of mercy, as a mild Judge and Ruler, He allows grace to rule rather than the principle of a tooth for a tooth (*Lehr. d. ev. Dogm.*[3], 1912, 467 f.). That God does in fact allow gentleness to prevail will have to be dealt with under the heading of God's patience. But Aristotle is quite irrelevant in this context. In the biblical account of God's exercise of justice there is never any question of a regard for individual circumstances, or a limitation of His justice by His gentleness, or allowing grace to precede strict righteousness, but it is everywhere stated that He unconditionally maintains right as right and wrong as wrong, judging, rewarding and punishing according to this standard without deviating a hair's breadth either to the one side or the

[EN65] forgiving father
[EN66] just judge
[EN67] distributive justice

other. Only when we admit this unreservedly do we understand what it means that God's justice is also in fact a determination of His love, and His judgment an expression of His grace. To grasp this it must be realised that the communication of His grace is an expression of His judgment. It is as God forgives sins in His mercy that He judges. We have to take it quite literally when Paul declares (Rom. $1^{16f.}$) that the Gospel is the saving power of God to every believer because in it the righteousness of God is revealed. And it is not a weakened, qualified righteousness, but, as the continuation makes clear in vv. 18 f. (concerning the simultaneous revelation of wrath upon all the ungodliness and unrighteousness of men), the unconditional eternal righteousness of God which it is impossible to evade or warp and which must be understood strictly as *iustitia distributiva*[EN68]. The mistake of the orthodox dogmaticians was not that they held fast to this concept, but that they did not follow the direction of Scripture and include and explain in their understanding of this concept the mercy of God. When Jesus Christ is set forth to be a *ἱλαστήριον ἐν τῷ αὐτοῦ αἵματι*[EN69] as the basis of free justifying grace, it is not, as is twice emphasised in Rom. $3^{24f.}$: *πρὸς τὴν ἔνδειξιν τῆς δικαιοσύνης αὐτοῦ*[EN70], in execution of a divine will discordant with divine [383]
righteousness, but in execution of the one righteous will of God: *εἰς τὸ εἶναι αὐτὸν δίκαιον καὶ δικαιοῦντα* (in justifying) *τὸν ἐκ πίστεως Ἰησοῦ*[EN71] (v. 26). For this reason it is not a later and inconsequent reservation, but the most consistent explanation of the grace which forgives sins, that a few verses later, after an express distinction in v. 28 between righteousness by faith and the righteousness of works, Paul rejects with horror in v. 31 the idea that this might imply the suspension of the Law: *μὴ γένοιτο. ἀλλὰ νόμον ἱστάνομεν*[EN72]. And as it is unconditionally the righteous government of God which makes this basis of grace, it is a full and true righteousness which is imputed to the believing sinner (the godless according to Rom. 4^{5}), who for his part cannot refer to any justifying works (and does not pretend to be able to perform them). This imputation as such (*λογίζεσθαι*) is not to be understood as what we usually call an act of grace or an "amnesty." On the contrary, it follows from the fact that righteousness really accrues to the sinner and therefore must be reckoned to him by right. He is in fact in the right against any accusation. He has fulfilled the Law. The godless, as H. Cremer rightly says (*Die Lehre von den Eigenschaften Gottes*, 1917, 49), is not saved from the hand of God, but by His hand, and by His righteous hand.

God cannot affirm Himself more strongly as the righteous God, He cannot more effectively attest and implement the Law as the most proper and characteristic revelation of Himself, He cannot bind the impious more closely to Himself as righteous and to His Law, than by His grace which pardons the sinner. For this grace is through and through the proof of the existence of the righteous God. It is so from every point of view: its foundation in the will of God, its execution in the death of Jesus Christ, and its application to believers. God does not need to yield His righteousness a single inch when He is merciful. As He is merciful, He is righteous. He is merciful as He really makes demands and correspondingly punishes and rewards.

[EN68] distributive justice
[EN69] mercy-seat in his blood
[EN70] for the demonstration of his justice
[EN71] so that he might be just and the one who justifies by faith in Jesus
[EN72] By no means! Rather we uphold the Law

That God winks at the times of ignorance (Ac. 17^{30}) does not mean, any more than the ἀνοχή[EN73] of Rom. 3^{26}, that God accepts ignorance or sins or even that He ignores and condones them. But what is described in Rom. 3 as the demonstration of God's righteousness in which God confronts sin as the Judge is pictured in Ac. $17^{30f.}$ as the dawning of the day when by the resurrection of Jesus Christ God offers faith (πίστιν παρασχών[EN74]) to all. Why? As a back door through which they can escape the demands of His righteousness? No, but in this way He "commandeth all men everywhere to repent; because he hath appointed a day (the day of faith) in the which he (according to Ps. 96^{13}) will judge the world in righteousness." Here we can and must look back to the Old Testament where, for example in Is. $1^{24f.}$, the prophet speaks with the same absoluteness of the gracious action of God towards Jerusalem: "Therefore saith the Lord, the Lord of hosts, the mighty One of Israel, Ah, I will ease me of mine adversaries, and avenge me of mine enemies: and I will turn my hand upon thee, and purely purge away thy dross, and take away all thy tin: and I will restore thy judges as at the first, and thy counsellors as at the beginning: afterward thou shalt be called, The city of righteousness, the faithful city. Zion shall be redeemed with judgment, and her converts with righteousness. And the destruction of the transgressors and of the sinners shall be together, and they that forsake the Lord shall be consumed." This is spoken no less concretely and directly to the contemporary situation because it confronts the latter with the coming day of the Lord. On the contrary, it is because this is the case that the prophet
[384] addresses this Word to his contemporaries. And this day of the Lord is no less the day of grace and salvation because it must clearly be described as the day of judgment. On the contrary, it is because God asserts His righteousness as against men and establishes a new righteousness. His righteousness, among them—it is in and through the terror which this implies, that He acts in mercy towards them. He is not merciful if He is even a jot less righteous. It is not the kingdom of heaven, imminent as the kingdom in which sins are forgiven and redemption is offered, if it does not have to be proclaimed with the summons to repent as, according to Mt. 3^{2} and 4^{17}, John the Baptist and Jesus did in the selfsame words. And the proclamation of this kingdom has not been heard, and it is not entered, if this proclamation is understood to cancel the Law and the prophets or even the smallest part of their message, if the new kingdom does not introduce a righteousness which is better than that of the scribes and Pharisees (Mt. 5^{17-20}). Israel always misconceived the righteousness of God and of the kingdom of heaven (Rom. 10^{3}). When the day of the revelation of God's righteousness dawns, when in the epiphany of Jesus Christ, in the proclamation of the Gospel the kingdom of heaven draws near, penitence is the one thing which Israel needs. In the parallel passage in Mark 1^{15} we read: "Repent ye, and believe the Gospel;" but even in this expanded form repentance is interpreted as faith and faith as repentance. As is still very plain in the later New Testament witness (2 Pet. 1^{1}), in faith it can only be a question of recognising and obeying the revealed righteousness of God.

For according to the Scriptures of the Old and New Testaments what constitutes the demonstration and exercise of God's righteousness, what makes penitence and obedience necessary on man's side, is precisely the fact that God enters into a covenant with him and promises that his sins are to be forgiven and eternal life assured. According to the witness of the Old and New Testaments, the love and grace and mercy of God, Jesus Christ, are the demonstration and exercise of the righteousness of God. And it is only in this way that

[EN73] patience
[EN74] offering faith

the divine love and grace and mercy can be truly recognised and felt and appropriated. It is only in this way that Jesus Christ can be believed. He is the righteousness of God. Any other kind of faith, any faith which does not refer consistently to God's righteousness and rest upon it, any kind of piety which is not for its part the righteousness of man, according to what is in this respect the quite unequivocal witness of both Old and New Testaments, necessarily lacks in seriousness, assurance and joy because it obviously has as its object another god than the God whose self-revelation is unfolded to us in Scripture as the being and basis and substance of the Church. For in the very fact that God founds and maintains this covenant with man He distinguishes His action from all caprice and contingency, from all confusion and unrighteousness. He does what is in the highest sense the right: that in which He Himself is righteous; that which befits Him and is worthy of Him as God. In this covenant He reveals Himself as the One He is, the One who is bound to His own nature, the One who is true to Himself.

It is not the case that in Jesus Christ there has, as it were, been an unforeseen episode in our favour. It is not the case that God in His love and grace and mercy has performed as it were a *tour de force* and brought about an altogether exceptional state of affairs. But it is [385]
rather the case that He is wholly Himself and true to Himself in the fact that He is true to us. And the point of faith is to trust wholly in the God who is true to Himself in the fact that He is true to us. For this reason in the first biblical passage in which these two ideas emerge (Gen. 15^{6}) faith and righteousness stand in an intrinsically necessary and indissoluble connexion. Therefore biblical faith consists in penitence and obedience, ὑπακοὴ πίστεως (Rom. 1^{5}, 16^{26}), ὑπακοὴ τοῦ Χριστοῦ (2 Cor. 10^{5}), ὑπακοὴ τῆς ἀληθείας [EN75] (1 Peter 1^{22}), a returning and a submission. From this derives its seriousness but also its joyous confidence. It is in the revelation of the righteousness of God (Is. 56^{1}; Ps. 98^{2}) that faith has its life. To it the heavens declare God's righteousness (Ps. 50^{6}, 85^{11}, 97^{6}), and allow it to prevail (Hos. 10^{12}; Is. 45^{8}). It sees the justice of God towering like mountains (Ps. 36^{7}). It knows it to be eternal (Ps. 111^{3}, 112^{3}; Is. 51^{6}). It knows its God only as the One who makes firm His kingdom (Is. 9^{7}), who espouses His own in right and righteousness (Hos. 2^{19}), who clothes them with the mantle of righteousness like the bridegroom who adorns his head and like the bride who decks herself in jewels (Is. 61^{10}). It calls *Yahweh* Himself our righteousness (Jer. 23^{6}, 33^{16}, cf. Ps. 4^{1}). It therefore realises that righteousness and peace kiss each other (Ps. 85^{10}, cf. Is. 32^{17}). It prays to be led in God's righteousness (Ps. 5^{8}), to be saved by it (Ps. 31^{1}), to be heard (Ps. 143^{1}), to be led out of distress (Ps. 143^{11}), to see the face of God (Ps. 17^{15}), to be allowed to pass through the gate of righteousness (Ps. 118^{19}). According to the Book of Proverbs, it knows that righteousness makes man's way straight (11^{5}), that it is a certain good (11^{18}), that it preserves the innocent (13^{6}), guards a people (14^{34}), saves from death (10^{2}). Not only in the mouth of Job (27^{6}, 29^{14}), it glories in its righteousness. The pious man knows and understands himself to be just. What else can he be if—and in this his piety consists—he holds fast to God? How can he declare God's righteousness (Ps. 22^{31}, 35^{28}, 71^{15} etc.) if he does not take seriously and make his own this divine righteousness? This does not make it any the less God's own righteousness. It is God's righteousness in this way. For God's righteousness is that the man in covenant with Him should be righteous, that he should be such a one as is justified in God's sight because God has addressed him and dealt with him in

[EN75] obedience of faith, obedience to Christ, obedience of the truth

righteousness, putting him in the right. But again, it is impossible to see how faith in the God who reveals Himself and speaks and acts in righteousness will not necessarily have as such the character of a returning and a submission. For this God calls us to Himself and binds us to Himself, tearing us from ourselves and from all that wills to resist Him and transporting us into an identity of our will with His. This God and only this God is our God in such a way—as we have indicated—that He is our righteousness. *Prodest meditatio haec ad colligendos omnes sensus nostros ad unam Dei iustitiam, ne varie spes nostras partiamur, sed relictis omnibus pravis fiduciis, quibus totus fere mundus circumagitur huc et illud, prorsus defixi in Dei voluntate propensissima ad exhibendam nobis promissam salutem. Neque consilio proprio, neque industriae, neque virtuti inniti, neque ullis opibus, neque hominum auxiliis debemus, ut secure nobis salutem polliceamur, sed hoc unum nobis propositum esse debet, quia iustus est Deus, fieri non posse, ut ab eo deseramur ... Nihil est tutius quam sicut in clementia et misericordia, ita in iustitia Dei acquiescere ne alio nos quicquam rapiat: nam qui consilio destituti, sibi ipsis prospicere nequeunt, qui obiecti sunt iniuriis, qui cavendis iniuriis minime sunt solertes, qui denique a filiis huius mundi superantur astu et fraudibus, si solummodo in fiducia iustitiae Dei sint firmi, ne utiquam subvertentur. Iustitia Dei exseret se ad ipsos tuendos; iustitia Dei pericula, quibus salus ipsorum impeditur, depellet*[EN76] (Polanus, *Synt. Theol. chr.*, 1609, *col.* 1162 f.).

Faith in God's righteousness is at one and the same time the source of all comfort and the epitome of God's most jealous demand upon man. For in this
[386] faith it is a matter of cleaving to God who does what befits Him and what is worthy of Him. That doing this He espouses man's cause, covenanting and keeping faith with him, is the comfort of this faith. But it is also God's strictest claim in that it affirms and apprehends as the covenant-partner of man the God who in this covenant does what befits Him, what is worthy of Himself. We cannot, therefore, appropriate and understand His love and grace and mercy without at the same time hearing and considering the summons with which He lifts us out of all the being and doing in which we try to follow our own ideas of justice, i.e., what befits and is worthy of us. Faith in God's righteousness means necessarily and essentially a choice and decision in favour of His righteousness as opposed to our own; in other words, the choice and decision by which instead of our own righteousness we accept as our own the righteousness of God, or, according to the shorter New Testament definition, of Christ. To this extent the revelation of God's righteousness means in fact judgment upon us,

---

[EN76] This meditation is of use for collecting all our impressions into the one righteousness of God, lest we variously divide up our hopes. Rather, with all our perverse confidences by which almost the whole world it knocked about hither and thither left behind, we should be fixed directly upon the most favourable will of God to hold forth to ourselves our promised salvation. We should not set our salvation before ourselves as secure either through our own counsel, or by hard work, or by innate virtue, or by any of our resources, or by the help of men. Rather, this one point ought to be set before us, that, since God is righteous, it could not happen that we be deserted by Him ... Nothing is more secure than to rest both in his clemency and mercy and also in his righteousness, so that nothing may snatch us away to another. For those who are destitute of counsel cannot look out for themselves; they, who are in no way accustomed to be careful of injuries, are knocked down by such; those who in the end are conquered by the sons of this world in their cunning and deceits, if they be alone secure in the confidence in the righteousness of God, they will in no way fall. The righteousness of God stretches itself out for their protection. The righteousness of God will drive away the dangers by which their salvation is hindered

implying our condemnation and the death of the old man. To this extent faith means that we accept this condemnation, the death of the old man, and that as condemned sinners, divested of our own righteousness, we flee from ourselves and take refuge in God who wills alone to be both our righteousness and our life, who, making us righteous by Himself, wills that there should be no division between Himself and us.

In this connexion it is important to notice that the people to whom God in His righteousness turns as helper and Saviour is everywhere in the Old Testament harassed and oppressed people of Israel, which, powerless in itself, has no rights, and is delivered over to the superior force of its enemies; and in Israel it is especially the poor, the widows and orphans, the weak and defenceless. The branch out of the root of Jesse "will have his delight in the fear of the Lord. He shall not judge after the sight of his eyes, neither reprove after the hearing of his ears," which means obviously that he will not vindicate him who in the common opinion is already in the right, "but with righteousness he shall judge the poor, and reprove with equity for the meek of the earth: and he shall smite the earth with the rod of his mouth, and with the breath of his life shall he slay the wicked." And so "righteousness shall be the girdle of his loins and faithfulness the girdle of his reins" (Is. 11^3f.). For this reason the human righteousness required by God and established in obedience—the righteousness which according to Amos 5^24 should pour down as a mighty stream—has necessarily the character of a vindication of right in favour of the threatened innocent, the oppressed poor, widows, orphans and aliens. For this reason, in the relations and events in the life of His people, God always takes His stand unconditionally and passionately on this side and on this side alone: against the lofty and on behalf of the lowly; against those who already enjoy right and privilege and on behalf of those who are denied it and deprived of it. What does all this mean? It is not really to be explained by talking *in abstracto*[EN77] of the political tendency and especially the forensic character of the Old Testament and the biblical message generally. It does in fact have this character and we cannot hear it and believe it without feeling a sense of responsibility in the direction indicated.

As a matter of fact, from the belief in God's righteousness there follows logically a very definite political problem and task. But seen and understood *in abstracto*[EN78], the latter—i.e., the connexion between justification and law in all its relevance for that between Church and state—cannot really be evident and necessary of itself. It becomes so when we appreciate the [387]
fact that God's righteousness, the faithfulness in which He is true to Himself, is disclosed as help and salvation, as a saving divine intervention for man directed only to the poor, the wretched and the helpless as such, while with the rich and the full and the secure as such, according to His very nature He can have nothing to do. God's righteousness triumphs when man has no means of triumphing. It is light when man in himself lies in darkness, and life when man walks in the shadow of death. When we encounter divine righteousness we are all like the people of Israel, menaced and altogether lost according to its own strength. We are all widows and orphans who cannot procure right for themselves. It is obviously in the light of this confrontation that we have all those sayings in the Psalms about God's righteousness and the believer and his righteousness before God. The connexion between God's righteousness and mercy now becomes clear. The righteousness of the believer consists in the fact that God acts for him—utterly, because he cannot plead his own case and no one

EN77 in the abstract
EN78 in the abstract

else can represent him. Faith grasps this full intervention on the part of God and it is therefore *eo ipso*[EN79] faith in God's mercy, the faith of those who are poor and wretched before God. According to the Gospel of Luke and the Epistle of James, as also according to the message of the prophets, there follows from this character of faith a political attitude, decisively determined by the fact that man is made responsible to all those who are poor and wretched in his eyes, that he is summoned on his part to espouse the cause of those who suffer wrong. Why? Because in them it is manifested to him what he himself is in the sight of God; because the living, gracious, merciful action of God towards him consists in the fact that God Himself in His own righteousness procures right for him, the poor and wretched; because he and all men stand in the presence of God as those for whom right can be procured only by God Himself. The man who lives by the faith that this is true stands under a political responsibility. He knows that the right, that every real claim which one man has against another or others, enjoys the special protection of the God of grace. As surely as he himself lives by the grace of God he cannot evade this claim. He cannot avoid the question of human rights. He can only will and affirm a state which is based on justice. By any other political attitude he rejects the divine justification.

But this is not the point with which we are immediately concerned. Our concern is that at this point the truth emerges that God's righteousness does not really stand alongside His mercy, but that as revealed in its necessary connexion, according to Scripture, with the plight of the poor and wretched, it is itself God's mercy. Just because He is righteous God has mercy, condescending sympathetically to succour those who are utterly in need of His help, who without it would in fact be lost. God is righteous in Himself, doing what befits Him and is worthy of Him, defending and glorying His divine being, in the fact that He is our righteousness, that He procures right for those who in themselves have no righteousness, whose own righteousness is rather disclosed by Him to be unrighteousness, yet whom He does not leave to themselves, to whom rather He gives Himself in His own divine righteousness and therefore becomes the ground on which, against their own merit and worth and solely by His merit and worth, called away from themselves and summoned to surrender themselves to His will, they can truly stand and live. This standing and living of man is not, therefore, threatened but in the true sense established by the righteousness of God when in his confrontation by God man must necessarily confess that—in so far as he stands isolated from God's activity on his behalf—he is a sinner. There is, therefore, only an apparent contradiction between the prayer of Psalm 143[2]: "Enter not into judgment with thy servant: for in thy sight shall no man living be justified"; and that of Ps. 7[8]: "Judge me, O Lord, according to my righteousness, and according to mine integrity that is in me." If Ps. 7 expresses the con-
[388] fidence of the man whom God has justified and who has in this way established his case in the teeth of all his accusers and adversaries, Ps. 143 shows how he attains this confidence—namely, by allowing that God is in the right against him, and accepting God as his only righteousness, his own but his real righteousness. It is in this sense that Zion boasts of its hope in Micah 7[7f.]: "Therefore I will look unto the Lord; I will wait for the God of my salvation: my God will hear me. Rejoice not against me, O mine enemy; when I fall, I shall arise; when I sit in darkness, the Lord shall be a light unto me. I will bear the indignation of the Lord, because I have sinned against him, until he plead my cause, and execute judgment for me: he will bring me forth to the light, and I shall behold his righteousness. Then she that is mine enemy shall see it, and shame shall cover her which said unto me, Where is the Lord thy God?" On the other hand, consider how the righteous Job, who is known to be protected by God Himself against all accusations, speaks of his right as such and *in abstracto*[EN80]: "How

[EN79] by definition
[EN80] in the abstract

should man be just with God? If he will contend with him, he cannot answer him one of a thousand. He is wise in heart, and mighty in strength: who hath hardened himself against him, and hath prospered?" (Job 9^{2-4}). "Behold, he taketh away, who can hinder him? who will say unto him, What doest thou? If God will not withdraw his anger, the proud archers do stoop under him. How much less shall I answer him, and choose out my words to reason with him? Whom, though I were righteous, yet would I not answer, but I would make supplication to my judge. If I had called, and he had answered me; yet would I not believe that he had hearkened unto my voice" (9^{12-16}). "If I speak of strength, lo, he is strong: and if of judgment, who shall set me a time to plead? If I justify myself, mine own mouth shall condemn me: if I say that I am perfect, it shall prove me perverse" (9^{19-20}). "If I be wicked, why then labour I in vain? If I wash myself with snow water, and make my hands never so clean, yet shalt thou plunge me in the ditch, and mine own clothes shall abhor me. For he is not a man, as I am, that I should answer him, and we should come together in judgment. Neither is there any daysman betwixt us, that might lay his hand upon us both" (9^{29-33}). "Man that is born of a woman is of a few days, and is full of trouble. He cometh forth like a flower, and is cut down: he fleeth also as a shadow, and continueth not. And dost thou open thine eyes upon such an one, and bringest me into judgment with thee? Who can bring a clean thing out of an unclean? Not one" (14^{1-4}). The tone of complaint and accusation, the bitterness, the fierce irony with which all this is spoken in the context of Job's speech does not alter the fact that it expresses the truth. And on it is founded the possibility that Job can again say with regard to his right: "Behold now, I have ordered my cause; I know that I shall be justified. Who is he that will plead with me? for now, if I hold my tongue, I shall give up the ghost" (13^{18-19}). "Also now, behold, my witness is in heaven, and my record is on high. My friends scorn me; but mine eye poureth out tears unto God. O that one might plead for a man with God, as a man pleadeth for his neighbour!" (16^{19-21}). "But I know that my Redeemer liveth, and an Advocate arises for me over my dust. Even when my skin is torn from my body and my flesh has perished, I shall behold God (to salvation), and my eyes shall behold Him, not as an enemy .... If you say: How we shall persecute him, and find the root of the matter in him, be afraid of the sword, for wrath falleth on the guilty, that you may know there is a judgment" (19^{25-29}). Again, all this is not spoken without defiance and even arrogance. Again, it is true that the consoling and warning counter-arguments of Job's friends undoubtedly sound far better theologically, and do in fact serve to put him subjectively even more in the wrong than he himself has already done in his own speeches. But objectively it is still the case that in all this Job speaks the truth, so that according to $42^{7f.}$ the wrath of God is not kindled against him but against his friends: "For you have not spoken of me the thing that is right, as my servant Job hath." So in spite of his revolt and presumptuousness he has spoken that which is [389]
right about God because in fact, even though sullenly and scornfully, he has confessed himself to be a sinner before God and because again in fact, though not without an element of impudent conceit, he has claimed God's righteousness as his own. In the objectivity of this twofold recognition of truth Job is plainly the prototype of the poor in spirit whose is the kingdom of heaven (Mt. 5^{3}). "If we confess our sins, he is faithful and just to forgive us our sins, and to cleanse us from all unrighteousness" (1 Jn. 1^{9}). "Blessed are they which do hunger and thirst after righteousness: for they shall be filled (Mt. 5^{6}). It is always and necessarily a subjectively sinful and unrighteous people, confessing its unrighteousness, whose cause before God is just, whose just cause God protects, because He Himself is its just cause. It is the people whose righteousness is as filthy rags (Is. 64^{6}). It is the people that must confess (Is. $59^{9f.}$): "We look for light, but behold obscurity; for brightness, but we walk in darkness. We grope for the wall like the blind, and we grope as if we had no eyes: we stumble at noonday as in the night; we are in desolate places as dead men. We roar all like bears, and mourn sore like doves: we look for judgment, but there is none; for salvation, but it is far off

from us. For our transgressions are multiplied before thee, and our sins testify against us: for our transgressions are with us, and as for our iniquities we know them; in transgressing and lying against the Lord, and departing away from our God, speaking oppression and revolt, conceiving and uttering from the heart words of falsehood. And judgment is turned away backward, and justice standeth afar off: for truth is fallen in the street, and equity cannot enter. Yea, truth faileth; and he that departeth from evil maketh himself a prey." This is the people that can stand and live under the divine answer: "And the Lord saw it, and it displeased him that there was no judgment. And he saw that there was no man, and wondered that there was no intercessor: therefore his arm brought salvation unto him; and his righteousness, it sustained him. For he put on righteousness as a breastplate, and an helmet of salvation upon his head; and he put on the garments of vengeance for clothing, and was clad with zeal as a cloke .... And the Redeemer shall come to Zion, and unto them that turn from transgression in Jacob, saith the Lord. As for me, this is my covenant with them, saith the Lord; my spirit that is upon thee, and my words which I have put in thy mouth, shall not depart out of thy mouth, nor out of the mouth of thy seed, nor out of the mouth of thy seed's seed, saith the Lord, from henceforth and for ever" (Is. $59^{15f.}$). It is only by the forgiveness of sins that God manifests and exercises His righteousness towards this people, giving it a just cause and Himself espousing its just cause. For "thou hast not called upon me, O Jacob, thou hast been weary of me, O Israel. Thou hast not brought me the small cattle of thy burnt offerings; neither hast thou honoured me with thy sacrifices ... but thou hast made me to serve with thy sins, thou hast wearied me with thine iniquities. I, even I, am he that blotteth out thy transgressions for mine own sake, and will not remember thy sins" (Is. $43^{22f.}$). The message can then continue: "Yet now, hear, O Jacob my servant; and Israel whom I have chosen. Thus saith the Lord that made thee, and formed thee from the womb, which will help thee; fear not, O Jacob, my servant; and thou Jeshurun, whom I have chosen. For I will pour water upon him that is thirsty, and floods upon the dry ground: I will pour my spirit upon thy seed, and my blessing upon thine offspring: and they shall spring up as among the grass, as willows by the water courses. One shall say, I am the Lord's; and another shall call himself by the name of Jacob; and another shall subscribe with his hand unto the Lord, and surname himself by the name of Israel" (Is. $44^{1f.}$). It is only as they invoke the grace of God which forgives sins that Moses (Ex. $32^{11f.}$ Deut. 9^{23}), Solomon (1 Kg. 8) and Daniel ($9^{4f.}$) can intercede with God that He will still graciously accept this people. It is never their own being
[390] and doing which constitutes the justice of their cause, and for the sake of which the divine advocacy and action takes place. It takes place only for the reason that Israel's infidelity cannot suspend God's fidelity (Rom. 3^{3}), that God cannot repent of His gracious promises and calling (Rom. 11^{29}), and therefore only for the sake of God's own righteousness. Looking upon Israel's own ways and conduct, God can only judge, reject and punish. In the process of judging, rejecting and punishing, God does not break but keeps His covenant, and therefore comforts, helps and saves. He maintains the right of this judged, rejected and punished people against all other peoples. He does not cease to act towards it as His own people called and chosen by Himself. But this is not the result of any preference which Israel has or has acquired in His sight. It is through and through the *iustitia peccatorum*[EN81]. It is the triumph only of God's own righteousness. Only in faith in Him, only in that intercession of Moses, Solomon and Daniel for the forgiveness of sins, can Israel be subjectively in the right. But in faith, in that prayer, it is in point of fact subjectively righteous. If it seizes this promise of the divine advocacy and action, in this apprehension it already lives in its fulfilment, and it can and may and will stand before its enemies and in every misfortune. "If ye will not believe, surely ye shall not be established" (Is. 7^{9}). And this implies as its complement: "He that

[EN81] justification of sinners

believeth shall not be ashamed" (Is. 28^{16}), or in Luther's translation: "He that believeth shall not flee." With Job the believer can confidently await God's righteous judgment: in spite of and in all the merited and inevitable threat to his own existence as such; in spite of and in the recognition and confession of his guilt and sin. He can in fact appeal to this first judgment of God as the court before which he is already declared righteous and before which, when it is publicly revealed, he will be justified to all eternity against the accusations of men and of his own heart. For him the day of the Lord will not be, as it is described in Amos $5^{18f.}$, Joel 2^{11} and Zeph. $1^{14f.}$, a day of darkness and terror, but a day of light and joy. On that day—in accordance with the saying in Hab. 2^{4} which is cited in Rom. 1^{17} and which assumed such importance for Luther—he will remain alive in virtue of his faith: *iustus ex fide vivet*[EN82].

According to the witness of the New Testament the One in whom God's people has its righteous cause, maintained and protected by God, is Jesus Christ. It is in Him that God reveals and does what is worthy of Himself. It is in Him that He reveals and exercises His own righteousness in favour of those whom He has called and chosen, even though their own righteousness is as filthy rags. It is He who had compassion on the people, for they were faint and exhausted like sheep without a shepherd (Mt. 9^{36}). It is His call which is the call to repentance and therefore to faith and therefore to the kingdom of heaven, and at the same time a blessing upon the poor in spirit, upon those who mourn, upon those who hunger and thirst after righteousness, upon those who are persecuted for righteousness' sake, etc. His is the invitation: "Come unto me, all ye that labour and are heavy laden and I will give you rest" (Mt. 11^{28}). It is He who is the righteous Advocate of sinners with the Father (1 Jn. 2^{1}). It is He who saves "them to the uttermost that come unto God by him, seeing he ever liveth to make intercession for them" (Heb. 7^{25}; Rom. 8^{34}). It is He who is made righteousness for us (1 Cor. 1^{30}). And it is faith in Him, the *πίστις Ἰησοῦ Χριστοῦ*[EN83], which is the condition on which the righteous God justifies the ungodly. It is faith in Him which God reckons to the ungodly as righteousness, and in which he becomes and is truly righteous.

But this leads us necessarily to a further consideration. As we envisage and apprehend in Jesus Christ the righteousness of God, and therefore the fidelity which is grounded in and constitutes His very being, the fidelity to Himself in which He is faithful to us, we are warned against the too convenient and facile way of thought which has simply divested the concept of divine righteousness [391]
of the notion which is necessarily bound up with the concept of judgment, that of a decision about good and evil, about reward and punishment. As we envisage and apprehend in Jesus Christ the righteousness of God we shall not think that we have exhausted it by viewing it and interpreting it as comfort and help in the misery of human sin, as the promise and fulfilment of pardon for this sin. On the contrary, it is just because—and there can be no surrender or weakening of the righteousness of God, but only its assertion in its true character and rigour—it implies comfort and help in the distress of our sin, the promise and the fulfilment of its pardon, that, if we have really seen it at work in Jesus Christ, a place must be found for a consideration in which (in contradiction to modern interpretations) its character as *iustitia distributiva*[EN84] is

---

[EN82] the righteous will live by faith
[EN83] faith in Jesus Christ
[EN84] distributive justice

maintained. It is a righteousness which judges and therefore both exculpates and condemns, rewards and also punishes.

Orthodoxy had pushed this aspect of the matter too much into the foreground and thus imperilled the unity of God's righteousness with His mercy. Because, as the righteousness of the God revealed in Jesus Christ, it must be understood essentially as an expression of His love and grace, we have been trying to grasp and interpret it chiefly in its oneness with divine mercy. Its character as *iustitia distributiva*[EN85] was necessarily obscured in the process. We have seen it so far as a righteousness which decisively exculpates and rewards, that is, in the case of faith. But if it is real righteousness, the essential righteousness of the God revealed in Jesus Christ, we must now see too that it is a righteousness which condemns and punishes. Even as such, of course, it is God's mercy and grace and love. But as mercy and grace and love it is now a righteousness which condemns and punishes. Otherwise its unity with the holiness of God is obscured and we have learned from our introductory references to Anselm that this obscuration is no more legitimate than that of which Ritschl is guilty. We shall have to arrive at a deeper understanding of the mercy of God, and of Luther's insight that God's righteousness is His mercy, as we now address ourselves to the concern which has led orthodoxy into this error (which we have avoided). This concern is rather more than the attempt to complete a purely human idea of righteousness and therefore to apply it in its other aspect. On the contrary, we are plainly compelled by the testimony of Scripture and in particular by the Christian testimony of Scripture, to go a step further than Ritschl did. We have already pointed out more than once the unity of the Gospel with the Law, and the character of faith as penitence. We have understood the distress and poverty of Israel, whom God in His righteousness assists, as the spiritual distress and poverty of the people who must confess their sin and failure before God. We have seen how the understanding in faith of the saving righteousness of God implies that man in himself must perish before God, to live only in Him and with Him. But all this requires special emphasis and explanation if it is to be seriously grasped and affirmed.

We can begin here with the prayer of Solomon uttered on the occasion of the consecration of the temple. Its first petition is (1 Kg. $8^{31f.}$) that justice should be proclaimed in the temple and the judgments of God awaited. When this takes place, then, as Solomon prays: "Hear thou in heaven, and do, and judge thy servants, condemning the wicked, to bring his way upon his head; and justifying the righteous, to give him according to his righteousness." This is obviously an appeal to the *iustitia distributiva*[EN86] of God. Obviously the righteous God
[392] is like this and acts like this even in His mercy. He adjudges guilt to the guilty and causes his deeds to recoil on his own head. Though His fidelity is endless and cannot be suspended by the infidelities of Israel, that is not to deny that it clashes with the offences of Israel. And what then takes place is the condemning and punishing operation of His righteousness. Does this mean that it ceases to be merciful? Certainly not. His mercy does not cease to be righteousness and His righteousness does not cease to be His holy essence and to show itself as such in conflict with human disobedience. In this clash God is and does what is worthy of Himself. This necessarily means condemnation and punishment where He finds disobedience, and pardon and reward where He finds the obedience of faith.

The witness is unequivocal: "In the day that thou eatest thereof thou shalt surely die" (Gen. 2^{17}); "Cursed is he that confirmeth not all the words of this law to do them" (Deut. 27^{26});"For thou art not a God that hath pleasure in wickedness: neither shall evil dwell with thee. The foolish shall not stand in thy sight: thou hatest all workers of iniquity. Thou shalt

EN85 distributive justice
EN86 distributive justice

destroy them that speak leasing: the Lord will abhor the bloody and deceitful man" (Ps. $5^{4f.}$); and "The face of the Lord is against them that do evil, to cut off the remembrance of them from the earth" (Ps. 34^{16}). The threats of the Law and prophets against sinful Israel and against the impiety of the heathen, and the accounts of the actual execution of these threats, also have a place in the Bible, forming in their severity and relentlessness an integral part of its witness to the revelation and therefore the essence of God. Nor do we have here a specific Old Testament concern which was later superseded. That the wages of sin is death is still the message of Rom. 6^{23}. Even in the Gospel the man who has no wedding garment at the marriage of the King (Mt. 22^{13}), and the unprofitable servant who has buried the talent entrusted to him instead of exploiting it (Mt. 25^{30}), are cast out into outer darkness where there is weeping and gnashing of teeth. The fig tree bearing nothing but leaves is cursed by Jesus and withers (Mt. $21^{18f.}$). The foolish virgins knock at the closed doors of the bridal chamber and are told: "I know you not!" (Mt. $25^{11f.}$). To those who have not given food and drink, and lodged and clothed and visited the Son of Man in His lowly brethren, it is said: "Depart from me, ye cursed, into everlasting fire, prepared by my Father for the devil and his angels" (Mt. $25^{41f.}$). We read expressly in 2 Thess. $1^{6f.}$: "It is a righteous thing with God to recompense tribulation to them that trouble you ... when the Lord Jesus Christ shall be revealed from heaven with his mighty angels, in flaming fire taking vengeance on them that know not God, and that obey not the gospel of our Lord Jesus Christ: who shall be punished with everlasting destruction from the presence of the Lord, and from the glory of his power; when he shall come to be glorified in his saints." Revelation speaks to the same effect; and on what page of the New Testament is not the same message directly or indirectly proclaimed? Certainly both the Old and the New Testaments summon Israel and the Church to have faith and in that way to trust in their deliverance from this operation of God's righteousness. But they do not conceal the fact—on the contrary, the whole impressiveness of their summons to faith is that they so powerfully show that the operation of the righteousness and therefore the mercy of God is the judgment which we certainly will not escape without faith. It is the abyss from which we are held back by faith alone. It is the damnation from which we are preserved only by faith, which in ourselves we have merited and which on our own merits we cannot escape, from which we have refuge only because (and this is the essence of faith) we are no longer expected to live in our own strength, because we see ourselves and act as those who have thankfully found the centre of their being in the faith that God lives for them.

It should be understood that we are not summoned in faith to look past the God who lives for us and stare into this precipice. We have not to fear that it might again threaten us, that
we might again be swallowed up by it. We apprehend by faith God's justifying and rewarding [393]
righteousness, and it is the unbelief of Lot's wife to try to look back and again reckon or even trifle with the reality or the possibility of damnation and death. For this is not a serious calculation but a wanton trifling. It can only be a false Christian earnestness which causes a man to suspend his faith as it were, to lay aside for a moment the decision about his salvation contained in God's revelation, and to place himself at the critical point where it is seen that the end of one way is eternal glory and of the other way everlasting fire. All heathen eschatology thinks in this symmetrical way, but Scripture never puts these two ways before our eyes. We are not called by its summons to faith to stand at this critical point.

On the contrary, we are clearly invited by this summons to give ourselves to the God who lives for us and saves us by His life for us. But the reference to the condemning and punishing operation of God's righteousness means (and this is why it is essentially a call to faith) that we are to understand God's life for us and therefore our deliverance from judgment as His mercy by which there comes to us that which we have not deserved and of which we are not worthy. It is the negative side of the matter. What we have deserved and what we are worthy to receive in our intrinsic being and conduct is always and will always be the condemning and punishing operation of divine justice. For in our intrinsic being we find ourselves in collision with the faithfulness of God. When we are confronted by the faithfulness of God, our own characteristic reaction to it is always unfaithfulness. We are revealed as foolish virgins, as unprofitable servants, as the murmuring stiff-necked idolatrous people of Israel. "No flesh is just in thy sight" (Rom. 3^{20}). "God saw that the wickedness of man was great in the earth, and that every imagination of the thoughts of his heart was only evil continually" (Gen. 6^{5}). This is the statement made before the Flood, and it is expressly repeated after the Flood (Gen. 8^{21}) as the presupposition for the suspension of further divine punishment. "The Lord looked down from heaven upon the children of men, to see if there were any that did understand, and seek God. They are all gone aside, they are all together become filthy: there is none that doeth good, no, not one" (Ps. 14^{2-3}). It is necessary that faith should remember the abyss from which it has been saved and over which it is poised in order that as effective faith it may praise God as the One who has found man in his utterly lost condition, snatching him from the grip of death and translating him into life; in order that it may give honour to free mercy in the freedom in which it has accomplished the unexpected and incomprehensible; in order that it may be bound in total obedience to the God who owed it nothing and to whom it owes everything.

But if this worship of the merciful God is to be an unequivocal and worthy worship of the true and living God it must redound also to the glory of His righteousness. His mercy is not truly His, it is not a saving divine mercy, if it is not also righteousness, and we do not praise the mercy of God if in it we do not also praise His righteousness.

The question which we have still to answer, or rather the answer which we have here to ponder as already given in God's revelation and being, the answer to every question about the depth and power and might of His mercy, is as follows. How far is the mercy of God, which is to be apprehended in faith, at the same time the righteousness of His judgment? And how far is it recognisable in that fact as His, the divine and therefore the eternal and actual, saving and victorious mercy? God's revelation in Jesus Christ supplies to this question the answer that the condemning and punishing righteousness of God is in
[394] itself and as such the depth and power and might of His mercy. Where Holy Scripture speaks of God's threats and judgments, we do not in point of fact find ourselves on a periphery from which we have finally to look to a very different centre of its message. On the contrary, we find ourselves at the very heart of this message. We can only be overlooking or misunderstanding the biblical message if for one reason or another we try to be spared having to take quite seriously the fact that God is the God who for the sake of His righteousness is wrathful and condemns and punishes. He is not only this, but He is also this. If He were not also this He would not be for us the living God to whom we are summoned to listen when we are invited to have faith. If we are earnestly to cleave to Him, if we are to accept the salvation accomplished in Himself and offered to us through Him, if we are really to look forward in faith rather than backward, we cannot try to overlook or evade by reservations the essential realisation that God also is angry, condemns and punishes. If we truly love Him, we must love Him also in His anger, condemnation and punishments, or rather we must see, feel and appreciate His love to us even in His anger, con-

demnation and punishment. For we cannot avoid the conclusion that it is where the divine love and therefore the divine grace and mercy are attested with the supreme clarity in which they are necessarily known as the meaning and intention of Scripture as a whole, where that love and grace and mercy are embodied in a unique event, i.e., in Jesus Christ, that according to the unmistakable witness of the New Testament itself they encounter us as a divine act of wrath, judgment and punishment.

Not only as that, for there also takes place there the resurrection of Jesus Christ from the dead, and to that extent what takes place is God's righteousness in an act of divine pleasure, acquittal and reward. But we must not for one moment forget the full implication of the fact that it is the crucified Jesus Christ who rises from the dead. This means that the divine Yes of Easter Day presupposes a divine No from which it is inseparable, without which it is not the divine Yes of God's vindicating and rewarding righteousness. The event of Good Friday embodies the divine No, which contains in itself the divine Yes and is the presupposition of it, but which must not be any the less on that account understood as a definite divine No: as the judgment whose frightfulness causes even the most dreadful judgments threatened and executed by God in the witness of Old Testament Scripture to fade; or conversely, as the judgment whose continual fire is the light in which is first revealed the true terror of those Old Testament threats and executions of judgment. If we view the latter in themselves, in spite of the terrible contents of almost innumerable Old Testament texts of this kind we may ask whether their terrors cannot be classed with the far too many similar happenings which have been the more or less merited destiny of other ancient and modern and indeed all peoples. Or if on a closer investigation we admit that in spite of its general similarity with that of other peoples the destiny of Israel reveals a consistency and radicalness which makes it of exemplary force even to-day, we may ask whether the Christian Church of every age and people has cause for this reason to see its God in these Old Testament texts, in His wrathful dealings with this people Israel. Why should the terrible fate of this people in this age (or in our own) concern us who do not belong to it? We will no longer ask this question once we have seen and understood the terror of Good Friday. The fact is that we cannot regard God's [395] threats and executions of punishment on Israel and Israel's destiny in every time and place as indifferent facts. This is not independent fire shedding an independent light. All that we have mentioned, dreadful as it seems and in fact is in itself, is only a faint reflection compared with the infinitely more terrible happenings that took place on Good Friday. But the light of the fire of this event goes still further. This event is the judgment which reduces to insignificance the seriousness of all the other judgments which from the beginning of the world have been seen to sweep over peoples and individuals—from the great catastrophes of nature and history which have and will come upon thousands and even millions, to that which we all have sooner or later to bear in the deprivation of health, wealth and opportunities in consequence of our own and others' folly or wickedness, and finally in the unique form of our death. It can, again, be more effectively expressed the other way round. The meaning of illness and want, of the mental and physical suffering of each individual, of war, hunger, tyranny and revolution in the life of peoples, of the winding sheet of death spread unceasingly over everything and everyone, is revealed in its true frightfulness only on Good Friday. For we can always relativise and soften and finally forget the pain and suffering, not only of others but also our own. This is true even of the most world-shaking destiny. What is there that has not been forgotten? What will we not all one day have forgotten again? There is nothing so frightful as to be able permanently to affect us: curiously enough, not even the

thought that to-morrow we might be dead. But all this inevitably assumes a different complexion as soon as we see it, not in itself as we usually do, but in its inner connexion with the event of Good Friday, with the agony and death endured there. For then we realise that, while it has no profound significance in itself, it acquires it, and in such a way as finally to shake our apathy, from its connexion with the place—the cross of Golgotha—where the infinite weight and meaning of suffering and death has been borne. Our own suffering and death in all their bitterness cannot approach this death and suffering. But as a token of them they assume the character of a witness which we can no longer overlook, though we shall at the same time be thankful that they are only a token of that suffering and death, of the passion of Jesus Christ, His bearing of the eternal wrath of God. For the terrible thing, the divine No of Good Friday, is that there all the sins of Israel and of all men, our sins collectively and individually, have in fact become the object of the divine wrath and retribution. It must be clearly understood: there and there alone; and therefore not in the great slaughter after the setting up of the golden calf, not in the swallowing up of the sect of Korah, not in the defeat and death of Saul by the Philistines, not in David's sufferings through Absalom, not in the destruction of Samaria and Jerusalem, not in the deportation to Babylon, not in the final overthrow of the temple worship and the state of Judah in A.D. 70. The scale of the Old Testament portrayal of this persistent smiting by *Yahweh* of His own unfaithful people is far too large, and the accompanying fact that in and through all this divine punishment Israel is not blotted out but continually preserved in a remnant far too singular, for it not to be clear that in spite of the terrible reality in which it is proclaimed and executed, this punishment is not the real divine judgment, but merely points beyond itself to the latter as its adumbration. The Suffering Servant of God in his historical form—whether it be the prophet himself, or the whole people, or the king, or something of them all—is only the representative of Someone very different. The negative and positive predicates heaped upon this Servant are so much more than life-size that the historical embodiment of this figure cannot possibly sustain them. In Israel the really suffering One who bears the wrath and judgment of God is not Israel itself but He to whose advent Israel looks forward and who furnishes the clue to the inner meaning of its existence: Israel's Messiah in the one day of
[396] His passion. He and not Israel is also the One who really suffers in all that the Jews of to-day have to endure. He is the One who is intended, aimed at and smitten, hated and pushed aside. And what Israel undergoes up to the present time is undergone as an echo and aftermath of what the heathen long ago did to the Messiah of Israel and had to do as instruments of God, as an echo and aftermath of the one real outbreak, smiting and slaying, of the divine wrath on Golgotha. This is the reason for the ceaseless futility and inevitable ineffectiveness of all that human beings at any time have perpetrated against the Jews or can perpetrate even to-day. They can only set up again the token of the crucifixion of Christ and therefore of the real judgment of God. But the real judgment of God is alone the crucifixion of Christ, and the terror of this event is that it is the reality which all other judgments upon Israel, the world and mankind can only foreshadow or reflect. The awfulness of the crucifixion of Christ is that in it the real essence of all the Old Testament threats and executions of judgment, i.e., the revelation of the wrath of God against all ungodliness and unrighteousness of men (Rom. 1[18])—without which revelation is not divine revelation—was embodied in a unique event. For in the strict sense we can truly say that human sin and sinful man have become the object of divine anger and judgment only as we look at this event. The whole seriousness of man's situation, the effective individual and collective threat to it from both nature and history, the seriousness of the fact that it is man's lot to die, is not at all diminished but only brought out in its full force when it is realised that all that world-history and the life story of each single individual is able to show of slowly advancing or suddenly manifested distress, affliction and catastrophe, every kind of agony and dying (the outpouring of

the vials of wrath. Rev. 15 and 16), is not yet or no longer the judgment of God Himself. None of these plagues either was or is the merited end. We have always continued, and do continue, like Israel. Whether we make good or bad use of them is another question, but we always have time and space, and by disregard or interpretation or especially forgetting we can draw away from even the most terrible events which come upon ourselves or others. But could we do this even physically if in what came upon us we had really and ultimately and basically to do with the wrath and judgment of God? If God's wrath and judgment were really to strike us in all this, and not merely its token (Rev. 15^1), foreshadowing and reflection—where should we be, where should we have been long since? Fortunately for us the idea that in the ills we encounter we have to endure the wrath of God Himself is incorrect. The only correct view, i.e., in harmony with the biblical interpretation, is that expressed in the 14th articles of the *Heidelberg Catechism* that "no mere creature can bear the burden of the eternal wrath of God against sin." In face of a real outbreak of God's avenging and smiting wrath, the creature would be annihilated. God's real judgment would mean the end of us. But there is obviously not an end of us, any more than there was or will be of Israel. We obviously still have, and will always have, time and space. Therefore, even though what comes on us from time to time pierces us to the heart, it cannot yet be, or any longer be, the real judgment of God, but only a serious token of it.

The meaning of the death of Jesus Christ is that there God's condemning and punishing righteousness broke out, really smiting and piercing human sin, man as sinner, and sinful Israel. It did really fall on the sin of Israel, our sin and us sinners. It did so in such a way that in what happened there (not to Israel, or to us, but to Jesus Christ) the righteousness of God which we have offended was really revealed and satisfied. Yet it did so in such a way that it did not happen to Israel or to us, but for Israel, for us. What was suffered there on Israel's account and ours, was suffered for Israel and for us. The wrath of God [397]
which we had merited, by which we must have been annihilated and would long since have been annihilated, was now in our place borne and suffered as though it had smitten us and yet in such a way that it did not smite us and can no more smite us. The reason why the No spoken on Good Friday is so terrible, but why there is already concealed in it the Eastertide Yes of God's righteousness, is that He who on the cross took upon Himself and suffered the wrath of God was no other than God's own Son, and therefore the eternal God Himself in the unity with human nature which He freely accepted in His transcendent mercy.

We may rightly say that in fact the whole of the New Testament is concerned with this matter. This is especially true of the Gospels with their unmistakable emphasis on the passion story. It also applies to the Epistles with their many references to the cross or blood or sacrifice of Christ. It is even true of Revelation in which the dominating central figure is the Lamb that was slain. Nor are there lacking specific explanations as to how this happening is to be understood.

We may take as our point of departure the well-known text (Jn. 3^{16}) which tells us that God so (οὕτως) loved the world that in its revelation and exercise to us His love took this form: "that he gave (ἔδωκεν) his only begotten Son;" that he "delivered him up for us all:" ὑπὲρ ἡμῶν πάντων παρέδωκεν, as Rom. 8^{32} puts it even more plainly and strongly. Or Titus 2^{14}: He, our great God and Saviour Christ Jesus, gave Himself for us: ἔδωκεν ἑαυτὸν ὑπὲρ ἡμῶν (cf. Gal. 2^{20}). In this giving or self-offering is expressed (Gal. 4^4; Rom. 8^3) what the Fourth

Evangelist especially likes to sum up in the conception of sending, of the divine *πέμπειν* or *ἀποστέλλειν* of the Son. This sending means a self-offering grounded in the free will of the Father and the Son in fulfilment of the divine love turned towards the cosmos and the world of man. But it is the case that God in this offering or sending of His Son, and the Son Himself in accepting this mission and allowing Himself to be sacrificed, has exposed Himself to an imposition. In His love God has been hard upon Himself, exacting a supreme and final demand. "He spared not his own Son" (Rom. 8[32]). Christ was rich and for our sake He became poor (2 Cor. 8[9]). He did not snatch at being equal with God but humbled Himself (Phil. 2[6f.]). In what consists this sternness of God against Himself, this self-abasement of God in His only Son? According to Phil. 2[7] it consisted in the fact that in a self-emptying, in a complete resignation not of the essence but of the form of His Godhead, He took upon Himself our own human form—the form of a servant, in complete likeness to other men: *ἐν ὁμοιώματι ἀνθρώπων γενόμενος*[EN87], allowing Himself to be found in fashion as a man: *σχήματι εὑρεθεὶς ὡς ἄνθρωπος*[EN88]. Like all men He was born of a woman (Gal. 4[4]). But what does it mean to take the place of man, to be Himself a man, to be born of a woman? It means for Him, too, God's Son, God Himself, that He came under the Law (*γενόμενος ὑπὸ νόμον*), i.e., that He stepped into the heart of the inevitable conflict between the faithfulness of God and the unfaithfulness of man. He took this conflict into His own being. He bore it in Himself to the bitter end. He took part in it from both sides. He endured it from both sides. He was not only the God who is offended by man. He was also the man whom God threatens with death, who falls a victim to death in face of God's judgment. If He really entered into solidarity with us—and that is just what He did do—it meant necessarily that He took upon Himself, in likeness to us (*ὁμοίωμα*), the "flesh of sin" (Rom. 8[3]). He shared in the status, constitution and situation of man in which man resists God and cannot stand before Him but must die. How could God resist Himself? How could God sin? The Son of
[398] God knew no sin (2 Cor. 5[21]; Jn. 8[46]; Heb. 4[15]). But He could enter into man's mode of being, being in the flesh, in which there is absolutely no justification before God (Rom. 3[20]), but only sin. God could—and not only could but did—allow His Son to be in the body of the flesh (Col. 1[22]), and therefore make Him to be sin for our sakes (2 Cor. 5[21]), to become the object which must be the object of His own anger, the victim of His own condemnation and punishment. This is just what has happened. He who was equal with God has become obedient unto death, even the death of the cross (Phil. 2[8]). Where we the unjust should stand. He the Just now stands *δίκαιος ὑπὲρ ἀδίκων*[EN89] (1 Pet. 3[18]). Where we the weak, the godless, should stand, the Son of God now stands (Rom. 5[6]). Where we the sinners should stand, our Judge now stands (Rom. 5[8]). Where we the enemies of God should stand, God Himself now stands in Jesus Christ (Rom. 5[10]). And on Him there now comes what ought to come on us: the condemnation of sin in the flesh (Rom. 8[3]). In His body—our body of flesh has become His—He bears our sins upon the tree (1 Pet. 2[24]). He dies for our sin (1 Pet. 3[18]; Rom. 6[10]). He became a curse for us, as it is written: "Cursed is everyone that hangeth on a tree" (Gal. 3[13]). And all this happened in order that there should be no more condemnation for us (Rom. 8[1]), that we who are subject to the Law should be ransomed (Gal. 4[5]), delivered from the curse of the Law (Gal. 3[13]), saved from wrath (Rom. 5[9]), released from sin, healed by His wounds (1 Pet. 2[24]), redeemed from all lawlessness (Tit. 2[14]). For by the event in which God has reconciled us with Himself (*ἀποκαταλλάσσειν* literally "exchanged") in which He Himself has therefore become the object of His own severity. His own righteous condemnation and punishment in our stead—in this event it has not only become possible but necessary,

---

[EN87] coming in the likeness of sinful men
[EN88] being found in appearance as a man
[EN89] the righteous for the unrighteous

and above all actual, that "He does not impute unto us our trespasses" (2 Cor. 5[19]). By His blood Jesus Christ has justified us (Rom. 5[9]), procured us the freedom to live in righteousness (Rom. 6[16f.]; 1 Pet. 2[24]), so that—as He was made sin for us—we have become the righteousness of God in Him (2 Cor. 5[21]). This is the witness of the New Testament concerning the dreadfulness, and in its dreadfulness the liberation and comfort, of the event of Good Friday.

The same truth must again be expressed in the words of Polanus—if only to remind us how fearlessly and unequivocally the older orthodoxy, for all its defects, could speak of this, the heart of the New Testament message: *Nullum exemplum iustitiae, irae et comminationum divinarum est expressius, severius, horribilius quam in Christo. Nam quia omnes homines in Adamo peccaverunt, postulat iustitia Dei, ut, quod adversus summam atque infinitam Dei maiestatem commission est, id etiam summis atque infinitis, hoc est sempiternis cum animi tum corporis suppliciis luatur, ut sit proportio culpae et poenae. Huic iustitiae satisfaciendum est necessario. At quia nemo hominum satisfacere posset in aeternum ne totum, humanum genus interiret, sponsorem* (a guarantor) *se ultra fecit unigenitus Filius Dei pro illis, quos pater ipsi dederat et ipse sese exinanivit* ... (Phil. 2[7f.]). *Quoniam ergo Filius Dei homo factus constituit se pro electis sponsorem: Deus poenam, quae electis in sempiternum perferenda fuisset, in ipsum transtulit sponsorem et iram suam adversus peccata electorum in eum effudit* (*Synt. Theol. chr.*, 1609, *col.* 1166).[EN90]

1. The fact that it was God's Son, that it was God Himself, who took our place on Golgotha and thereby freed us from the divine anger and judgment, reveals first the full implication of the wrath of God, of His condemning and punishing justice. It shows us what a consuming fire burns against sin. It thus discloses too the full implication of sin, what it means to resist God, to be God's enemy, which is the guilty determination of our human existence.

What this means no Old or New Testament command in itself and as such can reveal even in its transcendence of the best that we can will and do. Nor can any divine threat and [399] execution of judgment. Nor can any confession of sin made by us, nor any painful consciousness of sin that we experience. Nor can any of the greater or less judgments which may come upon us. Nor can any repentance and despair, however deep may be our experience of them (but when were we really in despair?). At the worst, these things in themselves and as such can point only to a great finite act of disobedience and suggest the possibility only of a finite punishment and restitution. None of them has in itself the power to summon us to such penitence before God that we have to recognise and confess ourselves infinitely guilty before Him and infinitely lost sinners abandoned to eternal death. Considered from the standpoint of these things in themselves, our most serious confessions of sin—those corresponding to the insights and language of the Bible—always have an inevitable smack of exaggeration. And—necessarily almost—the question arises in regard to the Old and New Testaments,

[EN90] No example of justice, wrath and divine threats, is more obvious, more severe, or more terrible than that in Christ. For since all men have sinned in Adam, the justice of God demands that – because it has been committed against the utmost and infinite majesty of God – it be paid with utmost and infinity (that is, eternal) punishments of body and mind, so that the punishment might fit the crime. There must necessarily be a satisfaction for this justice. But since no man could in all eternity satisfy this, he came among the human race, and the Only-begotten Son of God furthermore made himself guarantor for those whom the Father had given him, and he emptied himself ... (Phil 2.7). Therefore, since the Son of God become man appointed himself guarantor for the elect, God transferred the punishment, which was to have been carried out upon the elect in eternity, upon the guarantor himself, and poured out on him his own wrath against the sins of the elect

whether God's reaction of wrath as it is attested to us in the Bible really stands in an intelligible relation to man's opposition to God, to man's sin and guilt? And how natural it is to propose this question especially when we find or feel ourselves affected by God's token judgments! "Is God not unjust to exercise His wrath?" (Rom. 3^{5}). Have we really deserved it? Are we really as guilty as all that, that we should have to suffer it? This murmuring, this question of Job's, is silenced—but only really silenced—when we remember how it is that God judges the world (Rom. 3^{6}), that is, His relentlessness against Himself as we have described it. His allowing Himself so to feel the pain of our sin that He spared not His only Son, but delivered Him up for us all. What do *we* know of God's righteousness, of what is worthy of Him, and therefore of what, when He confronts us as our Creator and Lord, He necessarily and rightfully has against us? It is here, where He guarantees—but in His love for us and therefore utterly on His own initiative—that He is not against us but for us (Rom. 8^{31}), that we have to learn what is His righteousness and our unrighteousness. And it is from this point of view, as a token of the righteousness of God manifested here, that we have to appraise and interpret the righteousness of the Law, of the threats and judgments of the Old Testament, and of those of world history and our own life. It is here that we come to know of what we are accused and guilty, what our trespass is and means. It consists in an alienation from God, a rebellion against Him, which ought to be punished in a way which involves our total destruction, and which apart from our annihilation can be punished only by God Himself taking our place, and in His Son taking to Himself and bearing and suffering the punishment. This is what it costs God to be righteous without annihilating us. The opposition to Him in which we find ourselves is so great that it can be overcome and rendered harmless to ourselves only by God, and indeed only by His entering Himself into this opposition and bearing all the pain of it. Our position is such that we can be rescued from eternal death and translated into life only by total and unceasing substitution, the substitution which God Himself undertakes on our behalf. When this is clear to us we shall no longer have any objections to raise against the appropriateness of what we may encounter in the Old Testament, in world history and in our own life as a token of God's judgment. What symbol can be plain and strong enough to indicate the enormity of our opposition to God when it has been indicated in this way by God Himself through what He has done in order to overcome it?

2. Because it was the Son of God, i.e., God Himself, who took our place on Good Friday, what had necessarily to happen—because God is righteous—could happen there. There could happen there—the "could" being understood primarily in a physical sense—that which could not have happened to us
[400] without causing our annihilation. That is to say, the righteousness of God in condemnation and punishment could take its course in relation to human sin.

Jesus Christ, in His solidarity with "human nature which has sinned, could pay the penalty of sin" (*Heid. Catech.* Qu. 16), and at the same time, in the power of His divinity, could "bear the burden of the wrath of God in His humanity" (17). Without any diminution of His divine majesty, in the exercise of the divine majesty of His love He could enter into this "likeness of sinful flesh" to bear, in the same majesty, the judgment of divine wrath without annihilation, to be and to reveal Himself supremely as divine majesty even in His humiliation, to rise from the dead as conqueror of the judgment to which He had subjected Himself, the first fruits of all who were to follow in His steps. He could drink the cup which had to be drunk. Because He was God Himself, He could subject Himself to the severity of God. And because He was God Himself He did not have to succumb to the severity of God. God had to be severe to be true to Himself in His encounter with man, and thus to be true also to man. God's wrath had to be revealed against the ungodliness and unrighteousness of men. But only God could carry through this necessary revelation of His righteousness without involving an end of all things. Only God Himself could bear the wrath of God. Only God's mercy was capable of bearing the pain to which the creature existing in opposition to Him is subject. Only God's mercy could so feel this pain as to take it into the very heart of His being. And only God's mercy was strong enough not to be annihilated by this pain. And this that could happen only by the divine mercy is just what did happen on the cross of Golgotha: that double proof of omnipotence in which God did not abate the demands of His righteousness but showed Himself equal to His own wrath; on the one hand by submitting to it and on the other by not being consumed by it. In virtue of this omnipotence God's mercy could be at one and the same time the deepest and sincerest pity and inflexible and impassible divine strength. He could yield to His own inexorable righteousness and by this very surrender maintain Himself as God. He could reveal Himself at once as the One who as the servant of all bore the punishment of death which we had deserved, and the One who as the Lord of all took from death its power and for ever vanquished and destroyed it. In this twofold sense God's righteousness triumphed in the death of Jesus Christ.

3. Because it was the Son of God, because it was God Himself who on Good Friday suffered for us, the destruction which took place there of the suffering and death which resulted from human disobedience to God could justly satisfy and indeed fulfil the righteousness of God. As a fulfilment of the righteousness of God it necessarily meant that in the conflict between God's faithfulness and man's unfaithfulness, the faithfulness of God Himself was maintained, and therefore His honour was not violated. It was only in this way that it could also be exercised as His faithfulness to man, for how could man be really helped by a God who actually surrendered His own honour? On the other hand, the faithfulness of God Himself could not and must not exclude and suspend His faithfulness to man, nor must His honour be safeguarded by the visitation upon man of that which he has properly deserved: eternal death and destruction. In the death of Jesus Christ God remained true both to Himself and to man.

The dilemma seems inescapable. *Either* there is not visited on man what ought to be visited on him in his conflict with God. But in this case permanent injury is done to God's glory. [401]
God is no longer God. His faithfulness—a faithfulness in which He is untrue to Himself—can be of no help to man. *Or* there is visited on man just what he deserves. And in this case God's honour is indeed safeguarded and God remains God. But because God is God, in this conflict the precipice yawns in which man can only cast himself headlong and be swallowed up in the abyss. What then becomes of God's faithfulness to man. His mercy? The solution of this dilemma lies in the interposition for us at Golgotha of the Son of God, and therefore of God Himself. Because God is God, and remaining such can do in this conflict only what is worthy of Himself, therefore this conflict cannot be resolved without the divine condemnation and punishment necessarily proportionate to the trespass which we have committed. The endless consequence of the endless disobedience of which man has made himself guilty towards God and continually makes himself guilty, must be borne by man. "Is God then not merciful? God is certainly merciful but He is also just. Hence His justice demands that sin which has been committed against the supreme majesty of God should be punished in body and soul with the supreme, i.e., eternal punishment" (*Heid. Catech.* 11). Now consider the following point. Man, who is God's creature and exists wholly by God and is in God's hand,

has sinned and sins, and is therefore God's opponent in this conflict. And he has sinned and sins against God alone. Therefore in this conflict the injured and the aggressor have no higher lord and judge. But the injured Himself is also the Lord and Judge. As the wounded and offended party, at the same time He is both the measure and the Subject of the judgment and punishment which are proportionate to the offence. He is not only the measure but also the Subject. That is, He is not only the just norm according to which judgment and punishment takes place, but also the Judge who judges and punishes in righteousness. Because He is the measure, the judgment is necessarily one of condemnation and the punishment eternal death. But because He is also the Subject, because only He can judge and punish in this matter, He cannot be denied the right to execute judgment and punishment according to His good-pleasure. Again God is not God if He does not enjoy this freedom of His good-pleasure in the choice of the fulfilment of His judgment and punishment. Just as God is not God if in condemnation and punishment His righteousness does not take the course which He must take in conflict with the disobedience of His creature, so again He is not God if He is not free to give His righteousness the course which it must take according to the dictates of His mercy. Even if in the execution of His judgment and punishment God is bound, as it were, to an abstract conception of right which is superior to Himself, so that He has to condemn and punish according to this conception, He obviously will not be and do what is worthy of Himself, and He will not therefore be the righteous God. He is this because He is free to be righteous in His mercy, free to be true to Himself and therefore to remain true to us as well. And this was the character of His righteousness in the judgment executed upon Golgotha. This righteousness clothed in mercy is the meaning of the fact that the Son of God took our place, that He went surety for us, so that our judgment and punishment do not have to be borne by us because they were borne by Him. Let it be clearly understood that it did not have to happen in this way if we mean by that that God was under an obligation to clothe His righteousness in mercy and therefore in fulfilment of His righteousness to give His only Son to die for us. God could have been true to Himself without giving His faithfulness the determination of faithfulness to us. It could easily have been God's good-pleasure to express His righteousness in quite another way, namely in the form of our destruction. God would not have been any the less God if this had happened. We had and have no other claim against Him than that which arises from the fact that in the event His good-pleasure was that of His merciful righteousness. In other words we can say that it had to be so only as we look at
[402] what God has in fact done in Jesus Christ, at the way in which His good-pleasure has in fact revealed itself in Him. Looking at Him we must of course say that what did happen had to happen. But doing so we acknowledge and magnify only the decision made in God's good-pleasure and its necessity not that of any recognisable principle existing apart from this decision. We therefore exalt the divine love and grace and mercy. But as we exalt God's mercy, it must not be forgotten that in His mercy God allowed righteousness to have sway; that He was merciful but He was also just; that as He was merciful everything had to happen which has happened, which was necessary for the maintenance and preservation of His glory; that therefore in Him who is so true to us according to His own free good-pleasure we have in fact to do with Him (and this is why His faithfulness is so effectual) who is always true to Himself. God was true to Himself when He gave His Son to die for us. He did not in this way conceal the conflict between man and Himself, let alone ignore or overlook it. He bore it, as it had to be borne, to the bitter end, as it affected Himself as the injured party and man as the violator of His glory. His mercy consists in the fact that He took this conflict to heart, indeed, that He bore it in His heart. But it was nonetheless a conflict between Himself and us that was borne. For in Him who took our place God's own heart beat on our side, in our flesh and blood, in complete solidarity with our nature and constitution, at the very point where we ourselves confront Him, guilty before God. Because it was the eternal God who

entered in in Jesus Christ, He could be more than the Representative and Guarantor of God to us. He could also be our Representative and Guarantor towards God. He could be the fully accredited Representative not only of the divine Judge, but also of the judged: of fallen Adam in his sin; of the whole of sinful humanity; of each individual sinner in all his being and sinning. Because He was God's Son, He could take humanity to Himself in such a way that in it He was the Advocate for God to us and to God for us all—this one man for every man. In this fully accredited representation of God to us all and of us all to God, Jesus Christ came into the midst to bear that conflict to the bitter end in righteousness, but in the merciful righteousness of God. In this fully accredited representation He really suffered our distress as the distress in the heart of God Himself. He therefore became the object of divine wrath and judgment and the bearer of our guilt and punishment. Thus we do not have here—as in the travesty in which this supreme insight and truth of the Christian faith is so often distorted—a raging indignation of God, which is ridiculous or irritating in its senselessness, against an innocent man whose patient suffering changes the temper of God, inducing in Him an indulgent sparing of all other men, so that all other men can rather shamefacedly take refuge behind his suffering, happily saved but quite unchanged in themselves. We do not have here an abstract justice of God which is later changed into an equally abstract compassion and indulgence. On the contrary, it is the actual and terrible wrath of God which rules according to God's free good-pleasure in the fulfilment of what is from the first His merciful righteousness, and it does not need any change of mood or weakening, but in its strictest fulfilment it is the self-expression of the eternal unchangeably good will of God. And it is not the fact that a man suffers in patience and innocence which is the motive force of this happening. There is no moving of God by the creature on the basis of which God can then decide on a universal amnesty. But it is God's own heart which moves in creation on the basis of His own good-pleasure. It suffers what the creature ought to suffer and could not suffer without being destroyed. It suffers it with omnipotent vicariousness in virtue of the fact that it is the heart of the almighty Lord and Creator, who, since it is His good-pleasure, cannot be prevented from Himself sustaining His creature (even in the face of His own divine wrath), as He has Himself created it. And if the creature accepts this vicarious suffering, accepts its own life on the ground of this divine substitution as a gift of the love and grace and mercy of its Lord and Creator, this cannot mean that before God it [403]
hides behind another. As we know, this is what Adam and Eve did in the Garden according to Gen. 3[8]. But it is the very thing which must not happen again. On the contrary, the meaning is that it is dragged out of its hiding place and put fair and square before the face of God as the face of Him before whom it is utterly lost and who alone can now be its Saviour from death and its life. It means, then, that the creature is cast wholly and utterly upon God and bound to God as to Him who alone has conducted its cause and will conduct its cause in eternity.

4. Because it was the Son of God, i.e., God Himself who took our place on Good Friday, the substitution could be effectual and procure our reconciliation with the righteous God, and therefore the victory of God's righteousness, and therefore our own righteousness in His sight. Only God, our Lord and Creator, could stand surety for us, could take our place, could suffer eternal death in our stead as the consequence of our sin in such a way that it was finally suffered and overcome and therefore did not need to be suffered any more by us. No creature, no other man could do that. But God's own Son could do it.

We have seen that He could do it physically and that He could do it lawfully. We must now add specifically that He could also do it effectually, i.e., in such a way that His suffering is in fact reckoned to us, that it need not be suffered any more by us, that we can be free from fear, that in view of the righteousness of God in necessary condemnation and punishment we may cling to Him as to the One in whom satisfaction is done to this necessity. Jesus Christ could take our place with this effectiveness because as the Son of God He became man and had therefore the freedom and power to be in His humanity as that individual the Head and Representative of us all, and therefore not only to speak to us in God's name, but also in our name, as flesh of our flesh, to speak to God. If we hear Him as the Word made flesh, we hear what God also hears as the blood of His own Son cries to heaven to Him. But in His own Word made flesh, God hears that satisfaction has been done to His righteousness, that the consequences of human sin have been borne and expiated, and therefore that they have been taken away from man—the man for whose sake Jesus Christ intervened. In the Word spoken by the blood of His Son God hears that for those whose flesh this His Son has made His own, for those who are in Him, in Jesus Christ, there is now no more condemnation (Rom. 8[1]). In this His own Word answering Him out of the depths of humanity, God hears the Word by which we are justified, which as surely as it is His own Word is also our pardon. As we for our part may hear this Word, as there is said to us what God in Jesus Christ His incarnate Word has said to Himself, we hear our pardon. Everything depends on whether we are present at this divine colloquy. Everything depends on whether this Word is also spoken also to us and we also hear it. If it is addressed to us and we hear it, we know that there is no longer an objective judgment passed on us and we need no longer fear such. This is not because God is not just, or not strictly just. It is because He has been strictly just once and for all, but according to the requirements of His mercy and therefore in the sacrifice of His only Son. It is not because we did not deserve His condemnation—we deserved it a thousand times—but because, as the judgment which we have deserved, it has already been executed and suffered. It is not because—as we are in and for ourselves—we did not need to fear it. As we are in and for ourselves we would have to fear it throughout eternity. It is because we now have to fear God only in such a way that we allow His incarnate Word to be addressed to us
[404] and hear it—the Word which God has addressed to Himself and by which we are justified in His sight, the Word of our pardon. By faith in this Word we fear God's judgment as it ought to be feared. Everything now depends on whether our primary fear is that we should arbitrarily try to fear God's judgment in a different way. Everything now depends on whether "I live by the faith of the Son of God, who loved me, and gave himself for me" (Gal. 2[20]). "How art thou just before God? Only by faith in Jesus Christ, that although my conscience accuses me, telling me that I have grievously sinned against all the commandments of God and have never kept a single one of them, but have always been inclined to evil, yet God, without any merit on my part, of pure grace has granted and imputed to me the complete satisfaction, righteousness and holiness of Christ, as though I had never committed any sin and had myself performed all the obedience which Christ has rendered for me, if only I will accept these benefits with a believing heart" (*Heid. Catech.* 60). That this faith should be awakened in us and not sleep again, that it should begin and not cease, that it should live and not die, is the victory of God's righteousness and therefore our own real righteousness before God. It is the proper effect of the proper fear of God, which alone is required of us and is possible. Everything depends on whether we attain this fear of God, not letting it go, earnestly and constantly maintaining it. Everything depends on whether we do not remain fixed or again sink into a fear of judgment which in Jesus Christ has become pointless—the fear of a judgment which can still come upon us ourselves even though it has affected God Himself in Jesus Christ, even though God Himself has borne it for us in His own heart, even though

God has once for all saved us from it. In view of Jesus Christ this fear of judgment can no longer be called fear of God. We really fear God only in the judgment which in its righteous execution upon the cross of Golgotha has finally procured our pardon. We really fear God only in so far as we allow this pardon to be spoken to us, to be true and valid. From our point of view, the effectiveness of the intervention of God's Son for us lies in the fact that it is the revelation of God by which we are gathered to Jesus Christ as to our Head and Representative, by which we are gathered to His Church, by which, that is, we are awakened and called to the fear of God by faith, and maintained in it. In the revelation of God we are drawn into God's colloquy with Himself. In the revelation of God there is said to us what God has said to Himself in His incarnate Word. This revelation consists, however, in the resurrection of Jesus Christ from the dead as a confirmation that He who suffered eternal death on the cross was the One who by suffering it was destined to overcome it, and also as a confirmation that by placing His own Son, Himself, under the judgment, God would necessarily be the goal and end of judgment. As this conquest of death and this righteous end of judgment, the resurrection of Jesus Christ is both the self-revelation as the Son of God and the revelation of the righteousness of God in its unity with His mercy, and the revelation of faith as our salvation by the righteousness which has been fulfilled in Jesus Christ. It is in this sense that we are to understand Rom. $4^{24f.}$: "We believe in him that raised up Jesus our Lord from the dead; who was delivered for our offences, and was raised again for our justification," i.e., for the revelation of our righteousness, the revelation of the fact that God's righteousness has prevailed, that according to 2 Cor. 5^{21} we ourselves have become the righteousness of God. We have become this because we are members of the body of which Jesus Christ is the Head: He who is God Himself taking our place. And that we accept this position, that we admit His Godhead and allow Him to be God for us, is faith in Him and therefore the proper fear of God required of us. If by His resurrection He discloses this faith to us, if by the power of His resurrection He awakens and maintains this fear of God in us, His intervention on our behalf, and therefore the righteousness of God, is effective as the love and grace and mercy in which once for all He has turned to us sinners without even the slightest self-betrayal; as His faithfulness which is powerful for time and eternity because, while evincing it to us, He [405]
first and foremost remains true to Himself.

From this standpoint we must look back—really look back—to the divine threat and execution of judgment on Israel, but also to the divine judgment continually taking place on the Church and in the world, and again to the divine judgment which always menaces and strikes each individual life—and does so finally in the death towards which each of us is hastening. Only in unbelief, only by overlooking God's revelation in the resurrection of Jesus Christ, only in the selfish fear which has to be overcome by the true fear of God, can it be thought and said that in all this we are already or again and in the same sense dealing with the judgment of God which took place on the cross of Golgotha, which God suffered and consummated in His own heart as both Judge and judged. Of course, even if we could escape by a trick of interpretation what we have in fact to experience, the unitary testimony of Holy Scripture leaves us in no doubt that we do in fact stand under these judgments. The people of God, Israel in the hidden sense of the Old Testament and the open sense of the New Testament, the Church of Jesus Christ, is not in fact immune from divine judgment, but openly or secretly, directly or indirectly, it is subjected to it in every age. Again, according to the unitary testimony of Holy Scripture, there does undoubtedly exist an inner, essential connexion between the one passion of the Son of God and the many sufferings which we see afflicting Israel, the Church, the world and ourselves. The fear of God, in which we must cling to the revealing righteousness of God as the revelation of the conquest of death and

the end of judgment, does not preclude that we should constantly be witnesses, and indeed conscious and frank and honest witnesses, of the fact that God is not mocked either in Israel, or in the Church, or in the world, or in our own lives; that whatsoever a man soweth that shall he also reap (Gal. $6^{7f.}$). We can best see the connexion which exists here when we think of the reality of the divine intervention for sinful man which has taken place in Jesus Christ. We saw that the effectiveness of this intervention consists in the salvation of the sinner from judgment and the revelation of the faith in which he may grasp this salvation, knowing and rejoicing in it, giving glory to the Son of God as his Saviour, and placing his whole trust in Him. This effectiveness of the divine intervention, however, stands or falls according as we are taken up into unity and fellowship with the Son of God, and may live in faith as in this unity and fellowship with Him our Head, as members of His body. As the gift and the exercise of this unity and fellowship faith is our reconciliation, our divine righteousness. Is it not inevitable that the effectiveness of God's intervention should involve our seeing and feeling and experiencing and suffering the judgment of God fulfilled and suffered for us in Jesus Christ as He Himself has suffered it for us? Not in the same way as He has suffered it, for He alone has suffered the eternal death which we have deserved. Our cross is not the cross of Calvary where satisfaction was done to the righteousness of God in condemnation and punishment. But we cannot believe in the righteousness of God triumphing for us on the cross without realising that there we have been justified apart from and against our deserts, and therefore without taking our cross upon ourselves and placing ourselves under the signs of the divine judgment. Faith has its life in the submission which this involves. This is the faith which triumphs in Jesus Christ over eternal death. This is the faith which stands in Jesus Christ at the goal and end of all judgment. Faith lives in the self-prostration before God which is necessary and self-evident by reason of the fact that God has intervened on behalf of men, taking up their cause and vindicating it. Man himself could not have done this. As an indication of this the life of the believer must run its course in the shadow of divine judgment. In this respect we cannot speak of more than signs and shadows. The afflictions of
[406] Israel, the Church, the world and ourselves are all announcements and echoes of the reality of the divine judgment. The divine judgment itself in its reality is only what happened at Golgotha. But it did really happen there. We therefore find its traces and tokens, its announcements and echoes, in the environs of Golgotha. These environs are Israel, the Church, the world, and our own lives. Therefore alongside the cross of Christ there is our own cross, alongside His suffering our suffering, alongside His death our death. They are not the judgment of God that we have to fear, but the judgment of God that we have to see as vanquished and ended if we are to continue in penitence and obedience. For to see judgment in this way—in the ineluctability in which we ourselves really see it, in the honesty in which we must be prepared to see it, in the readiness to bear the little suffering which seeing involves—this is the necessary exercise of faith. We do not believe if we do not live in the neighbourhood of Golgotha. And we cannot live in the neighbourhood of Golgotha without being affected by the shadow of divine judgment, without allowing this shadow to fall on us. In this shadow Israel suffered. In this shadow the Church suffers. That it suffers in this way is the Church's answer to the world on the question of a "theodicy"—the question of the justice of God in the sufferings inflicted on us in the world. That suffering should be learned in this shadow is in 1 Peter the problem of faith for every Christian community and individual Christian. "Nay, in all these things we are more than conquerors through him that loved us" (Rom. 8^{37}). The shadow would not fall if the cross of Christ did not stand in the light of His resurrection. We would not have to suffer if it were not that we are "begotten again unto a lively hope by the resurrection of Jesus Christ from the dead" (1 Pet. 1^{3}).

3. THE PATIENCE AND WISDOM OF GOD

We now emphasise two further biblical attributes of God, both individually and in their interconnexion. We must try to understand them as expressions of the perfection of His love. As we do so, we are again reminded of the fact that all further consideration of the divine attributes can but move in a circle around the one but infinitely rich being of God whose simplicity is abundance itself and whose abundance is simplicity itself. We are not speaking of a new object but allowing the one object, God, to speak further of Himself. We are continuing to contemplate the love of God and therefore God Himself as the One who loves in freedom. What end can there be to this development? We are drawing upon the ocean. We are therefore faced by a task to which there is no end. But a third affirmation must now be added to the first two if we are to gain at least the authorised and commanded view of this inexhaustible ocean. We first said that God is gracious and holy. We then continued that God is merciful and righteous. Now that we have developed these two affirmations along the lines indicated by the biblical revelation, a third affirmation necessarily follows which expresses the same truth again, but again differently, that God is patient and wise. The first two points are not left behind when we proceed to this third. They are not exhausted and abandoned. If we proceed to this third point, we acknowledge by this very act that the first and second are
not exhausted and abandoned, but that we must reaffirm them in a new way. [407]
We have again to pursue the movement demanded by the object and therefore the development of the knowledge of God occasioned by it. We have again to magnify the plenitude of the divine being by not lingering unduly over any one proposition or letting it become the final word or the guiding principle, but by proceeding from one to another, from the second to the third. As we do so, we realise that even if we make a provisional halt at the third, this does not mean that we have spoken the last word. It is simply an indication that we are on a human path where in the very face of God we cannot even try to rival His infinity.

In view of certain specific scriptural passages, there is a clear necessity that after speaking of God's grace and mercy we should consider the perfection of the divine patience as a special perfection of the love and therefore of the being of God.

There is a whole series of Old Testament texts (Ex. 34^{6}; Joel 2^{13}; Jonah 4^{2}; Neh. 9^{17}; Ps. 86^{15}, 103^{8}, 145^{8}) in which, with variations of order, but obviously a certain necessity which has almost become a formula, these three—*Yahweh*'s grace, mercy and patience (or long-suffering), usually completed by the comprehensive thought of His "great faithfulness"—are described as the distinctive marks of the God revealed and active in Israel.

If first and basically we ask what is to be learnt and understood under this concept of the patience of God, it will be helpful if in the first instance we make it clear that in this third stage, too, there can be no question of our inference from a general idea of love. We have already seen that love in

general does not necessarily bear the character of grace or of mercy. We must now continue that it does not necessarily bear that of patience. Love can be extremely honest, deep and passionate and at the same time extremely impatient. It may want to possess its object immediately or in a specific qualitative or quantitative way. It may wish to devour it, or, if it is frustrated, vindictively to destroy it. Similarly, grace in general or mercy in general may behave with great impatience. We can mean only the love and grace and mercy of the God revealed in Jesus Christ, and not of an imaginary god, if we confess and affirm that love and grace and mercy must also be patient. We saw that the love of God is necessarily grace because it expresses the condescension of the unconditionally superior to the unconditionally inferior—of the Creator to His creature. It is because this condescension—in the absolute freedom without which it would not be such—is manifest in the God revealed in Jesus Christ that we say that God's love is gracious love. And further, God's grace is essentially mer-
[408] ciful because the absolute subordinate in this relation finds himself, the creature as such and as a sinful creature, in a position of needy distress and misery, because God's turning to him, as that of the absolute superior, implies necessarily that God espouses the cause of the creature in all his need and distress, sharing it, making it His own, taking it to His own heart. The fact that He does this, that He is the One whose very being impels Him to do it, means that God's grace—the grace of the God revealed in Jesus Christ—is merciful grace. On the way of knowledge pursued so far we saw that our statements rested on an utterly factual and concrete necessity—that the God revealed in Jesus Christ loves in grace and mercy. The case is exactly the same now that we proceed to affirm that His love bears essentially the character of patience. Patience exists where space and time are given with a definite intention, where freedom is allowed in expectation of a response. God acts in this way. He makes this purposeful concession of space and time. He allows this freedom of expectancy. That He does so lies in His very being. Indeed, it is His being. Everything that God is, is implied and included in the statement that He is patient. But this is no more self-evident than our previous considerations. It cannot in any sense result from a simple development of ideas. God could be gracious and merciful in such a way that His love would consume His creature. He could take to Himself his distress in such wise as to leave him no further opportunities in space and time, but to strip him of both, recalling and annulling his corrupt and twisted existence, destroying the perverse and tortured will of the creature, and again substituting His own good will as the sole effective reality. Does not the condescension of the unconditionally superior to the unconditionally inferior, the activity of the Creator on behalf of the suffering creature, logically and necessarily imply this outcome? And could it not be the most wonderful, effective and generous proof of divine grace and mercy if God willed it to be all in all in such a way as to be it in Himself to all eternity without creation, the meaning and basis of everything other than Himself without its individual existence, its differentiation from God? Is not the very

existence of all that is other than God identical with its suffering, its suffering with its existence? Could there be a more radical form of love than that which does not first need the existence of the beloved, that in which the beloved exists wholly and utterly in the lover, that which leads the beloved back to this form of existence ? Could not, then, the possibility of God's annihilating wrath against His creature, which we have already had frequent occasion to consider, be the real fulfilment of divine love. Could not eternal death as the work of this divine wrath be in truth eternal peace, the eternal rest of the creature in God Himself, unviolated and in fact inviolable by all the assaults and torments which are obviously unavoidably bound up with space and time and with our existence as such?

We have only to listen to what heathen and ostensibly Christian mysticism of all times and countries says about God's love and grace and mercy. We have only to listen to its decisive and culminating utterances. At a pinch mysticism could perhaps have followed us so far—with certain reservations and special explanations. But at the very latest it would have to diverge at the point we have now reached, proclaiming as the culmination of its own teaching concerning God's love and grace and mercy, as the properly and ultimately redemptive word, a doctrine of God's impatience. Here at the very latest the real difficulty of the Christian knowledge of God in relation to every form of mysticism (and even every mystical perversion of the Christian knowledge of God) would be revealed as irreconcilable. [409]

It is a necessary characteristic of Him whom the Christian Church names God not to be impatient but patient. The necessity to which we refer is again a factual, concrete necessity. From the logic of abstract ideas we might equally well infer that God is impatient. If we had to think of God according to the standard of what we think is fine and pleasing and therefore godlike, we might easily suppose Him to be impatient (and we should find ourselves in the best of company). The result would be a fine and complete and satisfying doctrine of God and an equally fine and complete and satisfying doctrine of redemption. Here then we can actually speak of the necessary patience of God only if we take as the pure source and necessary determination of our knowledge the factual and concrete revelation of God in Jesus Christ in its factual and concrete attestation in Holy Scripture. If we adopt this point of view, if we think and speak in the Church and therefore from within the basis and essence of the Church in Jesus Christ, from the very outset our course is so fixed that we cannot journey in the direction desired and initiated by mysticism, i.e., in the direction of a doctrine of God's impatience. This is not because, generally speaking, it is impossible that God should be impatient. And it is not because an impatient God could not be a very fine and profound conception. It is simply because God is in fact patient. When He discloses Himself to our understanding, when alone it is worthwhile to talk of a knowledge of God in the strict and full sense, He gives Himself to be known as the patient and not the impatient God. God reveals Himself in such a way that we have to say that in the concrete context in which God's love and grace and mercy are actualised, they bear unmistakably the mark of patience. They bear it in such a way that we are forced to say that we can know them as divine love and grace and mercy only in so far as they have this characteristic. The divine patience must, then, be for us another differentiating sign between the divine and that which is only apparently so, the demonic.

We define God's patience as His will, deep-rooted in His essence and constituting His divine being and action, to allow to another—for the sake of His own grace and mercy and in the affirmation of His holiness and justice—space
[410] and time for the development of its own existence, thus conceding to this existence a reality side by side with His own, and fulfilling His will towards this other in such a way that He does not suspend and destroy it as this other but accompanies and sustains it and allows it to develop in freedom.

Patientia Dei est, qua iram suam erga homines ita moderatur Deus, ut conversionem et resipiscentiam eorum expectet vel poenam differat, vel iram suam totam uno momento non effundat[EN91] (Quenstedt, *Theol. did. pol.*, 1685, I, *c.* 8, *sect* 1, *th.* 33). Polanus defined the concept of divine *patientia*[EN92] in a very similar way (*Synt. Theol. chr.*, 1609, *col.* 1146), and he linked it with that of the *clementia*[EN93] of God: *benignissima eius voluntas, per quam etiam in ira misericordiae suae recordans, nobis est propitius parcitque nobis etiam si aliter meriti simus, malens resipiscentiam et conversionem nostram quam mortem*[EN94] (*ib.*, *col.* 1152). The addition and explanation will have to be accepted: *etiam in ira ... recordans*[EN95], and we can then extract from the orthodox definition at least the following point—that when God is patient, there is no question of a weakness of God in the exercise of His grace and mercy. Nothing can affect or change the fact that God is holy and just. And nothing is to be deducted from what this implies for the creature, for man, in his encounter with God. The fact remains that God's anger burns in this encounter and that it requires on the part of man a complete change of attitude. But the divinity of God's grace and mercy and therefore of His holiness and justice is seen in the fact that in this encounter and therefore in God Himself there occurs a *moderatio*[EN96] or *recordatio*[EN97]. The wrath of God is characteristically divine, and therefore a holy and righteous wrath, in the fact that it does not break out like any anger, and (as the anger of Almighty God) take an utterly destructive course, but that it is guided and shaped, that it has its own particular form and limit, not a determination, form and limit imposed upon it from outside but by God Himself who is Lord of His wrath in virtue of what He knows and wills. And that man for his part really has to do with God, with the grace and mercy, the holiness and justice, the wrath of God, and not with a demon to whom also in a certain sense all this could perhaps be ascribed, is revealed by the fact that his allotted part in the encounter with God is not death and destruction, but conversion, *resipiscentia*[EN98] and *conversio*[EN99], and for this purpose he is not deprived of space and time and existence, but as he has been given he

---

[EN91] The patience of God is that by which God moderates his wrath against men, such that waits for their turning and repentance; he either delays his punishment, or he does not pour out all his wrath in one moment

[EN92] patience

[EN93] clemency

[EN94] that most benign will of his, through which, remembering his mercy even in wrath, he spares us even if we deserved otherwise, preferring our turning and our repentance, rather than our death

[EN95] 'even in wrath, remembering'

[EN96] moderation

[EN97] remembering

[EN98] turning

[EN99] repentance

is also left them. It is to be noted that God is not more powerful in His action than in His forbearance from action. Indeed there is no antithesis here: God's forbearance is only a specific form of His always powerful doing and being. God is therefore no less effective in His patience than in His grace and mercy, than in His holy and just wrath which includes His grace and mercy. God does not repent when He forbears to act, but it is also—and properly understood, precisely—the unrepentant outbreaking of His whole divine glory that He is patient in His grace and mercy and therefore patient also in His holy and righteous wrath. Polanus is right when he emphasises (*ib.*, *col.* 1145) that the *patientia*[EN100] of God does not mean a *pati*[EN101]. We add in elucidation that it does not mean a *pati* to which He is subject as to an external cause, so that it diminishes His majesty. If God restrains Himself, as is implied in the New Testament term *ἀνοχή*[EN102], this self-restraint is also to be understood as the powerful act of God. God could not be more divine, indeed, He would be less divine, He would not be God at all, if He were not patient. "For my Name's sake will I defer mine anger, and for my praise will I refrain from thee that I cut thee not off" (Is. 4^{89}). If the other New Testament term for this thought is *μακροθυμία*, the word "long-suffering" is a bad translation if it suggests hesitation, weakness, indulgence, a stretching of the divine will. On the contrary, the term implies that God's will is great and strong and relentless and victorious. It is this as a gracious, merciful will, and therefore it waits patiently, giving man every freedom and opportunity. But this waiting, by which God grants us liberty, is itself and as such to be [411]
understood as a plus, not a minus, of God's freedom, power and activity. It too is to be understood as a specific form of the divine majesty—exactly like His mercy.

The idea of the patience of God expresses an enrichment, a clarification and an intensification of the idea of His mercy, which is itself to be understood in an active and dynamic sense. This enrichment, clarification and intensification by the concept which is for the moment our special concern, consist in the fact that God takes up the cause of the creature, the reality distinct from Himself, in such a way that He accepts it as a reality and intervenes for it in recognition, not in suspension, of its reality. For it as such, He is severe with Himself. He suffers for it. He sacrifices His only Son for it. He does it for the creature as such—which means that God's mercy does not act in such a way as to overpower and blot out its object. God does not take the place of the creature in such a way as to annihilate it. That He takes its plight to His own heart does not mean that He robs it of its independent life, making the latter a mere potentiality or recollection in His own life. The encounter of His eternal love with the creature existing in space and time does not imply the utter dissolution of its space and time and therefore of its existence as such. The fact that God in His mercy intervenes for it must be understood in the full sense of the two words "for" and "it" in such a way, therefore, that this divine intervention for the creature does not exclude but includes its independent life—whatever the encounter with God may entail for that life—so that the atoning will of God maintains His will and act as the Creator: "What our God has created He will also uphold, and sooner or later control by His grace." He will control it—but not in such a way that grace means the catastrophic destruction of nature.

EN100 patience
EN101 passivity
EN102 forebearance

It means radical judgment upon nature. It means its radical transformation and renewal. But it does not mean its violent end.

In this sense we must admit the truth of that maxim of Thomas Aquinas which is so often put to dangerous use and in the first instance was no doubt dangerously meant: *gratia non tollit* (*non destruit*) *sed* (*praesupponit et*) *perficit naturam*[EN103]. God deals with His creature in such a way as to share his wretchedness. This is the meaning of His mercy. In this way it is more powerful than if it had to kill and slay in order to arrive at its goal. It is so powerful that it can wait, allowing us to continue. The abyss in the heart of God is so deep that in it the other, the reality distinct from God, can be contained in all its wretchedness. It does not have to perish. It is allowed to live, i.e., to live as the object of divine mercy, to live under the divine righteousness, to live under the full and strict outworking of what is entailed by its encounter with God, by God's intervention for it. There can be no question of a neutral juxtaposition of God and creature and therefore of a restraint on the part of God which signifies inaction. The relationship between the two is a very definite relationship of action and reaction. It is in this, the God–creature relationship, that there happens to the creature what is in accordance with the will of God. This relationship is part of the full and strict outworking of that [412] encounter. It belongs to it as the will of God that God acts as the One who in His absolute freedom, power and activity maintains what He has created so that it may continue to live. This is the patience of God.

We shall see at once that this patience is the divine being in power and not in weakness if we consider in detail the testimony of Scripture to God's revelation from this particular standpoint.

We begin with the story of Cain (Gen. 4^{1-17}; cf. W. Vischer, *Jahve der Gott Kains*, 1929). Eve has "gotten a man from the Lord"—the first human birth, Cain in his greatness, but also under the threat which arises from the fall of Adam. It is worth noting that it is not his name but that of his brother Abel which points to this latter fact. That they must both live by God's grace, as they testify with their offerings, leads to the disclosure of human sin in the act and guilt of Cain. Cain, too, has sought grace: yet not as man has to seek the grace of God; not in upright conduct before God; not freely looking up to God; but, as the eventual outburst of his jealousy shows, with the object of gaining God for himself. Therefore he finds no grace. Sin lurks before his door and he cannot control it because, seeking grace, he repulses grace. Hatred of grace manifests itself as hatred of his brother, in the murder of his brother, in the lack of a sense of responsibility evinced in his affectation of ignorance: "I know not. Am I my brother's keeper?" But what he wishes to conceal from God is not concealed: "What hast thou done? The voice of thy brother's blood cries unto me from the ground." And Cain is cursed. He is driven away with curses from this ground, which shall no more give him fruit. "A fugitive and a vagabond shalt thou be upon the earth." This is the encounter of the creature with its God. This is the intolerable and impossible nature of its existence in this encounter. It cannot be said that in this story God's holiness and righteousness do not receive proper attention. But this is not the end of the story. God's holiness and righteousness seem to require a different interpretation and to be differently determined from what we might have supposed from the story so far. The mood of despair in which alone Cain himself can react to this judgment is not the final thing that is decreed even for him. In his despair he sees and confesses: "My punishment is greater than I can bear." Obviously this cry implies objectively, as does the similar complaint of Job, the truth which Luther has expressed by the translation: "My sin is greater than can be forgiven." But has not Cain now sought God's grace as it must be sought? Obviously, for now according to the unambiguous

EN103 grace does not destroy nature, but rather perfects it

statement of the story he has in any event found it. "Everyone that findeth me shall slay me," he thinks in his despair. *Yahweh* answers him: Not so! "Whosoever slayeth Cain, vengeance shall be taken on him sevenfold. And the Lord set a mark upon Cain, lest any finding him should kill him. And Cain went out from the presence of the Lord, and dwelt in the land of Nod, on the east of Eden. And Cain knew his wife; and she conceived, and bear Enoch." We see that the story has as its theme the patience of God which receives pointed expression in the decree that death must not be the punishment of the murderer. Cain the murderer is permitted to live. It is not that he could arrange this himself, but that God wills and allows it to happen. It is not that he did not deserve death, but that God does not will the death he deserves. It is not that he does not stand under the wrath and curse of God. This has come upon Cain and he must bear it. But Cain must not be killed. The sign which God sets upon him is undoubtedly the brand of the sin which necessarily arises from his contempt of grace. It is the mark of the homicide. But this very mark is a protective sign which God has given him. In fact it is a covenantal sign by which *Yahweh* admits Himself to be the Avenger and Saviour of this murderer; by which—for the first time in the Bible—God binds Himself to sinful man in a kind of treaty. God is holy and righteous in such a way that He sustains the life of the one who has forfeited his life before God. He sustains it with the intervention of His Word and the gift of a token of Himself as the Lord of man. God is holy and righteous to [413]
such effect that whoever is against Cain is not for but against God, the holy and righteous One, and will necessarily be the victim of an even heavier judgment. In God's patience, then, there triumphs the almighty, gracious and merciful, and therefore the holy and righteous, being of God.

The same is true in the story of Noah in Gen. 6–9. This relates an annihilating judgment of God, and yet surely its proper sequence and original meaning are rightly perceived in 1 Pet. 3^{20}, which places it under the heading of the patience of God. For its true content is not that God repented having created man and that He decided and fulfilled His decision to extirpate man and all living creatures. Its true and final Word is that God in His wrath and judgment finds and saves the one man Noah, again not because of Noah's intrinsic excellence, but because he found grace in the eyes of the Lord (Gen. 6^{8}) and was seen to be "righteous before him" (Gen. 7^{1}). The point of this story is that while God destroys the human race and all things living for the sake of His holiness and righteousness, He is at the same time concerned about the further progress and growth of the human race and of all other creatures, and so, after the catastrophic destruction of all flesh upon the earth, He accepts the sacrifice of the rescued Noah and promises him: "I will not again curse the ground for man's sake ... neither will I again smite any more everything living, as I have done" (Gen. 8^{21}, cf. 9^{11}) But: "While the earth remaineth, seedtime and harvest, and cold and heat, and summer and winter, and day and night, shall not cease." Again a sign is appointed, the rainbow, as the "token of a covenant between me and the earth" (Gen. $9^{12f.}$), which, according to Gen. 9^{16}, not only man can see, but God Himself "will look upon it," that He may remember His covenant. Again, as in the Cain story, it is a question principally—and in an abstract sense we might almost say, only—of man's life and its conservation, of the place which he is granted on earth, of the existence permitted to him in time and the inevitable revolutions of time, even in spite of the fact that the thoughts of the human heart are evil from youth. But in this very abstraction the story asserts all the more plainly that it also belongs to God's being and action, that it renders His holiness and righteousness divine, that even when He punishes and slays He can still grant place and time. To whom? To the creature? Is it a question of the creature and its life in itself and as such? Obviously it is also a question of the creature, but again obviously—because the creature's life is forfeit—it is primarily and properly a question of God Himself who has not yet finished with this creature; who wills to continue with it, to have further dealings with it; who therefore leaves it the gift of life in order that He Himself may have opportunity for what He wills to do and be in His continued future relations with it. Does not the whole story of God's covenant with man, the covenant with Abraham, and the covenant at Sinai, and everything that happens in connexion with them—above all does not the fulfilment of all the promises of all these covenants in Jesus Christ, depend upon the fact that this covenant with Noah was concluded and kept and will always be faithfully kept? Does not the grace and mercy of God depend upon the fact that there is also a patience of God, that He grants space to the sinful creature, thus giving Himself space further to speak and act with it? We should certainly have to venerate the omnipotent Godhead of God in the end which He could have willed finally to prepare for all creatures and could have prepared long ago. But since He has willed and wills it otherwise, since He has willed to provide us with the sign of Cain and that of Noah, do we not have to say that the omnipotent Godhead of the living God consists only in the fact that He is not impatient but patient?

An impatient God would be in fact a petty, human, weak and finally a false god. It is only the patient God who is the great, divine, strong and true God. This truth emerges with particular clarity in the Book of Jonah. Notice the relation between the two parts of the work.
[414] First (cc. 1–2) we have Jonah's own disobedience to his prophetic mission, the punishment of this disobedience and his gracious and miraculous deliverance from the belly of the fish as he pleads for it and celebrates it in advance in the Psalm of Jonah $2^{3f.}$. There then follows in cc. 3 and 4, the apparent obedience of the prophet. But the same man who in this mysterious way was the object of God's patience is slow to understand it. Indeed, we might say that he shows crass ignorance in respect of the message read to him. He is called to be the prophet of the fact that in consideration of the penitence of the Ninevites God will repent of His intention to destroy the city. And he, of all people, makes this complaint against God: "For I knew that thou art a gracious God, and merciful, slow to anger, and of great kindness, and repentest thee of the evil." Indeed, he justifies his own original disobedience, thus in a sense repeating the sin that had been so wonderfully forgiven:"O Lord, was not this my saying, when I was yet in my country? Therefore I fled before unto Tarshish" (4^2). This prophet, just rescued from death, wearies of life, and in his final words he, the psalmist of ch. 2, impatiently prays down even upon himself the impatience of God: "Therefore now, O Lord, take, I beseech thee, my life from me; for it is better for me to die than to live." There then follows in $4^{5f.}$ the exquisite repetition of the whole in the shape of an unmistakable burlesque. The prophet instals himself in the eastern part of the town to see what will happen. He rejoices in a gourd which gives him the necessary shade as he waits for the outburst of God's anger. "So Jonah was exceeding glad of the gourd." But as a symbolic judgment God sent a worm which smote the gourd that it withered, and Jonah experienced in a most unwelcome way the heat of the sun, and had fresh occasion to desire his own death and therefore God's impatience. The ironical question: "Doest thou well to be angry for the gourd?" does not help him. Yes, he answers: "I do well to be angry that life has been so spoiled for me." What more can be done? Who is in the right? The impatient prophet who raises such a lament for the gourd and thinks "that it is justified," or the patient God whose final word we hear in the question: "And should not I spare that great city, wherein are more than six score thousand persons that cannot discern between their right hand and their left hand; and also much cattle?" We are not told that the prophet learned his lesson. But we must obviously learn from his story who and what God is and is not. For again we are not told that Jonah's impatient prayer for the action of an impatient God found any answer. It would seem that with the 120,000 minors and other inhabitants of the town and the mass of cattle he himself did not perish but was left alive—with a life which both he and they had forfeited. The truth of God's patience with Nineveh and with himself for his own salvation is the ultimate message of this Scripture. And in this way does it not express, more powerfully than any

picture of judgment and punishment on the city and the prophet could ever do, the omnipotent holy and righteous Godhead of God?

God does not renounce His government when He exercises patience. If God gives further opportunity to sinful man and grants him life, it is perhaps because, as in the case of the Ninevites, he has already repented and converted. Ezek. $18^{21f.}$ is obviously to be understood on this presupposition: "But if the wicked will turn from all his sins that he hath committed, and keep all my statutes, and do that which is lawful and right, he shall surely live, he shall not die. All his transgressions that he hath committed, they shall not be mentioned unto him: in his righteousness that he hath done, he shall live. Have I any pleasure at all that the wicked should die? saith the Lord God: and not that he should return from his ways, and live?" Or else the patience of God is exercised with the aim and intention of inducing his future repentance and conversion. Paul seems to speak of this in Rom. 2^{4} when he asks the impenitent Jew whether he despises the riches of God's mercy, patience and long-suffering? "Dost thou not know that the goodness of God leadeth thee to repentance?" The same point
is made in Rom. $9^{22f.}$, where it is said that although God wills "to show his wrath, and to make [415]
his power known," He has "endured with much longsuffering the vessels of wrath fitted to destruction," in order at the same time "to make known the riches of the glory on the vessels of mercy, which he had afore prepared unto glory." Again in 2 Pet. 3^{9}: "The Lord is not slack concerning his promise, as some men count slackness; but is longsuffering to us-ward, not willing that any should perish, but that all should come to repentance." It was in this sense that in 1 Tim. 1^{16} Paul described himself, who later became by God's mercy the type of faith, as an object of the *μακροθυμία* of Jesus Christ. Under this heading we may also include the remarkable recapitulation of a constantly recurring situation in Israel's history at the beginning of the Book of Judges. According to this survey there is a repeated cycle of Israel's apostasy, God's wrath and Israel's deliverance to its enemies, followed by a new invitation to Israel to return to God, a new manifestation of God's help and deliverance, and then again a fresh apostasy, a fresh outburst of divine wrath and a fresh deliverance to the surrounding nations (Judges 2^{11-22}).

But this raises a problem which has so often involved lax and unworthy conceptions of God's patience. What is the real aim and intention of God when He exercises patience? What is this human penitence for the sake of which, in prospect or retrospect, God contains His anger, sometimes refusing to execute punishment, but giving men further opportunities of life, sometimes punishing only one, but leaving others the gift of life, sometimes mightily destroying but no less mightily saving? Indeed, is there anywhere or at any time a real act of human penitence for the sake of which it is worth while to God to spare men and to give them time and life? Was the human race any better after the Flood than before it? Did it not immediately think it right to build the Tower of Babel? Was not all its penitent zeal only too much like Israel's passing cry for help in the time of the Judges? Where is there in the presentation of the Bible itself a single penitent whose existence really justifies the patience of God and therefore the preservation of the creature? Abraham, Isaac or Jacob? Moses or David? Are there any genuine exceptions to what we read in Is. $65^{1f.}$ "I am sought of them that asked not for me; I am found of them that sought me not: I said, Behold me, unto a nation that was not called by my name. I have stretched out my hands all the day unto a rebellious people, which walketh in a way that was not good, after their own thoughts; a people that provoketh me to anger continually to my face; that sacrificeth in gardens, and burneth incense upon altars of brick; which remain among the graves, and lodge in the monuments, which eat swine's flesh, and the broth of abominable things in their vessels." What, then, is the meaning of the patience of God? Is it not the equivalent of weakness? Does it not mean that God allows Himself to be mocked? For when and where will not both the actual and the anticipated penitence prove a disappointment?

But conversely it might equally well be asked: Where is in fact the patience of God? How often do we not read that God "repented" not only of His anger but also of His kindness and mercy? How often, to how many people, and how destructively His impatience also seems to take effect! How radically His wrath, too, seems to take its course! In spite of everything, how much death and destruction does actually come upon Israel! And in any case, is not the final thing the catastrophic end of this people behind which, according to the New Testament, we see the final catastrophe which overtakes the whole of humanity and indeed the whole universe, a passing away of heaven and earth? (Mt. 24^{35}). Where, then, is the patience of God? What does it really mean when we read in Is. 54^{8}: "In a little wrath I hid my face from thee for a moment; but with everlasting kindness will I have mercy on thee, saith the Lord thy Redeemer"? Or in Ps. 30^{5}: "For his anger endureth but a moment; in his favour is life: weeping may endure for a night, but joy cometh in the morning." Is not this the very opposite of
[416] the truth? Will not a new night of weeping follow upon this morning and finally a night that is without end? Ultimately will it not be found that the kindness and grace of God have been only the affair of a moment, whereas His wrath is the constant and eternal factor and will necessarily have the last word? Has He not always waited and will He not always wait in vain for real penitence? When we keep to the biblical testimony to God's patience, we cannot avoid but we have to ask the question in all seriousness: Is it really possible for God to be patient? And is He actually so? And if we do not at once accept the biblical answer, if we do not frame the question itself in the light of the biblical answer (i.e., if we do not consider that we have not yet touched upon the decisive aspect of the biblical testimony), we can hardly avoid having to give a negative answer to this question. If we look at the human repentance and conversion which are presumably the aim of divine patience, we are forced to say that this patience—if we do not regard it as mere weakness, as a passing failure of God to be God—can in any event be understood only as a temporary and in the last resort external attitude, that it is not rooted in His real and intrinsic being, that it is perhaps a determination of His *opus ad extra*[EN104], but that *ad intra*[EN105] in the proper nature of God there corresponds to it His impatience, so that finally even *ad extra*[EN106] there will correspond to it His wrathful punishment and destruction; a *dies irae*[EN107] in which righteous and unrighteous, pious and impious, penitent and impenitent, will equally fail to stand. This will necessarily be the end, and if God is still to be understood as love, it will be only as a radically impatient love which consumes its object in fire. But if this is so, how strange it is that according to the witness of the Bible this necessary end, and with it the revelation of the inner being of God, is continually deferred! How strange it is that according to the biblical presentation there can be this long interplay of patience and impatience, of mercy and severity, on the part of God, and of repentance and recurrent apostasy on that of man! In the last resort is not this for both partners a needlessly cruel game? In view of the Old Testament, may we not ask whether it is not a cat-and-mouse game which—with an evil, despairing, Promethean defiance, but choosing the lesser of two evils—man may well prefer to decline and evade? Is it not a game in face of which—if it is to be played with us—the best part of wisdom is to close our eyes? This chain of thought—and for those who consider themselves strong enough even its final conclusion—is hardly to be resisted if the decisive moment of the biblical testimony to God's patience is not expressed. But it can and must be expressed, and then the real meaning and basis of the aspects so far touched upon will become clear, and this chain of thought will be arrested.

EN104 work outside of himself
EN105 within himself
EN106 outside of himself
EN107 day of wrath

The decisive moment of the biblical testimony to God's patience is that according to Heb. 1^3 God upholds all things by the Word of His power. By His Word! which means in any event that they are not occasioned by, and dependent on, what becomes manifest and actual from our side as penitence and conversion. What is manifest and actual here is in point of fact the alternation of penitence and impenitence which is sufficiently clear in Israel's example and the final outcome of which will be Israel's impenitence. To this outcome in our experience there could correspond on God's part only the judgment of wrath, and this is actually the case. God cannot sustain all things or the sinful creature in his wretchedness by means of our final word. This word is definitely not effective to uphold all things. But God upholds them by His Word. And this Word as such is powerful. According to Heb. 1^2 it is the Word of the Son by whom He has spoken to us in these last days, i.e., at the end of the days of the fathers and the prophets, whom He has appointed heir of all things, by whom [417]
also He created the worlds, who is the brightness of His glory and the express image of His person. By this His Word in His Son Jesus Christ, He upholds all things and upholds them with power.

"For as the rain cometh down, and the snow from heaven, and returneth not thither, but watereth the earth, and maketh it bring forth and bud, that it may give seed to the sower, and bread to the eater: so shall my word be that goeth forth out of my mouth: it shall not return unto me void, but it shall accomplish that which I please, and it shall prosper in the thing whereto I sent it" (Is. $55^{10f.}$). We have already pointed out in relation to the story of Noah that God obviously gives His creature space in order that in this way He Himself may have space: time for eternity. This fundamental meaning constitutes the invincible victorious power of the divine patience; the reason and the effectiveness by which its exercise is distinguished from the unworthy and cruel game which it would otherwise be. The Word of God has not been spoken to man in vain, and God's Son has not Himself become incarnate in vain. But God's Word was spoken for the sake of God Himself, and therefore, included in the will of God, for the sake of man, and therefore meaningfully and effectively. In other words, God's Son became incarnate for the sake of God Himself, and again therefore, included in the will of God, for the sake of man, and again therefore meaningfully and effectively. Because this happened for God's sake and therefore for man's sake, in spite of all its sinfulness human existence is justified before God by God Himself, and therefore the patience of God, which leaves man his existence and space and time for it, is both well grounded and effective. It is because God's Word goes forth out of God's mouth, because God's Word cannot return to Him void out of our impenitent penitence, that God is patient and grants space and time. Strictly speaking, He grants it to His Word and therefore to Himself. He has time. And the fact that He has time for us is what characterises His whole activity towards us as an exercise of patience. Included in this exercise of patience is both God's mercy and punishment, God's salvation and destruction, God's healing and smiting. This all takes place in the course and service of the revelation of His Word. By it all Israel is instructed in the divine Word. It all means that God always, and continually, has time for Israel. That Israel has time to hear God's Word, and therefore time to live for the sake of God's Word and by its power, is shown—only symbolically and provisionally but nevertheless truly—in the very stumbling-block of the alternation of penitence and impenitence in which Israel receives this instruction. And the predominating measure of impenitence reminds us that we have to do primarily and decisively with the will and being of the righteous and holy God and not

with the intrinsic merits of man, that man can appropriate this instruction and set up this symbol only in so far as he is justified and sanctified by God, that without the aid of God's Word he cannot and will not provide the token of penitence and repentance, and therefore that in himself he cannot and will not have time, he cannot and will not be the object of God's patience. That in all this, again, Israel receives time from God, time to hear God's Word and therefore time to live for the sake of God's Word and by its power, is shown—again only symbolically and provisionally but nevertheless truly—in the further stumbling-block of the alternation of grace and judgment, mercy and punishment, salvation and ruin, in which God gives this instruction to Israel. And again the apparent prevalence of judgment, punishment and ruin shews that it is God's Word which must be heard in these signs and tokens, and for the sake of which He has time for mankind, so that it must always appear a miracle to man that in this connexion, included in the will of God to speak with him, he too, man
[418] himself, continually acquires and has time and acquires it again. It is in this way, however, in the language of God's Word characterised and made unequivocal by this very alternation, that man receives time from God and lives in virtue of God's patience—certainly in order to repent and convert, yet not in virtue of his penitence, but in virtue of God's patience.

But to see and hear and feel and recognise the power of this patience means to believe in Jesus Christ. As regards the question where and when genuine fruits of penitence have been brought forth, in consideration of which it is worth God's while to have patience with man and therefore to grant him space and time, the answer must be that such fruits have never been brought forth at any time or place except in Jesus Christ, but that they have been produced genuinely and finally and in sufficient measure for us all in the perfect obedience which He, the one and only direct and true hearer of God's Word, has rendered in human flesh. For His sake, as it is said in Rom. 3[25f.], the divine *ἀνοχή*[EN108] deemed it worth while to overlook sins committed in times past—and in comparison with the time of Christ all other time is past time, an old aeon—in which sins had remained unpunished through the forbearance of God (*διὰ τὴν πάρεσιν τῶν προγεγονότων ἁμαρτημάτων ἐν τῇ ἀνοχῇ τοῦ θεοῦ*[EN109]). For the sake of these times and the sins committed in them God has manifested His righteousness in Jesus Christ. But obviously the converse is also true. For the sake of manifesting His righteousness in Jesus Christ, God exercised *ἀνοχή*[EN110] in these times. In these times, therefore, there was a *πάρεσις τῶν ἁμαρτημάτων*[EN111]. Certainly there was judgment, punishment and destruction. But in and through it all there was a divine patience, a living and letting live in relation to the creature.

The position is now clear that God's patience does not leave man to his own devices. His jealous zeal in and for the creature cannot be more powerfully manifested than in the incarnation of His Word. He has espoused the cause of the creature to the final depths. From this point of view the divine patience certainly cannot consist in an indifferent self-withdrawal of God in relation to its being, action and destiny. If He allows the many to go their own ways, if He leaves them their freedom, if He gives continual time (and food for it), if through it all He constantly waits for them, He does so for the simple reason that He has already overtaken them in the One, His only Son, that in Him He has already walked with them in His own way and at His own time, and to the

---

[EN108] forebearance
[EN109] because God in his forebearance had overlooked sins previously committed
[EN110] forebearance
[EN111] an overlooking of sins

very end. He does so because, in the One in whom He has given Himself utterly to all, they have already fallen into His hand. He does so because this One stands in place of them all and for them all has accomplished the genuine penitence which was expected from all. For the sake of this One, God has patience with the many.

For the sake of this One, there is space and time for the many. It is not that they have deserved this or ever will or can deserve it by their ambiguous and, in the last resort, insincere penitence. Nor is it, of course, that space and time have been granted to enable them to continue in their impenitence. It is rather that they might have space and time to appropriate the life which has been secured for them by the sincere penitence of that One—space and time to believe in Him in whom as their Head their penitence becomes sincere and acceptable to God. Because there, in the One, the zeal of God is so powerful and attains its goal, therefore the others, the many who are summed up in Him, who in Him are conducted to the goal and have already attained it, can as the many be at their various times on the way—the way of faith on which their footsteps follow His, their freedom is an acknowledg- [419]
ment of His freedom, their time a sharing of His time, and therefore contemporary with Him. To go the way of faith is what God's patience leaves to them and concedes to them. Therefore the meaning of the divine patience is a summons to have faith. We have only to think of the object of faith, of the one Jesus Christ, to believe in whom the many are called by the patience of God, to realise that in the tarrying of the divine patience there can be no question of the indifference of God to His creature, but that this very tarrying of God is His decisive action and work in relation to it.

It is also clear that there can be no question of disappointment or self-deception on the part of God with respect to the sincerity, or insincerity, of the human penitence for which He waits in His patience. God is not short-sighted, nor is He subject to any optimistic illusions, when again and again He saves and preserves Israel only to reap continually wild grapes instead of grapes. God does not, then, experience any disillusionment with regard to His people, the many. He knows very well what is our frame. But because He knows it, He has good ground for being patient with us—the ground which He Himself has created and laid down. His self-restraint in regard to the many is justified by the fact that in the midst of the many, in the person of the One whom He Himself has appointed Head of these many and their Representative before Him, that which He awaits has taken place and is fulfilled, the obedience which He demands from His creature has been rendered.

Because this has happened, because in this happening God Himself has taken action on behalf of the many, something has happened which makes it possible for God in faithfulness to Himself to be faithful to us too; faithful even in the sense that He can leave us our existence although we ourselves in our own strength, i.e., apart from what has taken place on our behalf in Jesus Christ, cannot produce any justification of our existence. We are reminded of the fact that we cannot do so by the judgment, punishment and destruction to which, tacitly or openly, our existence is continually exposed. These things recall to us our true limits, i.e., refer us to that by which alone we are preserved from the outbreak of the objective anger and judgment of God. They refer us to Jesus Christ and to faith in Him. But in Jesus Christ and by faith in Him we are able in supreme reality to produce a justification, the justification of our existence. In the midst of the judgments and punishments which smite us we can and should find comfort and, indeed, glory in the fact that it is not all up with us. This is not because we have not deserved such an outcome. It is because rightfully—not by denying but by fully asserting His holiness and righteousness—God Himself has seen to it that this cannot be the final outcome for us, that our preservation is meaningful and necessary. It is necessary because God has linked His own life with ours, and has sacrificed Himself for us so that as truly as God Himself lives we cannot perish. As we are summoned by the patience of God to the life of faith, we are invited to seize and affirm this objective divine justification of our existence and with it the justification of the divine patience itself, for our own part giving God the glory which He has assured Himself by creating and establishing this ground for His patience.

Again, it is clear that even the judgments and punishments of God, the whole severity of His conduct towards Israel, do not contradict the truth that [420] He actually wills to maintain and not destroy His creature. They are all temporary and as such symbolic judgments and punishments. They are not the outbreak of the genuine wrath and judgment of God. They are not the eternal death, the abandonment and precipitation into nothingness, which Israel and with Israel all humanity has deserved. They are all to be included in the sway of God's patience. That which we all deserved has been suffered in our place and in Israel's place by the only righteous One, who achieved a perfect penitence—although He had no need of it for Himself—by not refusing to take upon Himself the genuine wrath and judgment of God. Because He has done this in His function as the One who could take our place and suffer for us as our Head, all that which we with Israel have to suffer is shown to be included in the government of God's patience, a reminder of our own incapacity to justify ourselves but also a reminder of the God who justifies us by Himself.

By His own suffering He has characterised our suffering as a token of life and not of death, as a token of His friendship and not of His enmity, as a token which is meant to awaken and maintain and not destroy our faith. It is the shadow of death under which our life stands, the shadow of the eternal death which Jesus Christ has suffered for us. It is this which lends it its seriousness, but takes from this seriousness its absoluteness, thus preventing it from giving rise to fear. It is only the shadow of eternal death. We shall not have to drink this cup. And it is the shadow of the eternal death suffered by Jesus Christ. Thus, although it is a real and a serious shadow—and this cannot be contested or argued away—it is the token of life, eternal life. And it is also the token of the continual maintenance of our life in time by Him and for His sake: that we might have time and space to believe in Him, to believe in His penitence, and in His penitence in the sincerity of our own intrinsically imperfect penitence.

Therefore, as all this becomes clear to us, as we apprehend the Word of God and Jesus Christ to be the power which sustains all things, the power which supported Israel for forty years in the wilderness (Ac. 13[18]), the power of the self-restraint in virtue of which God overlooked the times of ignorance (Ac. 17[30]) and was able to forgive the sins committed in these times (Rom. 3[25]), as we hear this Word as God's eternal Word spoken to us, we hear the decisive Word, the central truth of the biblical testimony to God's patience.

We had to ask first: What is the meaning of God's patience in view of our own proven impenitence? And again: Where is His patience in view of the manifest judgments and punishments of God which come upon us too? Can God be patient? And is He really so? Well, these questions can and necessarily will have to be asked so long as we have not heard the Word of God among the words of the Bible. But the open secret of the whole Bible is precisely the Word of God itself. In His Word God becomes the Protector and Avenger of the murderer Cain. He saves Noah and concludes a covenant with him and his heirs, although they are no better and become no better than the people destroyed in the Flood. He remains patient when Jonah the prophet would call down His impatience over godless Nineveh and his own head. In His Word He is patient even where He strikes and slays, for as He does so He utters His Word and establishes a sign of fellowship between Himself and the creature. Put the two questions side by side. In the light of the central answer and truth of the Bible it is clear that they cancel out each other.

We must accept the fact that God can be patient because He is patient in His Word. While we can still hear it, He keeps time and space for us who have forfeited our existence in His sight and are unable to justify ourselves. We must also learn that God is patient from the fact that He can be patient in His Word which is Himself, that is to say, He can have time and space for us, i.e., for faith. If we believe in His Word, we can no longer doubt either the reality or the possibility of His patience. [421]

From the point of view of faith in His Word there can be no justification for the conception, to which these questions seem to point, of a finally and essentially impatient God, or of the impatient love which consumes its object. For the same reason there can be no question of a game which God plays partly with Himself and partly and even more with us. Nor can there be any place for a possible Promethean defiance in which man tries to evade this game. Ideas like this can arise only outside the sphere of faith in God's Word, i.e., only where the central truth of the biblical testimony to God's patience has not yet been spoken to us or appropriated by us. Belief in God's Word, i.e., in Jesus Christ, will necessarily destroy at its root this whole sequence of thought. The truth which it distorts is, rightly expressed, that we have not deserved God's patience, and that His patience is effectual towards us even in judgment and punishment. But the former does not mean that God cannot be patient, nor does the latter mean that He is not so, or only partially so. On the contrary, His Word is the ground of our confidence, and in His Word He gives us His pledge that He can be patient and is so in fact. In His Word He waits for us to give Him the glory in faith, accepting both the possibility and the reality of His patience. God is the One who lives in His Word and He is no other. In Him is possible and real what is possible and real in His Word. If God reveals His patience to us in His Word, God is the very possibility and reality of patience itself. The way is thus closed both to a God of impatience and also to the Promethean defiance of a man who presumes to lose patience with God. The only way open to us now is the way of gratitude for our life which has been undeservedly left to us; the way which will become and be of itself the way of the patience that we now have to show in suffering the judgments and punishments which strike us. The fact that, in spite of our infinite guilt, we are permitted to suffer them in the fellowship and shadow of the innocent suffering of Christ, by which we have been spared the suffering of the eternal wrath and judgment of God, is sufficient reason for us to suffer them patiently and to allow them to serve the purpose which they have for us: the conversion from every illusion of our own worthiness ; the return to the One who has made us worthy of God, to faith, therefore, in which we can give ourselves to the God who in His Son has taken our cause into His own hands. The relationship with Jesus Christ in which we must suffer is sufficient to over-rule our suffering and the gift of our whole life for good

(Rom. 8^{28}). In this relationship the worst and the harshest thing that we can encounter, and do encounter, is our inevitable death in time, with which we must finally profess this relationship. But even this, the imminent end of all things, is not only not unbearable—for in its unbearable reality it has all been borne for us by Jesus Christ—but is in fact the outwardly bitter, yet inwardly sweet, promise of the eternal life which has been won for us by Him. To grasp this promise, to be permitted to live with it already in this life as with the certainty in comparison with which everything else pales into uncertainty—this is what is meant by believing in God's Word. From this standpoint we can see the truth of Is. 54^{8} and Ps. 30^{5}: the outburst of God's anger is only the affair of a moment. We do not have to endure and suffer even this moment. It is in truth the moment when Jesus cried with a loud voice: "My God, my
[422] God, why hast thou forsaken me?" (Mk. 15^{34}). But has not this moment in all its darkness all the attributes of that other moment when the trumpet shall sound and the dead shall be raised incorruptible? In any case, there corresponds to this very moment the eternal loving-kindness, the lifelong enduring grace and favour of God. The sufferings of this present time, which reflect both the light and shadow of this moment, are nothing in comparison with the glory which shall be revealed in us (Rom. $8^{17f.}$). If we suffer with Him in this hope, and we believe according to God's Word that we have to suffer with Jesus Christ in this hope, we can and may and must suffer in patience: answering His patience with our patience; giving the right answer to the waiting of His wrath with our waiting for redemption.

If now, coming to a provisional conclusion, we balance or confront the idea of the patience with that of the wisdom of God, the meaning of this juxtaposition is essentially the same as that of the juxtapositions which we have already made. In God wisdom is related to patience as is holiness to grace, and righteousness to mercy. All these ideas express and translate the love of God. But the second set of ideas—holiness, righteousness and wisdom—express with greater distinctness than the first (grace, mercy and patience) the fact that it is His free and therefore distinctively divine love. That God in Himself and in all His works is gracious and therefore holy, merciful and therefore righteous, patient and therefore wise, is the proof and essence of the divinity of His love according to the main theme of the section and the explanations already adduced. We have taken care to speak of the ideas of the grace, mercy and patience of God in such a way that there cannot arise any material antithesis to the ideas of the second category, but that the depth and majesty of all these perfections of the divine love in the divine freedom should, as far as possible, be visible in their proper content. Yet Holy Scripture itself does not allow us to stop here, but leads us at once to survey and think about the same matter from the other side, which is not opposite but in the one hidden being of God distinct. The recognition of the depth and majesty of divine grace called for a special consideration of the divine holiness. The recognition of the depth and majesty of the mercy of God called for a special consideration of His righteousness. Our experience would have been the same if we had begun with the second set of ideas. In our next section we shall in fact begin with the ideas which more definitely characterise and describe the freedom of God as His love. And we shall then find the same thing. The recognition of the attributes of the divine freedom in their depth and majesty will require a special consideration of those attributes which, on the other hand, characterise and describe the divine freedom as the freedom of divine love. The distinctive feature of the knowledge of God and of God Himself is that He is all that He is in particular, apart, newly and differently in the inexhaustible plenitude of His [423] one being, so that in all that He is He wills to be considered and apprehended in particular, apart, newly and differently.

So now, in connexion with the perfections of the divine love, the depth and majesty of God's patience call for a special consideration of His wisdom. The depth and majesty of God's patience, as we have seen, consist in the fact that He upholds all things by His powerful Word. In this it is distinguished from all impatience, but no less from all the weak, non-divine and therefore false patience which derives from indifference or weakness or shortsightedness. In this it is one, not only with the grace and mercy, but also with the holiness and righteousness of God. But, as is evident in the central biblical witness, this secret is a special characteristic in God requiring special consideration. God's Word, revealing the depth and majesty of His patience, is God's will expressed and to be accepted as such from all eternity; subject to no higher appeal; thankfully and obediently to be accepted because it is His will. But again, God does not reveal Himself and is not God in such a way that His expressed will is not in itself and as such light and recognisable as light. God's will expressed in His Word is neither in itself nor in its manifestation of such a kind that it can even be comparable, let alone identical, with an abyss of what is ultimately chance or caprice. We are not being led to the edge of this type of abyss when we are invited to recognise the majesty and depth of the patience of God in the power of His Word. There is no magic about what God has performed and completed in His Son. No *sacrificium intellectus*[EN112] is required of us to know this happening, to know the divine being as the ground of the divine patience which we encounter. In this whole matter of recognising the activity and ruling of His love, it is not a question of our being blinded but of our becoming clear-sighted. If His Word is His declared will, it is of the very nature of its being as His Word that it is not merely truth—as such it could still be the disclosure of an abyss of ultimate chance or caprice—but also wisdom. That is to say, it is meaningful in itself, and it shows itself to be meaningful to us who hear it. The wisdom of God is that God not only wills but knows what He wills. And He knows not only what He wills, but why and wherefore He wills it. And He wills only that of which He knows the why and wherefore, of which the why and wherefore is then His own meaning, plan and intention. To this extent there is in it light and no darkness. Because His Word is His wisdom, because the power of His Word is, therefore, the power of His wisdom, His patience is wise, and the grateful recognition of it is at the same time the recognition and adoration of His wisdom. It is not a closing but an opening of our eyes. It is not suspension of the real knowledge of God, but the basis for it. All other secrets—secrets which are neither directly nor indirectly the secret of God's

[EN112] sacrifice of the intellect

[424] patience—are fortuitous and capricious. What the creature in himself, i.e., apart from God and His revelation, considers to be wise, intelligible and purposeful, is fortuitous and capricious. The Word of God, however, as the foundation of His patience is neither fortuitous nor capricious. The Word of God shines as light in the darkness. When we hear it, we hear the reason, meaning, purpose and intention of God. When we hear it, we are instructed, enlightened, knowing and wise. When we hear it, the darkness of chance is lightened. If, then, on the basis of the revealed Word we accept our existence as something conceded to us for the sake of the one Jesus Christ, and if we accept the punishments and judgments which threaten and mark our existence as necessary and redemptive for the sake of our fellowship with Jesus Christ, this very acceptance signifies the acceptance of reason, of the sense and purpose for our life, for which it is not only intended, as surely as we are God's creatures, but which as the sense and purpose of God are the only satisfying sense and purpose, the only reason which our life can accept, because in the last resort they are the only ones there are, and in comparison with them everything else that may be described as such is only senselessness, purposelessness and unreason.

The Word of God which determines us to accept our existence as a gift of God's patience, Jesus Christ Himself, is the one reason, sense and purpose. We repel all reason, sense and purpose and relapse into darkness if we refuse to accept the order of the divine patience. On rational grounds, i.e., the one ground that here and only here we have the possibility of accepting reason, we really cannot not believe. This is the wisdom of God in its general connexion with His patience. This is the special characteristic of God in the power of His Word which makes His patience possible and real.

Before proceeding further it will be useful to extend our lines of reference backwards. The fact that God knows why and wherefore He wills what He wills, that He wills only that of which He knows the why and wherefore, is something which is also to be said of His grace and mercy. These perfections of God and the fact that He turns to His creature and takes its misery to heart, could still stand perhaps in the shadow of a slight suspicion. They are true, no doubt, but it might easily be otherwise. The freedom in which we see God manifest these perfections and give Himself still bears some resemblance to chance or accident. Why is it that God is gracious and merciful? We cannot, of course, try as it were to climb over God Himself with this Why? We cannot try to justify Him from above, measuring Him by this or that standard of value and reasonableness. Nor is it as if there is no answer to this Why? in God Himself, or as if we ourselves cannot understand this answer or know God Himself as the One in whom there is an answer to this question. The answer is that God is wise. He knows why and to what end He is gracious. And this is not something dark in
[425] itself, but intrinsically illuminating, intelligible and purposeful. The recognition of it does not mean that we are plunged into darkness but, on the contrary, that we are delivered from the darkness of ignorance and brought into the light of a reason hitherto concealed from us, but now revealing itself as

something we have to accept. God is not guilty of impulsiveness or irrationality when He is gracious and merciful, any more than He is of a surrender of His holiness and righteousness. He is not, then, overcome by a whim or a chance inspiration. He is not capricious. But in this as in every other respect He is the God of order. And His order, the order of His wisdom, is that in Himself and in all His works He is gracious and merciful. He would not be gracious, but ungracious; He would not be merciful, but unmerciful ; or He would be gracious and merciful only weakly and ineffectively, like a creature, if He were not wise. But He is gracious and merciful just because and as He is wise. Again, a connexion must be made with His perfect holiness and righteousness. Here too, perhaps, there remains the shadow of a suspicion. Must we evade the question why God is so zealous to affirm Himself in His holiness or to vindicate Himself in His righteousness? Could it perhaps be otherwise? Is the unity between His grace and holiness or His mercy and righteousness only a kind of freak or accident, a *factum brutum*[EN113] which is simply there and has to be accepted by us as such? Why is God holy and righteous? Why as such is He also gracious and merciful? Here again, of course, there is not as it were a Therefore which we can pronounce about God from without or above. But here too there is the Therefore of wisdom in God Himself. His holiness has nothing to do with defiance nor His justice with tyranny. And the unity of the grace and holiness and the mercy and righteousness of God has nothing to do with a "paradox," as has often been alleged. But the mystery with which these things confront us is that of the reason, meaning and purpose which God has in Himself, which He Himself is. It is the mystery of His wisdom. If He were not wise He would not be holy and righteous, nor gracious and merciful, and still less both in one. He is holy and righteous just because and as He is wise. Strictly speaking, there is no confidence or freedom in our knowledge of God apart from what we have to learn at this final stage. For if God is for us an abyss of chance and caprice, if as far as possible we regard the irrational as the essentially divine, we neither have nor can have any real confidence in relation to God. For confidence is based on the appreciation of reason, meaning and order. So long as we do not have this, the knowledge of God cannot give us any freedom. For freedom comes only from the recognition of reason, meaning and order, and not from the consideration of chaos, chance or caprice. We can only say once again that it all depends absolutely on how far we recognise God as wisdom. God is wise in so far as His whole activity, as willed by Him, is also thought out by Him, and thought out by Him from the very outset with correctness and completeness, so that it is an intelligent and to that extent a reli- [426]
able and liberating activity. We have to say of His activity in His works and also of His inner activity, of the essential actuality of His divine being, that God is wise, that in Him is wisdom. God Himself is wisdom.

EN113 brute fact

Polanus and Quenstedt, whom we have so far consulted for the orthodox doctrine of God, fail us at this point. For Polanus (*Synt. Theol. chr.*, 1609, *col.* 998 ff.) the wisdom of God seems to be dissolved in the general idea of divine knowledge as omniscience. It is, of course, true that God's all-powerful knowledge is the knowledge of His wisdom. But it must be realised first of all that wisdom constitutes the intelligence and rationality of God's love. It is only in this way that it can be understood as the source of God's all-powerful omniscience. Again, Quenstedt (*Theol. did. pol.*, 1685, I, *c.* 8, *sect.* I, *th.* 26) can really say about the wisdom of God only that as divine and therefore hidden wisdom it surpasses all human knowledge and understanding. This is also true; but it does not alter the fact that, like all the divine perfections, it forms the substance of His self-revelation and is therefore an object of faith, and to that extent of human knowledge. It safeguards the truth that God's wisdom surpasses our insight and understanding. But in a Christian doctrine of God the truth must also be safeguarded that God's wisdom is as determinative of His love as are His holiness and righteousness. H. Cremer (*op. cit.*, p. 69 f.) defines the wisdom of God at once as the transcendence of His saving counsel in contrust with the law of logical consistency current in the world. This again is true. But just because it is so true, it is advisable to pause and consider further that this God who vindicates the validity of His saving counsel in opposition to the world is Himself as such the source of all true logical consistency. More helpful in this connexion is the view of H. Heidegger. He, too, subordinates the *sapientia Dei*[EN114] to the idea of divine knowledge. But he gives the fuller definition that it is the quality of the divine being *per quam novit, quibus rationibus res ab eodem producendae gloriam suam illustrare queant, ut eas convenienter suae naturae, perfectioni et gloriae vocare et velle possit*[EN115]. It is the *moderatrix consiliorum Dei, per quam sic ad decentiam divinam gloriae suae attendit, ne veritati, ordini, pulchritudini in ulla verborum vel operum eius parte desit*[EN116] (*Corp. Theol.*, 1700, III, 65, quoted from H. Heppe, *Dogm. d. ev. ref. K.*, 1935, 49 f.). The allusion to the divine *convenientia*[EN117] or *decentia*[EN118] obviously reminds us of the connexion between the wisdom and the holiness and righteousness of God. In God's wisdom, too, it is a question of what is worthy of God as God, what befits Him as He loves. It befits Him to affirm Himself and to carry through His plans. In this reside His holiness and righteousness. But in both these *moderatio*[EN119] is also proper to Him (and here we are reminded of God's patience). By this they are both conjoined with His divine glory, rooted in it and related to it. In this relationship His holiness and righteousness, His whole being and doing, have truth, order, beauty, meaning, purpose and reason. In this foundation and relationship consists His wisdom.

The wisdom of God is the inner truth and clarity with which the divine life in its self-fulfilment and its works justifies and confirms itself and in which it is the source and sum and criterion of all that is clear and true. It is in this inner truth and clarity that God loves, and this is the source of the dignity with which He is free in His love. In it He also demonstrates the legitimacy, necessity and the sufficiency of His divine existence and action. God is glorious in His wisdom. He attests Himself as God by attesting His wisdom.

[EN114] wisdom of God

[EN115] by which he knows in what ways things can be arranged by his person for the extension of his glory, so that he can know them and will them more conveniently to his nature, perfection and glory

[EN116] moderator of the counsels of God, by which he is concerned with the divine propriety of his glory, so that no part of his words or deeds is not lacking in truth, order, or beauty

[EN117] convenience

[EN118] propriety

[EN119] moderation

The basic meaning of *sapientia*[EN120] is taste, that of σοφία[EN121] tact and skill, that of "wisdom" a right orientation. All such words obviously offer correct interpretations of the wisdom of God, for they all emphasise certain qualities which are integral to it. But the root meaning of *chokmah* is that of firmness and steadfastness, and we must think primarily on these lines if we are to speak of the wisdom of God and not another wisdom. The divine taste and skill and right orientation can be known only from the indication given by the Old Testament word. The truth that God is wise must, like His holiness and righteousness, mean primarily that He is steadfast and self-consistent. It is in this that He shows His intelligence, He who needs to apprehend nothing outside His own being, whose apprehension of realities distinct from Himself is already an exercise of His grace, mercy and patience, but who can also and does apprehend what is outside Himself, grace and mercy and patience being His most inward and proper being. The fact that God apprehends Himself and is therefore eternal reason, that He lives and is active in Himself in truth and clarity, attesting Himself, magnifying His own glory and to this extent being firm and steadfast and self-consistent—this is the wisdom of God which in His activity, His works *ad extra*, is revealed as His taste or sense for what will serve its supreme and ultimately its only purpose, His skill in making it contribute to this purpose, His orientation and therefore His guidance, the controlling providence and rule which He exercises in and over this activity. It is to be noted that the wisdom of God characterises His whole activity as reliable and liberating, as something in which we can have confidence, just because His wisdom consists in and finally evinces itself as His firmness and self-consistency, the satisfaction of His *decentia*[EN122] or *convenientia divina*[EN123]. When God is apprehended as the One who under all circumstances is intelligence and reason in this way, purposing and deciding and speaking and acting on this basis, the knowledge of God means that we can have confidence in Him, that we can be free, that all the uncertainty and darkness of the capricious and irrational is ended. [427]

That according to biblical insight the wisdom of God is actually bound up with His patience is clear from the fact that just where the idea is to some extent clearly unfolded in the Bible it is defined as a wisdom which creates, maintains and rules the world and therefore as the proper instrument of divine providence. Because God is Himself the truth and clarity which justifies, confirms and attests itself, He can allow time, space and existence to another beside Himself without uncertainty, danger or infidelity, as the Lord of this other, and to the praise of His own glory. And He does all this with the same truth and clarity. In this way His wisdom is the meaning of His patience and forbearance. In this way it is the meaning of the world.

But note—in this way and not in any other! God is not the immanent meaning of the world. The world has meaning as it acquires meaning from Him who alone has and is meaning. The difference between biblical wisdom and the world-idea of the Stoics and Philo and others is quite clear when we realise from the more immediate and wider context of the relevant passages that in the Bible wisdom is related not only to the divine patience but to the divine grace and mercy, and that it is also far too closely related to God's holiness and righteousness to allow the emergence of the idea to be explained by reference to the pressure of the Hellenic need to find a principle of world-interpretation.

EN120 wisdom
EN121 wisdom
EN122 propriety
EN123 divine convenience

That the main wisdom passages belong to the third part of the Canon of the Old Testament, and shew more or less clearly the historical contact between Israel and Greece, does not imply an acceptance of foreign interests and ideas, but that there has been here a confrontation of the Israelite conception of God with these alien concerns and ideas. If the God [428] of Israel is the God of grace, mercy and patience, it must be said on the one hand that God creates, maintains and governs all that is in His patience and therefore for His own sake and for the sake of His glory. He has determined everything that is as an arena for His activity. Therefore it exists by Him. This connexion of its determination by Him with its creation, maintenance and ruling by Him is the wisdom of God. And, on the other hand, in the actual being and nature of the creature we do not see the reign of chance and caprice, but of God's patience which has determined it as a theatre for His action and therefore created it out of nothing and still preserves and governs it. Therefore, the connexion between the actual being and its nature, and this its determination, is the wisdom of God.

Because it stands in this unity with the divine patience and therefore with all the other attributes of the God of Israel, because then it is really the wisdom of this God, it can and must appear as it actually does in Prov. $1^{20f.}$, and again $8^{1f.}$, not as a logical-ethical principle but as a person, and obviously indeed as a prophetic person: "Wisdom crieth without; she uttereth her voice in the streets: she crieth in the chief place of concourse, in the openings of the gates; in the city she uttereth her words" (Prov. 1^{20-21}). And therefore it comes about that the content of what it cries, preaches and proclaims is clearly nothing other than the well-known preaching of repentance, judgment and salvation, and even the wording might easily be that of a prophet: "How long, ye simple ones, will ye love simplicity? and the scorners delight in their scorning, and fools hate knowledge? Turn you at my reproof: behold, I will pour out my spirit unto you, I will make known my words unto you. Because I have called, and ye refused; I have stretched out my hand, and no man regarded; but ye have set at nought all my counsel, and would none of my reproof: I also will laugh at your calamity; I will mock when your fear cometh; when your fear cometh as desolation, and your destruction cometh as a whirlwind; when distress and anguish cometh upon you. Then shall they call upon me, but I will not answer; they shall seek me early, but they shall not find me: for that they hated knowledge, and did not choose the fear of the Lord: they would none of my counsel: they despised all my reproof. Therefore shall they eat of the fruit of their own way, and be filled with their own devices" (Prov. 1^{22-23}). Of the wisdom which acts and expresses itself in this way it is then said in Prov. $3^{19f.}$: "The Lord by wisdom hath founded the earth; by understanding hath he established the heavens. By his knowledge the depths are broken up, and the clouds drop down the dew." But do we not read the same in Jer. 10^{12}: "It is the Lord who hath made the earth by his power, he hath established the world by his wisdom, and hath stretched out the heavens by his discretion"? The full meaning of the cosmological determination of divine wisdom in Prov. $3^{19f.}$ may be seen from the rest of the chapter. Very simply it explains and emphasises both the threats and the affirmations made in regard to wisdom—that the merchandise of it is better than the merchandise of silver, and the gain thereof than fine gold (v. 14). "Length of days is in her right hand; and in her left hand riches and honour" (v. 16). "She is a tree of life to them that lay hold upon her; and happy is every one that retaineth her" (v. 18). "Then shalt thou walk in thy way safely, and thy foot shall not stumble. When thou liest down, thou shalt not be afraid: yea, thou shalt lie down, and thy sleep shall be sweet. Be not afraid of sudden fear, neither of the desolation of the wicked, when it cometh" (vv. 23–25). How far is all that true? To the extent that by the same wisdom everything has been created and is maintained (v. 19 f.). To the extent that it does in fact guard man and bring him continued life. And when its preaching of repentance, judgment and salvation is accepted, these its promises become true. Its preaching ? No, God's own preaching! For how can any other "hypostasis" than that of God's revelation

speak and preach and promise? How can even vv. 18 ff.—in what abstraction they would have to be read to be understood in this way!—suddenly have the character of an independent attempt at world interpretation, and wisdom therefore the character of an intermediary [429]
between God and the world? What we learn from this chapter is, in fact, that there is no such independent principle of world interpretation, but only the self-explanation of God, the explanation of His own wisdom which is effective because incidentally it does actually explain the world. And therefore it moves necessarily to the express conclusion: "For the Lord shall be thy confidence, and shall keep thy foot from being taken" (v. 26). It is in just the same context that we must read the even more famous passage (Prov. 8^{22-31}) where again wisdom itself speaks in the following terms: "The Lord possessed me in the beginning of his way, before his works of old. I was set up from everlasting, from the beginning, or ever the earth was. When there were no depths, I was brought forth; when there were no fountains abounding with water. Before the mountains were settled, before the hills was I brought forth; while as yet he had not made the earth, nor the fields, nor the highest part of the dust of the world. When he prepared the heavens, I was there: when he set a compass upon the face of the depth: when he established the clouds above: when he strengthened the foundations of the deep: when he gave to the sea his decree, that the waters should not pass his commandment: when he appointed the foundations of the earth: then I was with him, as one brought up with him: and I was daily his delight, rejoicing always before him; rejoicing in the habitable part of the earth; and my delights were with the sons of men." Even more plainly than in ch. 3 we find here that as God's eternal work produced before all other works as His first attestation and therefore as His witness, intermediary and companion in the creation of all other works, wisdom is equated with God Himself, so that again and more emphatically than before we are told that all the works of God testify to His wisdom as to His first and original work. Here, too, we have only to read the beginning and end of the chapter to be convinced that there is no independent attempt at interpreting the universe even in this exalted cosmological section. Why is it that wisdom has to be described in this way? Obviously to emphasise, for example: "I love them that love me; and those that seek me early shall find me" (v. 17). Or v. 35: "For whoso findeth me findeth life." Obviously to emphasise generally the exhortations of wisdom which precede and follow. The emphasising of these exhortations of this practical revelation of wisdom, i.e., the emphasising of this divine address, consists in the fact that the same wisdom, the same God whose exhortations are summed up in the beginning and end of the chapter, is characterised as the One who has created the world and sustains and rules it in His patience, who therefore has every right to expect that His exhortation will be needed in the sphere of this world, the ground which has been created and is maintained and ruled by Him alone. Those who do not heed it cut the only possible ground from under their feet. Those who do heed it live in accordance with the meaning of every creaturely possibility of life. If we doubt this inference from Prov. 3 and 8 because there it can "only" be drawn from the context and is not made explicit, the desired plainness is to be found at the close of Job 28, which is just as relevant in this connexion. In what is an exact parallel to Prov. 8 we read there: "To make the weight for the winds; and he weigheth the waters by measure. When he made a decree for the rain, and a way for the lightning of the thunder: then did he see it, and declare it; he prepared it, yea, and searched it out." And the immediate continuation is as follows: "And unto man he said, Behold, the fear of the Lord, that is wisdom; and to depart from evil is understanding" (Job $28^{25f.}$). But the very same verse stands at the beginning of Proverbs itself: "The fear of the Lord is the beginning of knowledge; but fools despise wisdom and instruction" (Prov. 1^{7}). It is also repeated in Prov. $9^{10f.}$: "The fear of the Lord is the beginning of wisdom: and the knowledge of the holy is understanding. For by me thy days shall be multiplied, and the years of thy life

[430] shall be increased. If thou be wise, thou shalt be wise for thyself: but if thou scornest, thou alone shalt bear it." Lady Folly, on the other hand, is "clamorous, simple and knoweth nothing" (9^{13}). She obviously bases her message on the assumption :"Whoso is simple, let him turn in hither" (9^{16}), and failure to understand life is what she brings to the man whom she invites into her house: "But he knoweth not that the dead are there; and that her guests are in the depths of hell" (9^{18}). The "sum of the matter" at the close of Ecclesiastes is in similar terms: "Fear God, and keep his commandments: for this is the whole duty of man. For God shall bring every work into judgment, with every secret thing, whether it be good, or whether it be evil" (Eccl. $12^{13f.}$). What is the meaning of all this? Divine wisdom is obviously the meaning and ground of creation and therefore of the sphere in which man can live. The whole art of living and understanding life consists in heeding and accepting divine wisdom and in this way becoming wise. But what is this heeding and accepting of the divine wisdom which distinguishes the wise man from the fool and which alone promises the possibility of life in this sphere? It is here that we have the apparent *μετάβασις εἰς ἄλλο γένος* which differentiates the Old Testament from all Greek teaching about wisdom. For this heeding and accepting in the fear of God, which alone can save and maintain, consists in an attitude to the divine wisdom active in the creating, ruling and sustaining of the world which is determined by the fact that this wisdom is at the same time holy and just, that it is the meaning and the basis of God's patience with man. The wisdom which man must strive to attain and which is required of him according to the Old Testament is an attitude which corresponds with this divine wisdom. For the further elucidation of this matter, notice that we have the same saying in Ps. 111^{10}: "The fear of the Lord is the beginning of wisdom: a good understanding have all they that do his commandments : his praise endureth for ever." But here the exhortation forms the conclusion of a recalling of the works of God which have taken place and still take place in His covenant with His people: "He sent redemption unto his people: he hath commanded his covenant for ever: holy and reverend is his name" (v. 9). If to fear this Lord is the beginning of wisdom, His wisdom is obviously something very different from an abstract world principle and the recognition of it. Similarly the human wisdom corresponding to it is very different from abstract assent to a particular explanation of the universe. On the contrary, it is settled that He and He alone is the world principle who in His revelation to Israel acts as the holy and righteous One. And the only world-explanation lies in the recognition that in the world we are given space and ground to learn how to live in the presence of this holy and righteous One and in covenant with Him a life which is in keeping with His being revealed in the establishment and execution of this covenant, to the end that we might thus live the only possible life. In Job 28 the possibility is unambiguously eliminated which has sometimes been (falsely) detected in the famous passage in Proverbs 8: the conception of an immanent divine wisdom accessible to and recognisable by man of himself. We are given a concrete picture of man's ability to extract silver and gold and iron and brass from the bowels of the earth: "There is a path which no fowl knoweth, and which the vulture's eye hath not seen: the lion's whelps have not trodden it, nor the fierce lion passed by it. He putteth forth his hand upon the rocks; he overturneth the mountains by the roots. He cutteth out rivers among the rocks; and his eye seeth every precious thing. He bindeth the floods from overflowing; and the thing that is hid bringeth he forth to light" (Job 28^{7-11}). But it is very different with divine wisdom: "But where shall wisdom be found? and where is the place of understanding? Man knoweth not the price thereof; neither is it found in the land of the living. The depth saith, It is not in me: and the sea saith, It is not with me. It cannot be gotten for gold, neither shall silver be weighed for the price thereof. It cannot be valued with the gold of Ophir, with the precious onyx, or the sapphire" (Job. $28^{7f.}$). In short, it cannot be possessed by man as in the last analysis all other

treasures can be possessed by him. "Whence then cometh wisdom? and where is the place of understanding? Seeing it is hid from the eyes of all living, and kept close from the fowls of the air. Destruction and death say, We have heard the fame thereof with our ears. God understandeth the way thereof, and he knoweth the place thereof. For he looketh to the ends of the earth, and seeth under the whole heaven" (Job 28[20f.]). And this leads to the conclusion already quoted: "And unto man he said, Behold, the fear of the Lord, that is wisdom; and to depart from evil is understanding" (v. 28). [431]

From this point of view it is necessary, but only from this point of view is it possible, to see why in the Old Testament the reference to the unfathomable wisdom of God is adduced as a proof of the impossibility, and therefore the utter folly, of all idolatry. If the wisdom of God and therefore God Himself could be known by man in the created world, if the flood, the sea, the deep and death disclosed to him what according to Job 28 they do not disclose, if there were not concealed from the eyes of all living creatures that which according to Job 28 is concealed, there would be no real reason why the adoration of God in images of all kinds should not be a justifiable and even necessary result of this natural knowledge of God. But the Old Testament says, quite rightly from its own standpoint, that all idolatry is folly. It is not of course sin, but only sin in the sense of folly. It is the work of those who do not understand life—not the work of the worldly wise, but the work of fools, of those who utterly fail to appreciate the only possible ground on which man can exist, viz., the recognition of God as Creator, Sustainer and Lord of the world. For they foolishly imagine that they can find the place of understanding just as men find the place of gold or brass in the hills. "Who hath measured the waters in the hollow of his hand, and meted out the heaven with the span, and comprehended the dust of the earth in a measure, and weighed the mountains in scales, and the hills in a balance? Who hath directed the Spirit of the Lord, or being his counsellor hath taught him? With whom took he counsel, or who instructed him, and taught him in the path of judgment and taught him knowledge, and shewed to him the way of understanding? Behold, the nations are as a drop of a bucket, and are counted as the small dust of the balance" (Is. 40[12f.]). "To whom then will ye liken God? or what likeness will ye compare unto him?" (v. 18). "Have ye not known? have ye not heard? hath it not been told you from the beginning? have ye not understood from the foundations of the earth? It is he that sitteth upon the circle of the earth, and the inhabitants thereof are as grasshoppers; that stretcheth out the heavens as a curtain, and spreadeth them out as a tent to dwell in ... To whom then will ye liken me, or shall I be equal? saith the Holy One. Lift up your eyes on high, and behold who hath created these things, that bringeth out their host by number: he calleth them all by names by the greatness of his might, for that he is strong in power; not one faileth" (v. 21 ff.). From this point of view, because God is this unfailing and perfect Creator, Sustainer and Lord of all that is, it is obviously impossible to go back to the work of heathen craftsmen and goldsmiths. For this reason, too, there are no images of God. From this standpoint—that of the true knowledge of God the Creator—there is only the way forward to confidence in Him who discloses Himself and gives Himself to be known as Creator, not in His creation in general, but in His spiritual and merciful dealings with Israel. "Why sayest thou, O Jacob, and speakest, O Israel, My way is hid from the Lord, and my judgment is passed over from my God? Hast thou not known, hast thou not heard, that the everlasting God, the Lord, the Creator of the ends of the earth, fainteth not, neither is weary? there is no searching of his understanding. He giveth power to the faint, and to them that have no might he increaseth strength. Even the youths shall faint and be weary, and the young men shall utterly fall: but they that wait upon the Lord shall renew their strength; they shall mount up with wings as eagles; they shall run and not be weary; they shall walk, and not [432]
faint" (v. 27 ff.). We started with the confession and worship of God as the real and only source of wisdom in and above all that He has created. We then moved to the knowledge of

His unfathomableness and incomparableness and therefore His transcendence of all images. We have now reached the knowledge of Him at the place where He has permitted Himself to be heard by Israel, His recognition as the One who as the Creator and Lord of all things has not forgotten but vindicates, saves and strengthens Israel—and conversely, as the One who, remembering and vindicating and saving and strengthening Israel, is also the Creator and Lord of all things. From the one point to the other it is a direct path in Is. 40. These things are all a unity in the Old Testament knowledge of God, and in order to attain this insight we have only to leave it in its original unity and accept it as expressed in this text, and of course others too (for example, we find the same sequence of thought in Jer. 10[1–16]). The place where we discover the wisdom of God, the place where it really exists and is known in the fear of God, is, if we give due weight to the Old Testament witness in its context and specific utterances, the place where God gives Himself to be recognised as Creator, Sustainer and Lord of the world. And that place is His holy and righteous, gracious and merciful dealings with Israel.

The new truth imparted by the concept of wisdom as compared with those of grace and holiness, mercy and righteousness, or rather its special contribution to the clarifying of these other ideas, is that God is not the slave of His patience when in the dealings of which these other ideas speak He gives Himself time, and also gives us time, and therefore allows space and ground as the Creator, Sustainer and Lord of the world. What moves Him to exercise patience is His holy and righteous, gracious and merciful meaning, His will to unfold to us this meaning, to lead us to penitence, and therefore to make our own lives meaningful. This meaning behind His patience is His wisdom. It is the wisdom of His being and His works. And as the wisdom of His works it is world-wisdom properly understood. It is the philosophy of the created universe and the philosophy of human life. This "philosophy" is certainly not to be derived from reflection upon the universe or upon the being of man. It can be appreciated only by the bearing of God's own Word which as such gives us the right philosophy of the universe and of our own human life. In this connexion it should be clear at once that the testimony to God's wisdom in the Old and New Testaments is not a divided but a united testimony. We shall not, therefore, be surprised to read in Col. 2[3] that in the mystery of God called Christ "are hid all the treasures of wisdom and knowledge," and in 1 Cor. 1[30] that Jesus Christ is made not only our justification, sanctification and redemption, but with a special emphasis our wisdom: ὃς ἐγενήθη σοφία ἡμῖν ἀπὸ θεοῦ[EN124]. That Jesus Christ is the meaning of God's patience is the result at which we have really arrived in discussing the perfection of the divine patience.

"The divine wisdom is the principle which orders and determines the world for the divine self-communication active in our redemption" (Schleiermacher, *Der Chr. Glaube*, § 168). This separation between the divine self-communication and a special principle ordering and fashioning the world to that end is untenable. "All things were made by him; and without

[EN124] who has become for us wisdom from God

him was not anything made that was made" (Jn. 1^{3}). The definition must be corrected to [433]
read as follows: "The divine wisdom is the divine self-communication ordering and determining the world for itself."

The Old Testament has already in King Solomon a supremely wise man, endowed by God Himself with wisdom, and therefore made the image and exponent of God's own wisdom upon earth. Tradition has unanimously ascribed to him the wisdom teaching of the third part of the Canon. We are told in 1 Kings $4^{29f.}$ that God gave him "wisdom and understanding exceeding much, and largeness of heart, even as the sand that is on the sea-shore. And Solomon's wisdom excelled the wisdom of all the children of the east country, and all the wisdom of Egypt. For he was wiser than all men." "And he spake of trees, from the cedar tree that is in Lebanon even unto the hyssop that springeth out of the wall: he spake also of beasts, and of fowl, and of creeping things, and of fishes." We read in 1 Kings $10^{1f.}$ how the queen of Sheba heard of his fame and came to him to prove him with riddles. "And when she was come to Solomon, she communed with him all that was in her heart. And Solomon told her all her questions: there was not any thing hid from the king, which he told her not." And because at God's offer: "What shall I give thee?" he had asked for wisdom and not for long life, wealth or the life of his enemies, God granted him also what he had not asked for. "Riches and honour: so that there shall not be any among the kings like unto thee all thy days" (1 Kings $3^{4f.}$). His wisdom thus became manifest in his wealth, in the splendour of his palace and of the temple built by him, in the whole earthly brilliance of his kingdom. We recognise at once the connexion which we have met already in the Book of Proverbs. Human wisdom means the art of living. The wise man as distinct from the fool knows how to make a use of his life and of the whole universe which is in harmony with its creation and preservation by God and therefore meaningful, rich in promise and redemptive. The man who makes this use of his life and of the universe can and will live, and, as the life of Solomon shows, he will do so in unparalleled fulness and dazzling splendour. But there emerges from the Solomon story of the First Book of Kings a second point beyond that of the wisdom teaching of the Ketubim. This is that human wisdom of this kind is not a possibility which man can intrinsically realise. It is a gift of God which has to be sought. It springs from a special divine grace and favour. And as a wonderful divine gift of grace it acquires at once in the human sphere an unparalleled expression and brilliance which casts everything else into the shade. Therefore, and above all, the wisdom of Solomon is not a kind of knowledge or worldly shrewdness which has its meaning and purpose in itself, or in the existence of the individual Solomon. On the contrary, as recorded in I Kings $3^{7f.}$, Solomon's prayer for wisdom, which was so richly answered, is as follows: "And now, O Lord my God, thou hast made thy servant king instead of David my father: and I am but a little child: I know not how to go out or come in. And thy servant is in the midst of thy people which thou hast chosen, a great people, that cannot be numbered nor counted for multitude. Give therefore thy servant an understanding heart to judge thy people, that I may discern between good and bad: for who is able to judge this thy so great a people?" The wisdom of Solomon is not, then, a private wisdom, but a public, official wisdom of kingship and government. In a remarkable inversion of what, according to Gen. 3^{5}, was the sinful private desire of Adam at the suggestion of the serpent, it consists (cf. also Is. 7^{15}) in a gift which marks the competent judge, the power of discrimination between good and evil, the possession of the criterion which the ruler of a people needs to establish justice and peace in his kingdom. What this criterion is, is seen from the singular story of Solomon's judgment (1 Kings $3^{16f.}$) which follows directly upon this prayer and its answer. Which of the two women who appear before Solomon's seat of judgment is the mother of the living child? The answer is—the one who would rather give up
the possession of it than sacrifice its life. Solomon judges that she is in the right and to her [434]
the child is now awarded. On the other hand, the woman is in the wrong who would rather

sacrifice the child's life than renounce the claim to its possession. What is the meaning of this story? In fact it is the people of God who are being judged here. Two mothers, that is, two peoples, are secretly hidden and must again and again be distinguished in its midst. The one cherishes a living, the other a dead hope. But which is the one, which the other people? This question and the divine answer to it is the red thread which runs through the whole of the history of Israel. Does not the people with the dead hope constantly lay claim to have a living hope? Does it not stealthily creep into the possession of this hope, self-confidently refusing to renounce its claim and passing itself off as the true people of God? And how does the other stand, which is the true people of the living hope, but cannot prove its possession? Well, God knows, and King Solomon, endowed by Him with wisdom, will declare, what is good and evil! Between the two peoples comes the threat that even the living hope will become dead; there will be an utter end of Israel. The decision might be carried out at once in this terrible way. But the threat of this frightful decision, the sword already drawn against the living child, the threatened destruction of the living hope of Israel, is only Solomon's means of bringing to light right and wrong in his people, and therefore between the two peoples contained in his people. For now it is shown that the people of the dead hope looks on indifferently at the imminent destruction of the living hope to which it had falsely laid claim and still lays claim. In face of this threat the people of the living hope wills only one thing: may the fulfilment of the hope come to whomsoever it will, may the false pretender enjoy it, so long as it only remains and remains alive. The people vindicated in Solomon's judgment is the people which would rather resign its just claim, which would rather renounce the possibility of experiencing salvation, than renounce the life of hope itself; which would choose hell rather than impiety. It is the people of motherly love which loves not itself in the child but the child for its own sake. And it is revealed in face of the drawn sword as the people which in fact has the true claim to the living hope, as the people to which this hope properly belongs, and which will not have to be deprived for ever of its salvation. This, then, is Solomon's wisdom. This is how it rules in the midst of God's people. This is the criterion which it knows and applies—the living child as a question concerning the true mother, the living hope as a question concerning the true people of God. Solomon's wisdom knows and decides that the true people of God will reveal itself and be known as such in the fact that the living hope in God is dearer to it than its own life. And for that reason it will always retain this hope.

Jesus Christ, who is greater than Solomon (Mt. 12^{42}), stands in the midst of the people of God with all the wisdom of Solomon, and indeed as its embodiment. Again, and this time critically, the question is asked: Which is the true mother? Again the threat appears—will it again be divisive and decisive? Again it is possible—and in the strict sense inevitable—that neither is right, i.e., that they are all mothers only of a dead child. Again the wisdom of Solomon, which is divine, pursues a different course. But a greater than Solomon is indeed here. For now the sword is not only drawn. It strikes. The Judge Himself suffers Himself to be both the dead child, the annihilated hope of Israel, and also the true mother bereft of her child, the Israel that has lost all hope. He does so in order that as the sacrificed victim (crucified but risen from the dead on the third day) He may be the living hope which wills to be loved in faith for its own sake, but which rightly belongs to all those who believe, who, like the mother of the child, protest and maintain and desire only that He should live, that He should be always who He is, and who for the sake of this desire are justified. The action of Jesus Christ as King of His people is that as the Judge who pronounces and fulfils this threat,
[435] but also as the mother and child who must suffer its fulfilment, He continually looks for faith in Himself, continually distinguishing and separating as justified those who have faith in Him. For them and for all of us there remains the threat, the drawn sword, the sword that has not yet smitten or that smites no longer. The only course open to us all, if we wish to be

vindicated and revealed as God's people, is that of faith in Him, the faith in which He Himself will necessarily be dearer and more precious and more significant for us than any claim and expectation we might have in Him for ourselves, the faith which does not find its object in itself but in Him. Again, in faith in Him we retain that which we cannot even try to procure for ourselves as we believe in Him: our justification, our membership of the true people of God, and therefore the promise of life for time and eternity. As we subordinate ourselves to Jesus Christ in faith, or rather as He subordinates Himself to us by giving Himself to us as the object of our faith. He is made unto us wisdom (1 Cor. 1^{30}). Under the patience of God which is shown us for His sake, and in the time which is granted us for His sake, He is the meaning of this patience and this time—He Himself present with us and making us wise as well.

It is from this standpoint that we must read the whole argument of 1 Cor. 1^{18}–2^{10}. This tells us that the Word of the cross is foolishness to them that are perishing but the power of God to them that are being saved (v. 18). How is this? Because the foolish are without faith in Him and therefore do not belong to the true people of God, they can obviously see in the news of the death of Jesus Christ (either with or without that of His resurrection, and even more so with it) only the news of a further demonstration of the meaninglessness of human life; and probably indeed the proclamation of the paradox that the meaninglessness revealed here too is as such its true meaning. So then, as is described in Acts 17^{32}, they turn away in impatience or alarm from this foolish Gospel. But they do not realise that by doing this, and by making this judgment, they are already condemned, exposed and revealed as the mother of the dead child. For what happens when they pass this judgment? "For it is written, I will destroy the wisdom of the wise, and will bring to nothing the understanding of the prudent" (v. 19, Is. 29^{14}). What happens, then, is simply that in this judgment they and their wisdom are superseded and destroyed and eliminated. This is what is revealed and confirmed when they consider this news to be folly. "Where is the wise? where is the scribe? where is the disputer of this world? (v. 20*a*). There is none. By the very fact of what God has done through this Gospel He has made *tabula rasa*[EN125] of all that is published in the world as wisdom but is not. "God has made foolish the wisdom of this world" (v. 20*b*). Whatever this wisdom may be in itself, confronted with what God has done in this Gospel it is clear that it is assuredly not what it claims to be, the art of living, worldly wisdom, but the exact opposite. For what happened at this point? *Διὰ τῆς σοφίας*[EN126], applying its own supposed wisdom, the world failed to recognise God *ἐν τῇ σοφίᾳ αὐτοῦ*[EN127], i.e., where His wisdom actually was and acted and revealed itself. But it pleased God by the supposed folly of this preaching to save them that believe (v. 21): by the preaching of the crucified Christ, unto the Jews a stumbling-block, unto the Greeks foolishness; but unto them which are called, both Jews and Greeks, not only the power of God, but also the wisdom of God (v. 23 f.). Even this supposed folly of God is in fact wiser than men—so much wiser as Solomon was wiser than all men—and even this supposed weakness of God is in fact stronger than men (v. 25). For this reason, it is not a bad sign for the Church, but an indication of the genuineness of its calling, that not many wise after the flesh, not many mighty, not many noble are in it. In keeping with the presumed folly of this Gospel, God has chosen the so-called foolish ones of this world to confound the wisdom of the wise, the weak to confound the strong, the trivial and contemptible, the things that are not (*τὰ μὴ ὄντα*) to bring to nothing those that are
(*ἵνα τὰ ὄντα καταργήσῃ*), in order that it may be manifest that no flesh can glory in His [436]
presence (vv. 26–29). From this God, in whose presence no flesh can glory, Christians have

EN125 blank slate
EN126 through its wisdom
EN127 in his wisdom

their life in Jesus Christ: *ἐξ αὐτοῦ δὲ ὑμεῖς ἐστε ἐν Χριστῷ Ἰησοῦ* [EN128]. They have it by the power of His resurrection from the dead. Therefore, on the one hand, they clearly participate in the supposed folly, weakness and contemptibility of the divine action which has taken place in Jesus Christ. They must be content, with Jesus Christ, i.e., with God Himself, as His children, to fall under the judgment of that Greek world. But for this very reason, they participate, on the other hand, in the triumph of real divine wisdom over the false human wisdom from which this judgment stems—a judgment which can only reveal the actual folly of this wisdom. For them, Jesus Christ the Crucified, in whom they have their being from God, as God's children, has been made by God Himself by His resurrection, not only justification, sanctification and redemption, but also and above all wisdom (v. 30), in order that in them may be fulfilled the words of Jer. $9^{23ff.}$: "He that glorieth, let him glory in the Lord." The exact wording of the passage runs: "Let not the wise man glory in his wisdom, neither let the mighty man glory in his might, let not the rich man glory in his riches: but let him that glorieth glory in this, that he understandeth and knoweth me, that I am the Lord which exercise loving-kindness, judgment and righteousness, in the earth: for in these things I delight, saith the Lord." If a man boasts in the Lord, there are three reasons why he cannot at the same time boast also in his own wisdom, the human wisdom of this world. 1. Since he boasts in this other, the real wisdom of God, he has no more room for his own, human wisdom. 2. By this wisdom in which he may now glory human wisdom is for him unmasked as unwisdom, as utter and contemptible folly in his eyes. 3. He cannot wish to withdraw from his solidarity with divine wisdom even in regard to its supposed folly and the judgment to which it must be content to submit in this world.

A passing reference may be made to Mt. 11^{16-19}. It describes this generation as angry with John the Baptist because of his asceticism ("He hath a devil"), and with Jesus because of His freedom from asceticism ("Behold, a man gluttonous, and a wine-bibber, a friend of publicans and sinners"). True wisdom is always different from what this generation has expected and desired, and therefore the latter, like the disappointed children in the market-place, believes itself to have reason to complain: "We have piped unto you, and ye have not danced; we have mourned unto you, and ye have not lamented." What are the representatives of wisdom to do? Should they accept these complaints? Should they determine their conduct accordingly, dancing when there is piping and lamenting when there is mourning. No, but as they continue to do undeviatingly in face of these complaints what as wise men they must do, it happens that wisdom is justified and justifies itself in its works, i.e., in that which the wise as such must faithfully do: *καὶ ἐδικαιώθη ἡ σοφία ἀπὸ τῶν ἔργων αὐτῆς* [EN129]. For the true works of wisdom are the works of its representatives so long as the latter—and what else is to be expected when they are John the Baptist and Jesus?—will only remain faithful and obedient. They, too, do not need to look for any other justification for their works. They are justified as wisdom justifies itself in and by their works.

But this brings us back to the argument of 1 Cor. 1–2. What was Paul trying to prove by his exposition in 1^{18-31}? According to the first verses of the second chapter it was simply this. He could not come among them *καθ' ὑπεροχὴν λόγου ἢ σοφίας* [EN130] (v. 1), or *ἐν πειθοῖς σοφίας λόγοις* [EN131] (v. 4), to declare his testimony to God. He could not then, in accordance with their expectation, dance after the pipings of a human wisdom or lament after its mourning. As one whose mission it was to glory in the Lord and only in the Lord he could not please them by glorying at the same time in what was still a human wisdom. He could not

[EN128] by him you are all in Christ Jesus
[EN129] and wisdom has been justified in her deeds
[EN130] in lofty words or wisdom
[EN131] with wise and persuasive words

declare to them the testimony of God in such form as would have been in keeping with their ambitions as children of this "generation." He could declare it to them only as it actually ran. [437]
When he was among them, he could know nothing but Jesus Christ and Him crucified (v. 2). Inevitably, then, he appeared among them in "weakness, and in fear, and in much trembling" (v. 3). His word could have only one foundation, and this of course it had: the ἀπόδειξις πνεύματος καὶ δυνάμεως[EN132] (v. 4), i.e., obviously the justification of wisdom by its works which takes place whenever the work of man consists solely and supremely in the fact that he yields himself wholly as an instrument at the disposal of God's wisdom, allowing it to say unreservedly, without subtraction or addition, what it wills to say. When this happens we have the demonstration of the Spirit and of power, about the effectiveness of which no one need have any anxiety, but the effectiveness of which again cannot be replaced or completed by that of any other sort of wisdom. And this is just what took place in Corinth, to please no one and to harm no one. Nothing else could take place or could be allowed to take place. For the faith of the Corinthian Christians would not have ripened into genuine faith if Paul had tried to adduce even provisionally any other proof. He could not base his position on the wisdom of men, but only on the power of God with its self-justifying wisdom. And as far as Paul was concerned, such a foundation could be achieved only by one thing, that is, the preaching of the crucified Christ (v. 5). It is with this preaching that Paul speaks wisdom. That is, for the τέλειοι[EN133]. But again, these are not, as in the mystery religions, the esoterics, the initiates of a human wisdom, who from the point of view of this preaching ($1^{20f.}$) could only be the most foolish of all fools. They are simply those who accept the Word of the cross in faith. Those who do this do not deceive themselves or go astray. They are no fools. They are not like the weeping children in the market-place. They do not adopt the judgment of folly, or determine their conduct accordingly. The demonstration of the Spirit and of power has become effective with them because they are wise enough to hear wisdom where fools think to hear folly and, because they are fools, can in fact only hear folly. Certainly what those who are righteous in faith hear when they hear the Word of the cross is not the wisdom of the world, nor the higher wisdom of those angelic powers which are at present the rulers of this world, the ἄρχοντες τοῦ αἰῶνος τούτου (v. 6). But what Paul proclaims only by the Word of the cross, and what they hear, is God's own wisdom: His wisdom which in this mystery (that of the cross of Jesus Christ) is just as concealed (for the world) as it is revealed (for believers); the wisdom which before all worlds God has appointed and foreseen for our glorification, as it has already served, and will further serve, to this end in the resurrection of Christ, by which He was made wisdom for us. For this is already our glorification. We already have actually and visibly something of the splendour of Solomon. We live here and now with all joy and gladness in Solomon's temple. For by the resurrection of Christ we have received our life from God as life in Him, the risen Lord. He has been made wisdom for us, God's children, and we ourselves may now be wise in faith. We! For this wisdom is not only a wisdom apart, alien to all the human wisdom of this world as such, and to that extent, where there is no faith, alien to all who live within it. Not only is all human wisdom unmasked and compromised by its judgment that as so-called wisdom it is folly, and supreme folly in those who justly perhaps can boast that they are perfect in this human wisdom. It is also alien to the higher or supreme wisdom of the angelic powers which rule this world and humanity. Obviously these too have incurred condemnation. For as represented by the governmental authority of the Roman state, they shared in the rejection and murder of Jesus Christ. If they had been alive to the wisdom of God at the point where it lived and spoke, not merely in the form of testimony, but in its original reality; if they had

---

EN132 the demonstration of the Spirit and of power
EN133 perfect

been receptive of the demonstration of the Spirit and of power as it was given, not in the form of the apostolic word, but by the incarnate Word itself, "they would not have crucified
[438] the Lord of glory" (v. 8). They would have been wise enough to perceive His glory, the glory of divine wisdom as such. But they did not do so. It was they who in the last analysis crucified Jesus Christ. There is therefore all the less reason why Paul, in his witness to God, should consult the desires and expectations, the piping and mourning of any kind of human wisdom, and thus give his Gospel any other form than that in which it has clothed itself: the form of the Word of the cross. He must be content with the demonstration of the Spirit and of power, with the self-justification of divine wisdom in face of all the folly of men, as it takes place and will continually take place in the preaching of this Word. It is in this way that the Word of the cross becomes for those who are being saved the power of God—that God has prepared for those who love Him what eye hath not seen, nor ear heard, nor the human heart conceived (v. 9). What is this? In the wider context it is undoubtedly the revelation of the secret of the cross of Christ and therefore of the wisdom of God predestined and applied to us from all eternity for our future and indeed our present glory. This wisdom of His in its eternally concrete expression is what eye has not seen, nor ear heard, nor the human heart conceived. And God has revealed it to us by the Spirit: *ἡμῖν γὰρ ἀπεκάλυψεν ὁ θεὸς διὰ τοῦ πνεύματος* (v. 10).

It is evident that even in this New Testament context the wisdom of God is identical with the administrative and judicial wisdom of Solomon which awards to each what is properly appropriate. Folly to fools who do not have so great a love for wisdom that for the sake of it they prefer to be regarded as fools in their own eyes and in the eyes of the world; and wisdom to the wise whose love of wisdom is such that for the sake of it they are prepared to be able to glory only in the Lord and no longer in their own human wisdom. Folly to fools who in applying and exercising their own presumed wisdom do not hesitate, but are in fact compelled to destroy genuine wisdom, thus revealing their own real folly; and wisdom to the wise, for whom and in whom, contrary to any ostensible wisdom of their own, the wisdom of God is itself at work—alive, vindicating and justifying itself, as genuine wisdom, the wisdom of God, can and does. But in distinction from the Old Testament picture, or rather supplementing and clarifying it, we find that the three main aspects of the wisdom of God in Solomon's judgment are united in the New Testament presentation of the divine mystery called Jesus Christ. For He is (1) wisdom as the judge, alone knowing, deciding and disposing in sovereign power; (2) wisdom as the object of accusation and counter-accusation, rejected and destroyed, and yet ever living; (3) wisdom as the fulfilment of the verdict, imparting itself to the wise and denying itself to fools.

According to the New Testament God is the *μόνος σοφός*[EN134] (Rom. 16^{27}; 1 Tim. 1^{17}) in such a way that His wisdom coincides with His holiness and righteousness, and the recognition of it, i.e., man's attainment of wisdom, with his winning through to faith. That is why Paul can speak as he does (Eph. $3^{8f.}$, cf. Col. $1^{25f.}$) about the meaning of his apostolate. It is laid upon him to bring to light the economy (the order or structure) of the mystery eternally concealed in God, the Creator of all things, "to the intent that (*ἵνα*) now unto the principalities and powers (*ἀρχαί* and *ἐξουσίαι*) in heavenly places might be known by the church the manifold wisdom of God (*πολυποίκιλος σοφία τοῦ θεοῦ*) according to the eternal purpose which he purposed in Christ Jesus our Lord." In accordance with this Paul had already told the Church in Eph. $1^{7f.}$: In the riches of His grace exercised in our redemption through the blood of Christ and in the forgiveness of our sins, God has abounded toward us *ἐν πάσῃ σοφίᾳ καὶ φρονήσει*[EN135], for He has made known to us the mystery of His will which is to

---

[EN134] only wise
[EN135] in all wisdom and insight

gather together all things in heaven and on earth in Christ as their Head—their Representative and recapitulation, their core and substance (ἀνακεφαλαιώσασθαι)[EN136]. He had also prayed in Eph. $1^{17f.}$ (cf. Col. 1^{9}) that "the God of our Lord Jesus Christ, the Father of glory, may give unto you the spirit of wisdom and revelation in the knowledge of him: the eyes of [439]
your understanding being enlightened; that you may know what is the hope of his calling." He also invites them later in Eph. 5^{15} to walk ἀκριβῶς[EN137], "not as fools, but as wise"; or, as we have it in the parallel in Col. 4^{5}, "to walk in wisdom toward them that are without." Paul understands his own task to be that of preaching Christ the hope of glory and therefore instructing and warning every man in all wisdom and presenting him perfect (τέλειον[EN138]) in Christ (Col. 1^{28}). In Colossians and Ephesians wisdom is plainly enough identified with Jesus Christ Himself. But exactly the same wisdom is meant in James $3^{13f.}$. The question is asked: "Who is a wise man and endued with knowledge among you?" and the answer is that he will show it by walking ἐν πραΰτητι σοφίας[EN139]. Again, in Jas. $3^{17f.}$ the wisdom which is from above is described as "first pure, then peaceable, gentle, and easy to be intreated, full of mercy and good fruits, without partiality, and without hypocrisy." Again, in Jas. $1^{5f.}$ the man who lacks this wisdom is exhorted to pray to God for it in faith. It is instructive to see that the freedom from doubt, which in 3^{17} is a criterion of the wisdom for which we have to pray in faith ($1^{5f.}$), is defined in this latter passage with great emphasis as the fundamental determination of faith and therefore of a right prayer for wisdom. Wisdom to the wise! this rule clearly applies here, as it did in the case of Solomon, who had to be already wise in order to pray for wisdom, and in that of Jesus Himself, of whom Lk. $2^{40\ 52}$ does not tell us that He received wisdom or became wise, but that He "increased" in wisdom and stature and in favour with God and man. It is clear that in all these New Testament passages wisdom is nothing more nor less than God Himself turning to man in grace and mercy, God in His love but also in His freedom, in the fulness of His love but also in the fulness of His freedom.

The observation with which we opened our discussion of the wisdom teaching of the Old Testament may be repeated in relation to that of the New. It is perhaps a stumbling-block that here too the concept of wisdom is explicitly mentioned only in a relatively small part of the Canon. And there can be no real objection to the historical explanation that—as in the case of Israel's encounter with older Hellenism—this was the necessary consequence of the contact and conflict of the New Testament community with the philosophical and religious movements which gave rise to so-called *Gnosis*. But it should be carefully noted how radically critical this contact was, and how completely the conceptual material perhaps received in the course of this contact was assimilated to the apostolic testimony, not weakening or transforming but underlining and sharpening the Christian message when assumed into the context of other concepts and viewpoints and applied, of course, only in this context—I know of no passage where it could be said to be broken or even disturbed. But whatever may be our attitude to the historical question, there can be no doubt that in the New Testament Canon, as in that of the Old Testament, the wisdom teaching has become an integral part of the apostolic preaching. Paul would not be Paul without 1 Cor. 1–2, and the whole context of Colossians and Ephesians would disintegrate if for some reason it were desired to remove this stone from the edifice. Jesus Christ, our righteousness, sanctification and redemption, is also our wisdom, and faith in Him is our instruction by the wisdom of God. In substance, the

---

[EN136] to bring together
[EN137] with insight
[EN138] perfect
[EN139] in the poverty of wisdom

witness of John's Gospel is the same, although surprisingly it avoids the use of the term as such. Instead, more penetratingly than any other New Testament document, it brings faith and knowledge into juxtaposition and conjunction.

INDEX OF SCRIPTURE REFERENCES

INDEX OF SUBJECTS

INDEX OF NAMES